"Colin Coulson-Thomas has done a first-rate job of co-ordinating the contributions of a group of authors whose backgrounds range from accountancy through ancient philology to philosophy and whose perspectives tend to reflect that diversity."

Modern Management

"Reading this book should certainly help organisations make an informed choice about whether BPR is right for them."

Personnel Today

"Overall the book's strength lies in its multiplicity of voices and viewpoints. . .Consultants will find much that is edifying. . ."

Management Consultancy

"A critical and balanced appraisal of BPR."

Lloyds List

"Coulson-Thomas and his colleagues have put together a useful commentary on BPR topics and their contexts."

IPR Journal

"This is an interesting book for IT managers and management students."

Computing

Dedication

To all those unsung heroes who are creating and building organisations that are humane, fulfilling, and fun as well as efficient, productive and profitable.

Business Process Re-engineering:
myth
& reality

edited by

Colin
Coulson-
Thomas

KOGAN
PAGE

First published in 1994
Paperback edition published in 1996

Kogan Page Limited
120 Pentonville Road
London N1 9JN

© Colin Coulson-Thomas, 1994, 1996

British Library Cataloguing in Publication Data

A CIP record for this book is available from the British Library.

ISBN 0 7494 2109 6

Typeset by Saxon Graphics Ltd, Derby
Printed and bound in Great Britain by
Biddles Ltd, Guildford and Kings Lynn

Contents

Preface

Professor Colin J Coulson-Thomas

Creativity and imagination are at a premium. According to its theory and rhetoric Business Process Re-engineering (BPR) is concerned with step change rather than incremental improvement; revolution not evolution. However, while BPR is being used to 'improve' existing situations, ie cut costs, reduce throughput times and squeeze more out of people, what does it contribute to radical change and innovation?

COBRA (Constraints & Opportunities in Business Restructuring — an Analysis), an initiative of the European Commission, is designed to cut through the hype and examine what is actually happening. It has involved a pan-european study of: (1) BPR experience and practice; and (2) the relationship between BPR and new forms of organisation and new patterns of work. COBRA has led to reports with case studies and methodologies for ensuring that issues relating to new ways of working (*The Responsive Organisation*, Policy Publications, 1995) and supply chains (*The Competitive Network*, Policy Publications, 1996) are fully addressed during re-engineering.

A new mode of working such as teleworking, with its emphasis on the use of information and telecommunications technology to overcome barriers of function, organisation, location and time, can be a very good indicator of whether or not a so-called 'radical' change programme is reaching down to the roots of an organisation. BPR and new ways of working should be complementary. They may both result from common 'drivers', for example a desire for greater flexibility, and examining the relationship between them provides new insights into the nature and contribution of BPR.

The purpose of this book is to share the 'picture' of BPR which is emerging from the COBRA project. Its authors have all contributed to and/or participated in COBRA activities. The book also complements an earlier work of the author, *Transforming the Company: Bridging the Gap Between Management Myth and Corporate Reality* (Kogan Page, 1992).

Other COBRA outputs deal more specifically with the relationship between BPR and teleworking. Both were found to exist in many organisations, but causal links between them are the exception.

While more of the potential and commitment of people can be harnessed by means of more creative and satisfying work environments, the emphasis of BPR tends to be on working people harder rather than smarter. Even where new ways of working are applicable, appropriate and actually demanded, they are either not adopted, or play a minor role, in most BPR 'solutions'. In comparison with such factors as cost and speed, new ways of working and learning are given a low priority. Without continuing learning, BPR outcomes that are quickly imitated by competitors cease to be 'differentiators'.

No-one seeking radical change should feel compelled to undertake BPR. Many organisations that have introduced new patterns of work have achieved more radical and fundamental changes than comparative organisations that have relied instead on BPR. Creative thinking, benchmarking, culture change, innovation, etc, can all be undertaken quite independently of BPR. Many other frameworks and approaches exist, along with models of organisations that make it much easier for people to be true to themselves and to work in ways, and at times and places, that enable them to give of their best.

BPR is often little more than a 'cover' for downsizing or some other form of restructuring. People become victims of BPR rather than its beneficiaries. The 'negative' focus upon internal cost cutting, headcount reductions and driving people harder is causing widespread alienation, and can lead to a negative spiral of descent to the status of a low margin supplier of commodity goods.

To reap the full benefits of BPR, and if more civilized lifestyles and inspiring work environments are to be created, attitudes and behaviours will have to change. 'Positive' BPR goals and more vision-led, balanced, strategic, sensitive and holistic approaches to BPR are needed as a matter of urgency. BPR could be undertaken with the express purpose of improving the quality of thinking or working life, introducing new ways of working and learning, or widening job opportunities; while a focus upon external relationships could lead to the building of capability, market or network innovation and more profitable partnerships with customers.

Professor Colin J Coulson-Thomas
Leader and coordinator of the COBRA project
Chairman of Adaptation Ltd and of Attitudes Skills and Knowledge Ltd
Professor of Corporate Transformation, Dean of the Faculty of Management and Head of Putteridge Bury at the University of Luton.

Acknowledgements

I would like to thank all the contributors to this book, Dr Peter Johnston and Professor Jean Millar of DG XIII of the Commission of the European Communities which has provided the core funding of the COBRA project, my COBRA colleagues from Adaptation Ltd, the University of the Aegean, CELSA SA, empirica Tekom, Euro PR, and The Home Office Partnership, our additional COBRA sponsors ACT Business Systems, A T Kearney, CCTA, Mercury Communications, 3Com, and the Learning Systems Institute, colleagues at the Faculty of Management of the University of Luton and City University Business School, and Philip Mudd and the team at our publishers Kogan Page for their help and encouragement.

List of Contributors

Hamid Aghassi is responsible for directing the Change Management services in the areas of Organisational Structures and Human Resource Management at ACT Business Systems. He has over 15 years of management and technical consultancy experience in the private and public sectors backed by his educational achievements in the diverse fields of engineering, marketing and business administration.

During his career as a management consultant, Hamid has helped organisations to develop an holistic view of their business strategy aimed at addressing the people, business and technology issues. He has conducted public briefing programmes on BPR key concepts and methods as well as speaking in the media and at major conferences on the importance of addressing the people issues at early stages of a re-engineering programme.

Eric Benhamou is president and CEO of 3Com Corporation, a leading global data networking company, a position he has held since 1990. He is also chairman of 3Com's Board of Directors. He co-founded Bridge Communications in 1981 and was its vice president until the company merged with 3Com in 1987. He was then promoted to chief operating officer of 3Com taking responsibility for all product operations including development, marketing and manufacturing.

Additionally, Eric chairs the American Electronics Association's National Information Infrastructure (NII) Task Force, which is working to provide the United States government and other interested groups with an end-user perspective on the NII.

He is also a member of the Board of Directors of Smart Valley Inc., a non-profit consortium seeking to revitalise the Silicon Valley economy through advanced telecommunications and networking technologies. As chairman of Smart Valley's telecommuting project, Eric is responsible for the initiation of pilot projects at organisations within Silicon Valley. Other positions include serving on the Board of Directors of Cypress Semiconductor, Legato, and Santa Clara University's School of Business.

Colin J Coulson-Thomas is leader and coordinator of the European Commission's COBRA project to examine BPR experience and practice across Europe. He is Professor of Corporate Transformation at the University of Luton. He is also Dean of the University's Faculty of

Management and Head of Putteridge Bury – one of Europe's largest management centres and a leader in the field of competence-based learning at post-graduate and post-experience level.

Colin is also Chairman of Adaptation Ltd and of Attitudes Skills and Knowledge Ltd. An international authority, counsellor and adviser on the achievement of corporate transformation and implementation of BPR, he is regularly called on to review change programmes and approaches to re-engineering.

In recent years he has held a portfolio of private and public sector directorships, and visiting appointments at Aston Business School, City University Business School, and the IT Institute of Salford University. He is the author of some 30 books and reports including *Transforming the Company* (1992); *Creating the Global Company: Successful Internationalisation* (1992); *Creating Excellence in the Boardroom* (1993) and *Developing Directors, Building an Effective Boardroom Team* (1993).

Nigel Courtney embarked on a career in project management after graduating from UMIST and gained five years experience on major infrastructure projects. Progressing into general management, he co-founded and directed a business which generated revenues of some £100 million with public and private sector clients over the next 15 years.

A growing interest in the use of IT to improve managerial productivity and organisational effectiveness led to the MBA in Information Technology Management at City University Business School where Nigel is now pursuing part-time doctoral studies in the field of BPR.

Courtney Consulting was established in 1990 and reflects the convergence of Nigel's project and general management and IT capabilities. The firm delivers business solutions to companies in the UK and EU mainly in the financial services, engineering and construction sectors. It also carries out research projects for government and university clients and professional and trade associations.

Wanda D'hanis studied ancient philology and philosophy in Antwerpen, UFSIA, Leuven, KUL (Catholic University of Louvain) and Frankfurt/Main, Johann Wolfgang Goethe Universität. In 1983 she obtained a doctorate in philosophy at the KUL. She has been an assistant in Philosophy at the Higher Institute of Philosophy, Leuven in the English Programme, and in the Translators' Programme at the Katholieke Vlaamse Hogeschool, Antwerpen.

As co-founder of Nikè Consult she has been manager of the Management & Reflection department since 1990. As such, she regularly publishes material on the common ground shared by philosophy and management and organises seminars and round-table conferences on these subjects.

Brian Fitzgerald is a lecturer in the Department of Accounting, Finance and Information Systems at University College Cork, and is also attached to the Executive Systems Research Centre (ESRC) where he is actively involved in research and consultancy in the areas of business process re-engineering, systems development approaches and executive information systems, and his work in these areas has been presented in international journals and conferences. Having worked in industry prior to lecturing, he has more than 15 years' experience in the computer field.

Clive Holtham is Bull Information Systems Professor of Information Management at City University Business School. An accountant by background, he spent six years as a Director of Finance and Information Technology before joining the Business School in 1988. He is the author of numerous publications. His research covers IT strategy, EIS, groupware and BPR. He is the inventor of the Business Flight Simulator (an intensively computer-supported environment for management work groups) which is currently the subject of a major UK government/industry founded collaborative project.

Matthias Maier is a scientific assistant and research fellow in the Department of Organization and Strategic Management, University of Trier, where he specialises in organisational transformation. He has studied business administration, sociology and media science at the Technical University, Berlin, the Ecole de Management Européen, Strasbourg, and the University of Trier.

Derek Miers joined the computer industry in 1978. Having worked in a variety of IT consulting roles, he started developing systems for his own use to control information and documents used within the business. By 1990 this had evolved into a generic work management system known as Office Engine, supporting knowledge workers with an accessible and extensible object-oriented repository to support the contact management requirements of the business, and integrating many third party technologies.

Over the last two years Derek has undertaken an exhaustive analysis of tools and technologies that support business re-engineering. He provides workshops on business and process modelling and has also provided direct support on the selection and implementation of work management technologies. The consultancy and research provided, builds on his extensive experience developing and implementing technologies to support process oriented working.

Ciaran Murphy is a statutory lecturer at University College Cork, where he is responsible for the MIS discipline. He is founder and Director of the Executive Systems Research Centre – a centre that undertakes research into the impact of information systems on the work of senior executives. The Centre undertakes collaborative research with industrial organisations and produces a series of research and discussion papers. He has published extensively in international journals, including *Accounting, Management & Technology*, the *Journal of Applied Expert Systems*, the *Journal of Information Technology* and has collaborated on the writing of a number of books. His research interests include decision support systems, executive information systems, inter-organisational systems and BPR.

Edna Murphy is a director of The Home Office Partnership, an innovative consultancy dedicated to developing new ways of working. Edna read Law at Cambridge before taking a post-graduate degree in Law at New York University School of Law. After a year working in a US law firm, she left the USA to become the Fundraising Director of a national charity. Following several years combining activities in the voluntary sector with freelance journalism, she joined The Home Office Partnership to develop the research and information aspects of the business. She started the newsletter *Flexibility: Business Innovation and Human Resource Management* in 1993.

Simon Robinson is Director of empirica communications and technology research in Bonn. Simon graduated from Cambridge in engineering and management science. He joined empirica in 1985, and in 1988 founded the communications and technology group, whose consulting and research activities range from advanced personal communications to groupware. Simon has researched the practice of telework extensively, with some results published in the Wiley Information Science Series *Telework – Towards the Elusive Office*. He himself practices telework and is currently looking to extend the use of telework within empirica. His company continues to contribute to research on the subject, having recently launched a survey of attitudes to telework across Europe, and actively supports telework development, eg by drawing up a European Code of Telework Practice.

Walter Schertler is professor at Trier University and holds the chair of Organization and Strategic Management. Before he continued his academic career, he spent several years with the Boston Consulting Group in Munich. His recent research, teaching and consulting areas focus on problems of strategic and organisational change within industries, co-operation and communication strategies in the aerospace industry, and the influence of information technologies on organisational strategies and structures in the service industry. In these research areas he has published several books and articles. He is also a member of advisory boards in different industries.

Karl A Stroetmann is senior research fellow at empirica communications and technology research in Bonn. He has a background in business administration and economics. His present research concentrates on flexible work through teleworking, telecooperation of small business, information management and policies, and related issues. He was a senior research fellow for information economics with the German National Research Centre for Computer Science, managing director of the German

Social Sciences Information Centre, speaker of the Board of the German Social Sciences Infrastructure Services (GESIS), and vice president and partner of Abt Associates – consultants. His professional activities include adjunct lecturer at the University of Trier and Councillor of FID and EUSIDIC. He is an active member of various national and international professional associations.

Rohit Talwar is the founder and Managing Director of The Centre for Business Transformation, Chairman of the Strategic Planning Society's Re-engineering and Radical Change Group, and a member of the advisory board for the Dutch Association of Business Engineers. He is editor of *Process Product Watch* – the review service for re-engineering tools and techniques as well as being a member of the editorial board for the *Journal of Business Change and Reengineering*.

Rohit teaches an MBA course on re-engineering and transformation at City University and has run several public and in-company workshops on re-engineering, learning and the management of change. His recent article, *Business Reengineering – A Strategy Driven Approach*, was published in *The International Journal of Strategic Management* in December 1993. He has worked with a number of major public and private sector organisations to help them develop and implement strategies for re-engineering and radical performance improvement.

1

Business Process Re-engineering: Nirvana or Nemesis for Europe?

Colin J Coulson-Thomas

Business Process Re-engineering (BPR) is one of the latest management buzzwords on the block. Although its main elements have been successfully utilised by internal change teams within certain corporations for several years before being 'packaged' for a wider audience, the impact of the first few articles and books on BPR has been dramatic. It required less than three years for the concept to take the US by storm and, more recently, interest in Europe has become feverish.

BPR is now in vogue. Hardly a day goes by without an invitation to a BPR event, or yet another article on BPR, arriving in the in-tray. The initial trickle of books on the subject has now become a flood. In some larger organisations, 'me too' exercises abound, as people jump onto the BPR bandwagon in order to keep up with colleagues and rivals.

While some worry that they may have missed the boat, others wonder whether the BPR boom will last. Will the BPR bubble burst leaving organisations stranded in mid-stream, locked into half-completed exercises? Will the fickle move on to the next fashionable term? Already conference organisers are having to differentiate their events in order to attract an audience, extending the application of BPR to ever more specialized and obscure fields.

Critics and critiques have started to emerge. Re-engineering is now frequently described as 'hype', a triumph of packaging, or as a cover for downsizing or some other form of restructuring. Already the term sends a shiver down the spines of many who learn they are about to be re-engineered.

How many companies face such a challenge, if not a crisis, that they actually need to undertake BPR? How long will it be before BPR triggers a backlash? Does it encourage creativity or lead to the avoidance of difficult choices? Will it stay the course, or be forced out of the limelight by a more alluring and better marketed alternative?

CONFUSION REIGNS

BPR has both its passionate advocates and its ardent detractors. Newly converted enthusiasts talk of nirvana, while earlier champions now warn of nemesis for the naive in view of the risks involved. Is BPR just a temporary gravy train for consultants? Or is it a management fad equivalent to a flu epidemic, quickly spreading and leaving people and organisations the worse for wear when it passes?

Those endeavouring to understand what is going on are operating in a sea of fog. Confusion is widespread. Many early applications of BPR have been functional rather than cross-functional. There are few independently validated and cross-functional examples of BPR that have run the full course from initiation to implementation and subsequent assessment. In any event, validation presents its own challenges in a dynamic organisational and market context. When various other corporate initiatives are being undertaken in parallel, how does one identify the contribution of BPR?

Suppliers of information technology (IT) and consultancy services have a vested interest in publicising and exaggerating success. Measurement criteria are carefully selected, for example, response time, or 'competing on speed', is often stressed as something that BPR can deliver.

The extremes are sometimes concealed. Success resulting in a competitive advantage is kept under wraps, and the embarrassment of failure is also hidden. The carefully packaged and self-contained case studies that have emerged often cover initiatives that were started before those involved had heard of BPR. These can sometimes be used to support both arguments for and against BPR.

Attitudes towards BPR vary between countries. In the UK, for example, almost any successful 'change programme', including those initiated prior to awareness of BPR, is now referred to as an example of re-engineering. In France where it is often referred to as re-configuration, the term may be viewed with some caution as an American import. This is despite the fact that elements of BPR occur in local approaches to radical change and where mangers are imaginative and questioning (eg teleworking in the case of France). Indigenous equivalents of BPR have also been developed (eg in Germany), but these have been generally pushed into the background under the onslaught of the better packaged US alternative.

PURPOSE OF THIS BOOK

The aim is to clear up some of the confusion surrounding BPR by presenting a balanced picture of what BPR is and how it can be successfully applied. Our hope is that it will encourage people both to think and, subsequently, adopt more balanced, holistic and humane approaches to BPR.

In the course of the book we will examine different views of BPR, how it can be used, what tools can support it, examples of its application, and the technology and people issues that need to be considered. The book complements other outputs of COBRA (1994–96); a project of the European Commission designed in part to subject the principles and practice of BPR to independent scrutiny.

The book does not attempt to present any final conclusions and recommendations of the COBRA project, as at the time of writing these have yet to be agreed. The various contributions have been selected from papers submitted by individuals who have contributed to the work of the COBRA team. No attempt has been made to impose a corporate view or style on the contributors. The opinions expressed are those of the individual authors and should not be taken as representing a statement of views of either the COBRA project team or the Commission of the European Communities.

THE BUSINESS ENVIRONMENT

To survive and prosper a business must adapt to the changing requirements of its customers and to other internal and external pressures. An organisation's response and the kind of change required will depend on its situation and circumstances.

A demanding and turbulent business environment, formidable competitors, technological innovation and low barriers to entry put a premium on learning, flexibility and responsiveness. The variety, scale and intensity of the challenges have made people receptive to talk of 'revolution'. Although not all enterprises face the imminent threat of extinction, some require more than mere evolutionary change.

The scaling back of internal resources to match declining external competitiveness can result in a negative spiral of cutbacks and layoffs. This may not be avoided by the incremental adaptation offered by Total Quality Management (TQM), or Kaizen. Companies are therefore turning to re-engineering, whether it be one or more of their business processes; their total organisation; or the way in which business is done within their particular marketplace.

ASPIRATIONS

The more ambitious managements are seeking 'corporate transformation' and 'breakout' to more flexible, responsive, 'horizontal' and team-based organisations. Networks of customers, suppliers and business partners are being developed to access resources irrespective of distance and time to meet the requirements of individual customers.

Virtually all the new models of more flexible organisation (and of different ways of working and learning) have been conceived and, in many cases, implemented quite independently of BPR. It would not have occurred to their creators to build-in most of the features and deficiencies of organisations (eg vertical functions) that BPR has been packaged to tackle.

Those 'organised by project' or offering tailored products and services may not have repetitive processes to re-engineer. It is paradoxical that most manifestations of BPR, with its rhetoric of radical change, depend for their survival on the continuing existence of traditional bureaucratic pyramids. Is BPR fighting yesterday's battles, rather than preparing us for tomorrow?

In time, re-engineering processes may come to be associated with attempts to keep alive activities, and the dying giants among organisations, that no longer have a compelling and distinctive rationale for existing. When these outdated forms of organisation, many of whose designs date from the 1940s and 1950s finally pass away, so too may many of the management techniques such as BPR that have derived from their problems.

RIGHT FOR THE MOMENT

We are in an era of transition between models of organisation with differing values and priorities. The desire for fundamental change could not have come at a better time. Due to the simultaneous availability of a number of complementary change elements, we have an unprecedented opportunity to transform the capacity of companies to harness the talents of people and deliver value to customers (Coulson-Thomas, 1992).

Where inspired by a vision of the future and properly used, BPR can represent a useful element in a corporate transformation programme or business excellence model. There is a danger that reaction against simplistic packaging, hype, and a focus on what BPR is not, may blind us to what it actually is and can do.

A sense of balance needs to be maintained. Best-practice experience of companies such as Rank Xerox suggests the thoughtful application of BPR at the level of an individual process can increase managerial productivity. This can be by a factor of ten or more according to such measures as throughput times. In Chapter 9 Brian Fitzgerald and Ciaran Murphy present an example of what can be achieved.

However, a word of caution is necessary. What little evidence there is (eg Hall, Rosenthal and Wade, 1993) concerning the impact of BPR on financial performance, suggests that most BPR projects result in little overall improvement.

In the rest of this chapter, we will examine what BPR is, its relevance, some of the principles from which it has been derived, and what is different and distinctive about it. We will look at the drivers of BPR, the choices to be made and some of the risks, concerns and danger areas that have emerged. Finally, some background is given on the COBRA project and the wider challenges and opportunities presented by the BPR phenomenon.

RE-ENGINEERING: A PROCESS VIEW

So what is BPR? There are almost as many answers to this question as there are commentators. In this book, Rohit Talwar (Chapter 2) presents a view of what BPR is and Clive Holtham (Chapter 3) focuses on what it is not. Karl Stroetmann and his colleagues Matthias Maier and Professor Walter Schertler (Chapter 4) examine the phenomenon from a German perspective.

People are at work re-engineering individual processes, organisations, markets, and even whole communities (Chapter 11). The wider the scope of the exercise, the greater the number of change elements that need to be brought under the BPR umbrella. Each generation has its radicals or social revolutionaries whose aim it is to re-engineer society. Re-engineering appeals to radicals and revisionists. It attacks the *status quo* and vested interests, and like other forms of revolutionary activity it can unleash unexpected forces and consume those who initiate it.

To appreciate what BPR is, and whether it is new, we need to go to its essence, the notion of processes and understand what these are. They normally consist of one or more inputs into one or more value adding activities that lead to one or more outputs. The boundary of a process defines its limits. Within a process there may be a number of sub-processes, and each activity may be made up of a number of tasks.

Business processes are sequences and combinations of activities that deliver value to a customer. Management processes control and coordinate these activities and ensure that business objectives are delivered. Support processes, as the name implies, provide infrastructural and other assistance to business processes.

Processes frequently cut horizontally across the vertical functional boundaries of the marketing, production, accounts and other departments found in traditional organisations. Various obstacles, barriers and sources of delay are encountered *en route*. In the past, these cross-functional paths have rarely been documented, and no one may have been responsible for them. Previous investments in training and IT are likely to have been departmental, rather than applied to the processes that actually deliver the outputs. Much past effort has been devoted to entrenching vertical channels of command and control, and to setting self-contained departmental procedures in concrete.

BPR takes a horizontal and process view. It is having the greatest impact where functional forms of organisation exist. The purpose of BPR is to radically improve the outputs or benefits of processes. Especially in relation to the resources they consume and the value they generate for the various stakeholders in an organisation.

THE RELEVANCE OF BPR

The opportunity to use BPR is least where most progress has been made in challenging and breaking down a functional form of organisation. In many creative organisations that excel in learning and flexibility of response, there is little scope for repeatable processes, or for the tools and approaches allied to them.

In practice, BPR is rarely associated with drives to introduce new ways of working and learning. There is little contact between those in personnel and elsewhere who are seeking to build learning organisations, and those who are undertaking BPR. Each group tends to attract different sorts of people. They usually speak different languages and they often live in different worlds.

In some instances, the use of BPR may so distort the focus and perspective of a review team as to act as a significant brake on creativity. Hence many of the more imaginative models of organisation and operation, and of working and learning, have emerged without any reference to BPR.

Some people are instinctive entrepreneurs and do not need a particular step in a management methodology labelled 'visioning' or 're-design' to encourage them to think creatively about identifying and delivering what represents value to customers. A different decor, a walk in the woods, a dose of rock music, even the use of a simple problem-solving tool can do more for creativity than ploughing through BPR methodologies.

IMPROVING PROCESSES

Processes vary in required-output production, cost-effectiveness, and flexibility. Ideally, there should be a process owner and clearly defined responsibilities. There should be measurement and feedback at each stage with continuous improvement built into the process. A process should also be documented. Where these conditions are not met, then *prima facie* there is scope for process improvement, even though more radical re-engineering may be rejected.

Processes can be assessed in various ways depending on the degree of change required. Thus:

1. Process simplification can yield significant but incremental improvements to what exists. This is done by cutting out non-value added activities, re-drawing departmental boundaries and empowerment to improve throughput times and save on resource requirements. It is not unusual to find 90 per cent or more of the non-value elapsed time occurring at the hot spots or hand-over points between functional departments.

2. In contrast, re-engineering involves radical change. This can mean the re-design or re-building of individual processes, a whole organisation, or the relationships between suppliers and customers. Such restructuring comes about after a 'blue skies' or vision led examination of the basic elements of people, processes, information and technology. This will look into new ways in which they can be brought together to achieve a fundamental transformation.

Some distinguishing features of simplification and re-engineering are shown in Table 1.1:

Table 1.1 *Simplification or Re-engineering?*

Process Simplification	Process Re-engineering
Incremental change	Radical transformation
Process-led	Vision-led
Within existing framework	Review framework
Improve application of technology	Introduce new technology
Assume attitudes and behaviour	Change attitudes and behaviour
Management led	Director led
Various simultaneous projects	Limited number of corporate initiatives

Source: Colin Coulson-Thomas, *Transforming the Company*, 1992

1. Simplification usually results in incremental rather than a major step change. Simplification exercises tend to take for granted an existing

framework, the limits of installed technology, and current attitudes and behaviour.

2. Re-engineering aims at fundamental or frame-breaking change. A re-engineering exercise would challenge the existing framework, question attitudes and behaviours, and might suggest the introduction of new technology.

In practice, approaches to change form a continuum (see Chapter 2) and the two can overlap. They are sometimes combined and are often confused. What is radical to some people could appear pedestrian to others.

. Many approaches to re-engineering are little more than process improvement or productivity tools re-named in order to capitalise on the growth of interest in BPR. These, and other approaches, should be used for the purposes for which they were designed and not be employed in contexts for which they are not suited.

Which approach (ie simplification or re-engineering) is best will depend on the situation and circumstances:

■ Over time, steady and continuing improvements could overtake the occasional big leap. In a dynamic marketplace, undertaking a BPR exercise every five years may not be enough. This is recognised by organisations that question and improve continuously. Occasional steps can be so significant as to be regarded as a jump from one improvement path to another.

■ On the other hand, as Matthias Maier points out in Chapter 10, the most committed incremental improver runs the risk of being leapfrogged by a creative innovator.

Breakthrough thinking leading to a step change can occur in both service and production environments, for example, First Direct introduced home banking. Lean manufacturing now replaces expensive stocks of components with deliveries from suppliers as and when they are required. It can also occur quite independently of BPR which, in itself, is neither a necessary nor sufficient requirement for organisational or marketplace innovation.

Most of what is termed BPR, and most of the (so called) BPR work that is undertaken is of the simplification variety. There are good reasons for this. Analysing and improving processes is laborious and time consuming. When radical change is required, the blue skies variety of BPR is often squeezed out. People go straight to a blank sheet of paper approach and realise that blue skies thinking does not necessarily require BPR, nor may it be helped by what has been packaged as BPR.

THE PRINCIPLES OF BPR

Various lists of points or principles of BPR and transformation (eg organise around outcomes rather than tasks) were produced as manuals or guidance notes within individual companies throughout the 1980s. Different compilations of these began to enter the public domain towards the end of the decade as major consultancies began to consolidate the experiences of their clients and strove to differentiate their offerings.

Individually, the principles that evolved during the 1980s have varied in their impact. Some now feature as elements of BPR, while others have been overlooked. For example:

- Externally, focus on end customers and the generation of greater value for customers. In contrast, some applications of quality appeared to put almost as much stress on internal customers as was placed on those who were external and who ultimately paid the bills.
- Give customers and users a single and accessible point of contact through which they can harness whatever resources and people are relevant to their needs and interests. This principle is driving many of the one-stop type BPR programmes within the public sector.
- Internally, focus on harnessing more of the potential of people and applying it to those activities which identify and deliver value to customers. This principle, and the next one, have tended to be overlooked in the packaging of BPR for public consumption.
- What matters is that people and other resources can be accessed and applied when required, not where they are located. Hence, the experimentation with teleworking in companies like Rank Xerox during the mid 1980s. (A decade later, a new generation of organisations is rediscovering the same lessons.)
- Encourage learning and development by building creative working environments. This principle has been almost forgotten, the current emphasis being on squeezing more out of people and working them harder, rather than improving the quality of working life and working more cleverly.
- Think and execute as much activity as possible horizontally, concentrating on flows and processes through the organisation. This concern led to the emergence of document management. However, in some of the flexible network and project based forms of organisation that are beginning to emerge, notions such as vertical or horizontal have little meaning.
- Remove non-value added activities, undertake parallel activities, speed up response and development times. Some consultants are placing great emphasis on competing on speed as this is an area in which significant and measurable improvements can be made.

- Concentrate on outputs rather than inputs, and link performance measures and rewards to customer related outputs. Customer and employee satisfaction surveys now provide key inputs into many corporate management processes.
- Give priority to the delivery of value rather than the maintenance of management control. The role of the manager is being redefined and an emphasis on command and control is giving way to empowerment, and the notion of the coach and facilitator.
- Network related people and activities. Various surveys undertaken in the late 1980s (summarised in Coulson-Thomas, 1992) revealed that the majority of chief executives aspired to a network form of organisation. More recently, 'virtual corporations' are becoming commonplace in some business sectors. The drivers here tend to be EDI, groupware, etc., rather than BPR *per se*.
- Move discretion and authority closer to the customer, and re-allocate responsibilities between the organisation, its suppliers and customers. The most visible expression of this is when people invert the pyramid in their diagrammatic portrayal of the corporation.
- Encourage involvement and participation. (Edna Murphy in Chapter 13 sets out the evidence and arguments in favour of participation.) Few today would question this principle, or the next two, but corporate practice does not always match rhetoric.
- Ensure people are equipped, motivated and empowered to do what is expected of them.
- Where ever possible, people should assume responsibility for managing and controlling themselves.
- Work should be broadened without sacrificing depth of expertise in strategic areas. The latter consideration tends to be overlooked today.
- Avoid over-sophistication. People are losing sight of this principle under a growing assault from suppliers of modelling and other BPR support tools that can encourage the collection and input of data at the expense of creative thinking.
- Keep the number of core processes in an organisation to a minimum. Some larger organisations have a bewildering array of processes. Many of these are operated by very able and committed people, but lack external customers. Management processes such as corporate planning processes which deliver too late to have any real impact can lack both internal and external customers.
- Build learning, renewal, and short feedback loops into processes. Where cursory attention is paid to this, and to the next principle, a re-engineered solution can become either commonplace, and no longer be a differentiator, or be overtaken by competitors.

■ Ensure that continuous improvement is built into implemented solutions. Experience of BPR can re-awaken interest in TQM, the two being natural complements.

The above list of a selection of BPR and transformation principles is intended to be illustrative rather than exhaustive. Different approaches and interpretations will generally not place the same combination of principles under the BPR umbrella. Certain principles could be given a priority in the context of a particular BPR exercise, while consultancies tend, naturally, to stress what they feel they can deliver.

BPR principles generally assume a bureaucratic form of organisation with functional departments. As transition occurs to forms of learning networks without traditional functional departments and with fewer repeatable processes, one can expect a repackaging and re-prioritisation of the elements included under the BPR umbrella.

WHAT DIFFERENTIATES RE-ENGINEERING?

Increasingly, BPR has come to mean all things to all people (see Nigel Courtney's selection of material on BPR in Chapter 15 which illustrates the diversity). Some consider BPR as one of a number of change elements that can be employed to transform organisations. Others use it as an umbrella term to embrace those change elements (eg empowerment, focus on process and customers) which they feel are particularly important.

Many of the individual elements of BPR are not new. Self-managed workgroups operated in Scandinavia long before they were discovered by enthusiasts of BPR. However, the combination of change elements under the umbrella of re-engineering does concentrate attention on processes and their outputs. As most organisations are still organised by vertical function rather than horizontal process, the potential benefits of such a focus ought to be considerable.

The rhetoric of BPR also encourages fundamental step, or frame-breaking, change. More management teams are now prepared to consider radical measures that may involve high risks. They have been emboldened by the dramatic (although localised or specific) increases in productivity which have been chalked up by well-publicised BPR exercises in US companies like Ford, GTE, Hallmark, Pacific Bell and Xerox. Response times have plunged from months to days, and from days to hours.

Buoyed up by some early successes with breakthrough (10x) levels of improvement, the hype and expectation now surrounding BPR are intense. If its advocates are to be believed, its impact could be as dramatic as that of the ironclad on Victorian navies. The race is on to transform bureaucratic organisations that are as inflexible and limited as wooden hulls and sails in comparison with other models.

DRIVERS

No-one should feel compelled to undertake BPR. Even where radical change is needed, activities such as creative thinking, benchmarking, corporate transformation, culture change and innovation can be undertaken quite independently of BPR. Many other frameworks and approaches exist, and these may or may not include the use of certain change elements that have been claimed by advocates of BPR.

Whether or not BPR is desirable will depend on the reasons for undertaking it. The motivations, or drivers, for considering or embracing re-engineering can be extremely varied. They could include survival, differentiation, competitive advantage, or a desire for early wins and quick fixes. Some of the drivers are negative, while others are positive.

BPR could be used as a cosmetic to demonstrate action, or to avoid difficult choices. It could be used to squeeze more blood out of managers already working harder than they have ever done before. Alternatively, it could liberate them from less essential and non-value added tasks in order to give them more time for creative thinking. Sadly, most BPR practitioners appear to achieve the former at the expense of the latter.

Other drivers of BPR include headcount and cost reduction rather than value to customers. In itself, BPR is a neutral instrument. We determine whether it turns out to be a help or a hindrance. Whether or not BPR is of central or marginal importance will depend on what it is applied to, how it is used and the goals that are set. (See Chapter 5 on initiating and preparing for BPR.)

THE CHOICE

Many organisations face a stark choice between evolution and revolution. Will incremental improvement be enough? Given the frame-breaking changes that are possible, the consequences for the laggards could be dire. Will gung-ho re-engineered US corporations sweep the board of their more hesitant European competitors? Or will they come a cropper.

In deciding whether to seek incremental improvements or a step change in performance, the following could be among the factors that are considered:

■ How well is the organisation performing, and how big is the gap between where it is and where it would like to be? Could the gap be bridged by improving or building on what already exists?

Alternatively, is the gap so large that the organisation needs to throw away and start again?

■ What else is happening? Have customers suddenly become more demanding? Are other similar organisations performing significantly better? Has an innovative development occurred which is revolutionizing existing ways of operating? Is there a need to respond to a radically different direction and strategy?

■ How stable is the environment, or framework, within which the organisation operates? Where the environment is relatively static or unchanged from one year to the next, a management team may not feel under any particular imperative to change. However, it might still opt to undertake some blue skies thinking about different ways in which an existing product or service might be delivered.

■ Is the model of organisation and mode of operation appropriate in the situation and circumstances? Does organisational capability match both organisational vision and customer requirements? If the answer to these questions is no, then a radical transformation may be required. If, however, an organisation is thought to be broadly appropriate, then all that may be required is fine tuning in areas of relative deficiency.

Much of what is termed re-engineering operates within an existing framework of attitudes and assumptions, and does not radically challenge them. To the purist, BPR is about revolution rather than evolution, fundamental change not incremental improvement. This book, and other outputs from the European Commission's COBRA (1994–96) project, is concerned with the radical change end of the spectrum.

RELATIONSHIP WITH TQM

The benefits of BPR largely derive from thinking, organising and acting horizontally, ie in terms of cross-functional processes, rather than vertically in terms of specialist functions and departments. Radical improvements result from challenging assumptions, breaking down barriers, innovative uses of technology, introducing new ways of working, changing relationships and re-drawing traditional boundaries. What is sought could be a longer term increase in capability and competitiveness.

TQM is more concerned with continuous improvement within an agreed framework. The benefits are more likely to be short term and limited to the immediate context. Various quality groups could work at points along a cross-functional process. Particular activities may be examined from a departmental perspective rather than considering the process as a whole from the perspective of an end customer.

TQM can complement BPR, as when subsequent learning and refinements are built into a re-engineered solution. Many of the tools and techniques of quality can also be, and are, used in the course of BPR exercises.

However, in comparison with BPR, TQM can be a blunt instrument. Thus quality improvement groups could be set up to examine all sorts of activities, whether or not these form part of a critical process. The author recalls helping the senior management team of one household-name corporation. It was discovered that not one of several thousand quality improvement teams in operation was focused on any of the top ten factors they believed would ultimately determine whether or not the company would live or die.

TQM should result in a focus on both internal and external customers. Thus it could be a useful precursor to BPR, which in turn has been spoken of as a successor to TQM. However, the primary focus of BPR is on end customers. Ultimately, the external customer is the source of all value and of the rationale of an organisation. On occasion, satisfying internal customers can be a distraction.

THE RISKS

Not for the first time there is a huge gulf between rhetoric and reality. Less well known than the benefits are the risks involved in radical change, the BPR exercises that have stalled and the revolutions that have failed. In spite of the potential and opportunity for radical change, few transformation programmes are bringing about the required changes of attitudes or behaviour.

Re-engineering can be risky and should not be undertaken lightly. Before jumping in, an organisation needs to clarify its motives, decide how much change is required and establish the scope of what it is trying to do (again see Chapter 5). For example, is it engaged in BPR or wholescale corporate transformation?

There are risks to be balanced, both of action and non-action. What are the alternatives? For example, what are the longer term implications of today's cost cuttings? If the rhetoric is to be believed, and US competitors are re-engineering, how come so many European CEOs sleep at night?

BPR is suffering from over exposure (and getting too early into the wrong hands). Already, in some applications, it is going off the rails, even before it is properly understood. Quite simply, even given a strong desire to succeed, many BPR exercises are failing to deliver the hoped-for benefits. Also, while BPR may suit a US culture with its faith in action, single solutions and fixing problems, in Europe many CEOs tend to be more cautious and guarded.

EMERGING CONCERNS

BPR may have been over-sold. The more aware BPR practitioners also warn of 'processism'. Whereas a focus on process can be healthy, an obsession with it and a belief that all one has to do is establish the right processes and nothing but good will follow, can be unhealthy. Judgement and quality of decisions are still needed. Rubbish flowing along world-class processes will just produce disappointment more quickly than before.

Outstanding processes will not save a group from the consequences of inadequate business judgement. Thus, having undertaken a role model BPR exercise did not prevent Mutual Benefit Life Insurance Company from filing for Chapter 11 protection.

Very often what is described as BPR turns out on closer examination to be process improvement or simplification. Such initiatives may result in worthwhile increases in performance, but they are unlikely to produce the dramatic transformations promised by advocates of re-engineering.

Over time, BPR practice may regress from the radical transformation end of the spectrum in the direction of simplification and improvement as the term becomes more widely appropriated by those working on processes or simply managing change.

DANGER AREAS

Some applications of BPR can be positively dangerous. Repeatable processes may not exist in creative, dynamic environments. In many fast moving contexts, each path through the organisation in response to an individual problem or opportunity may be unique. Establishing, documenting and supporting particular paths may create a new set of inflexibilities. These can be the organisational equivalent of turning the flexible responses of the human brain into the programmed approach of the robot.

Creative thinking has hitherto been discouraged by command and control and procedure based approaches to management. Some CEOs who would now like to attempt BPR are insecure. They doubt the ability of their people to deliver, and are uncertain about whom to trust externally.

The questions of confidence and trust are critical. Boards and senior management need to have confidence in the ability of their teams to deliver, and belief in the objectivity and competence of their advisers. Both are more likely to occur where there is openness and trust, a balanced view of BPR, the helps and hindrances have been thought through, and likely obstacles have been identified and assessed.

As I report in my book *Transforming the Company* (1992) most change programmes falter because they are incomplete. Where success occurs it is usually because other change elements are employed alongside BPR. A holistic approach is required, comprised of the critical elements that will make it happen in a particular context. By itself, BPR may not be able to deliver.

Re-engineering, as opposed to incremental improvement, requires a willingness to be bold. To get the full benefit of BPR, an organisation must want to change and be prepared to ask challenging and fundamental questions. Sustained top management commitment is also required. There is little point starting a BPR exercise if top management is complacent or does not have the fibre to see it through.

STAFFING LEVELS

Within Europe, some concern has been expressed about the employment consequences of more widespread adoption of BPR. Does it automatically equate with a headcount reduction? Advocates of BPR counter with reminders that a failure to remain competitive can lead to liquidation and the consequent loss of all jobs.

BPR exercises almost invariably result in fewer people being required to deliver previous levels of service. However, lower levels of employment are not inevitable. For example, customers may wish to have more direct contact with people providing a personal service and may be prepared to pay for this. Also a focus on improving the quality of working life could lead to developments such as job sharing.

Whether or not, and the extent to which, staffing levels actually are reduced will depend on the motivations underlying an individual BPR exercise:

■ If the intention is to find a more cost-effective way of delivering an existing service and to compete on price, then advantage may be taken of the opportunity to achieve a headcount saving or to move jobs off-shore to cheaper locations.
■ If the intention is to differentiate by doing more than has hitherto been possible, then staff released from traditional tasks may be redeployed to other activities that generate greater value for customers or create new business opportunities.

Much will depend on the extent to which an organisation is under pressure to reduce its budget or costs. Where the pressure is intense, an organisation may feel compelled to sacrifice a longer term competitive advantage in order to achieve a short term cost saving.

Where a BPR exercise helps to differentiate an organisation and improve its competitive positioning, the longer term consequence could be an increase of staffing levels in a number of areas. Increases in employment (or a slower rate of scaling down) may also be experienced by suppliers and business partners.

BPR that results in relative gains in competitiveness could mean some firms hire while less successful rivals fire. However, genuine innovation could generate new employment opportunities and create rather than move jobs.

CONSEQUENCES FOR SKILLS AND THE NATURE OF WORK

While BPR is likely to change skill requirements, it should not be assumed that skill levels will be higher or lower *per se* after a BPR exercise. Thus multi-skilling is more likely to be a requirement following BPR. On occasion, when it is introduced, breadth is secured at the expense of depth.

Some BPR solutions consciously set out to de-skill (eg perhaps by centralisation and the rule based automation of an activity), and certain specialist skills may be lost as a result of defining roles more broadly. Specifying the steps to be taken could increase the flow of work and reduce variation at the cost of de-skilling.

Solving one problem can create another. For example, specifying steps and automating processes can result in staff processing transactions and dealing with bits of paper, and forgetting the people behind the transactions.

BPR can have a significant impact on how work is done, if not on where it is done. Rather than working in isolation on individual tasks, people may, post-BPR, undertake related tasks together. This can be more rewarding for those involved, when considering a number of aspects together can result in a more balanced solution from the point of view of the customer, as well as allowing each person to see his or her contribution to the whole.

New ways of working can be at the heart of re-engineering, as the ambitious seek corporate transformation to the more flexible, responsive, horizontal and team based organisations mentioned earlier. In many organisations, the groups responsible for BPR exercises and for introducing new ways of working are quite separate and do not communicate. While those ostensibly responsible for BPR pore over the latest software package for modelling processes (see Chapter 8 on the use of tools and technology within a BPR initiative), people elsewhere (who may have little or no involvement with BPR) are radically changing how work is done, and hence could be said to be re-engineering.

THE EUROPEAN SITUATION

An examination of business restructuring across Europe suggests that many managements are approaching their tasks with all the subtlety of a butcher with a chain saw. The driver is headcount reduction, or reducing the cost base, rather than value to customers or employee satisfaction.

Greater openness and honesty are required. Many attempts at involvement and participation, especially in subsidiaries of US companies, are crude in the extreme. Speeches and videos are made about how middle managers need to put their backs into initiatives that are likely to result in the elimination of their jobs.

The European Commission has recognised that many change programmes are not working and that unthinking and uncaring restructuring leads to the crude downsizing and hollowing out of enterprises, with traumatic human consequences. The key to the Commission's interest in BPR lies in its White Paper *Growth, Competitiveness, Employment – The challenges and ways forward into the 21st century* (1993). Will restructuring lead to greater unemployment? Will the hollowed out companies be able to compete with the best from North America and Japan?

Is there a better way? How might innovative and enlightened implementation regenerate the capacity and capability of enterprises and communities to compete, deliver value and satisfaction, and offer people a richer variety of work and lifestyle opportunities?

COBRA

COBRA (Constraints & Opportunities in Business Restructuring – an Analysis), is an initiative of the European Commission designed to cut through the hype and examine what is actually happening. It is the largest such study ever undertaken of BPR across Europe. Members of the core COBRA team advise the governments of five EU member states on BPR and related work issues. The initiative is led and coordinated by the author.

COBRA (1994–96) has led to reports on current practice and future prospects, case studies and methodologies for ensuring that issues relating to new patterns of work and supply chains are fully taken into account during re-engineering projects. Additionally, the selection of submitted material presented in this book is designed to contribute to a more balanced and rounded understanding of BPR.

The main organisations involved are corporate transformation specialists Adaptation Ltd; The Home Office Partnership based in Cambridge, England; empirica GmbH of Bonn, Germany; two Brussels based companies Euro PR SA and CELSA SA; and the Department of Business Administration of the Greek University of the Aegean. Support has also been provided by a number of sponsoring organisations which include ACT Business Systems, A T Kearney, CCTA, Mercury Communications, 3Com, and the Learning Systems Institute.

Issues

There are many fundamental issues for the COBRA team to examine. For example:

- Is BPR leading people towards, or away from, the learning organisation? Does its nature inevitably lead to a focus on certain outcomes (eg cost and time saving) at the expense of others (eg creativity and time for reflection and learning)?
- Is BPR, in itself, leading to the introduction of new ways of working? (Simon Robinson examines the link between BPR and teleworking in Chapter 7.)
- Is BPR perpetuating outdated models of organisation and mechanistic attitudes and approaches? Is it helping to keep alive organisations that either no longer have a rationale for existing, or should be subjected to more radical treatment?
- How do the requirements for corporate transformation differ from those for re-engineering a particular process or for introducing TQM?
- How do transformation goals, for example, survival, differentiation, competitive advantage or a desire for quick fixes, influence success requirements?
- How many organisations actually need BPR? What are the implications of seeking radical rather than incremental change?
- Given the European cultural context is different from that in which quality and BPR initially took root, what might a European alternative look like?
- Are methodologies a help or a hindrance? How might they result in people thinking rather than acting like automata? (See Chapter 6 on implementing BPR.)
- Are individual BPR consultants facilitators or parasites? Who is learning from whom? How does the client distinguish the good from the bad?
- How does one address the human issues (see Chapter 12 by Hamid Aghassi), and especially the critical areas of attitudes, beliefs and behaviour?

- How should management processes be used to achieve focus, direction, and the application of BPR to what is strategically important?
- Can BPR deliver in time? What should one do when the timescale to achieve fundamental change may extend beyond the lifetime of the change requirement?
- Can flexible forms of organisations be created and thrive in a social context of restrictive attitudes, and a reluctance to challenge and change long established practices?
- Do approaches to BPR need to be modified to take account of the European business and cultural environment? There is, rightly, a suspicion in Europe of supposed panaceas that are imported from the US.

Impartial guidance does seem to be needed. Many of those leading European initiatives in pioneers such as Rank Xerox and Texas Instruments are strongly encouraged by, and can learn from, US colleagues. In contrast, those seeking to introduce home grown initiatives into, say, a German company might be stifled by cautious, if not cynical, and conservative colleagues.

THE CHALLENGE

BPR represents a challenge for both public and private decision makers. The evidence being examined by the COBRA team suggests the European Commission is right to be concerned about Europe's labour costs and the competitiveness of its labour market:

- Innovative firms often shed rather than create jobs. Companies that are transforming their organisations to new network forms are identifying a range of activities, especially back office tasks, that could be performed at almost any location that can be accessed by telephone. As a consequence, jobs are being lost in areas where the costs of employing or utilising people are high, and transferred to other locations where they are cheaper.
- The poorer peripheral regions of the community could be the gainers. This also applies to off-shore locations, such as the Caribbean, Far East, India or Mexico where skilled labour may exist in some quantity and at a fraction of the cost in Europe. Radical thinking could lead to a new division of labour and the export of jobs. The true scale of this phenomenon is hidden as greenfield investments elsewhere in the world do not appear in statistics of jobs moved.

The political debate concerning employment could itself benefit from a first-principles review. Perhaps what is perceived as a problem could turn out to be an opportunity. Re-engineering could so easily be used to re-think the purpose of the enterprise, or to introduce new ways of working and learning.

Also, what is so great about work when compared to working out, or walking in the woods, or listening to the blues? Due to advances in productivity we no longer need so many people to produce a wide range of goods. This offers us the prospect of lives built around hobbies and interests rather than work. Social attitudes and expectations need to adjust to both the realities and the alternatives.

If organisations and their people are to reap the full benefits of BPR, attitudes and behaviours will have to change. A negative focus on cost cutting or squeezing more out of people is causing widespread alienation. Fundamental changes need to occur within ourselves before more civilised living and working environments can be created. In Chapter 14 Wanda D'hanis argues that if BPR is to live up to its claims to be radical it must reach down to the 'radies' or roots of business life itself.

More positive approaches are called for. Improving learning or the quality of working life are key drivers of far too few BPR initiatives, yet BPR could enable us to obtain far greater control over our lives. Other outputs of the COBRA (1994–96) project will examine how a wider range of options for working at times and locations of our choice can be explored during the course of a BPR exercise.

Departmental and blinkered thinking and the protection of functional interests can reach all the way through an organisation into the boardroom. Many directors have narrow visions and little understanding of corporate transformation. Changes at the top are needed. These may be hastened by BPR as management boards come increasingly to consist of process owners rather than heads of functions.

A FATAL FLAW?

The very term re-engineering is an unfortunate one. Betraying its North American origins, it adopts an instrumental approach and tends to treat organisations as machines. What doesn't work gets fixed, pieces are taken out, changed and replaced. However, whatever is done to a machine it remains a machine. Unlike an organism, it cannot transmute into something else.

In reality, as my book *Transforming the Company* (1992) points out, organisations are living communities of people. They are sensitive organisms, reflecting our dreams and fears. Knowledge workers are increasingly attracted to those networks whose values they share.

The acronym 'COBRA', and its association with a snake, suggests danger. Much can be learned from the board game Snakes and Ladders. The player landing on the head of a snake moves down and back to its tail, while the more fortunate arriving at the foot of a ladder shoots up it to its top. BPR can be either a snake or a ladder depending on how it is used.

The aim of COBRA is to help reduce the risks involved with BPR and its harmful consequences, by encouraging its more thoughtful, sensitive, humane and inspired application.

THE OPPORTUNITY

In reality BPR is not out to get us. It is how we use it, to what ends, and to what it is applied that will determine whether or not it bites us. It could be undertaken with the express purpose of improving the quality of working life, introducing new ways of working and learning, and widening job opportunities.

BPR should not be allowed to become an alternative to creative thinking about ways of achieving policy outcomes. Neither should the limitations of some applications of BPR blind us to the value of blue skies thinking, of imagination and of creativity. There are models of organisations that make it much easier for people to be true to themselves and to work in ways, and at times and places, that enable them to give of their best.

BPR may mean little to the small business that cannot afford enough people to establish functional departments in the first place. However, BPR need not be a big company phenomenon. There are market sectors, such as the supply of spectacles, where small rather than large firms have been the innovators. They have simply harnessed more of the potential and commitment of their people and out-thought the competition.

We live in a world in which insight and initiative could allow almost any organisation, regardless of size, to become world-class. Already, the COBRA study is revealing that size and scale are not the guarantors of business success they were once thought to be. Being the best, remaining focused on what one does best, and improving the quality of life are becoming more significant as corporate goals. The organisation that knows what it is about, and does it supremely well is sought out as a business partner, while the lonely giant that is average at lots of things quietly dies.

FURTHER INFORMATION

The outputs of the EU COBRA project comprising methodology manual, 21 case studies, briefings and notes on 101 techniques are published as a three volume boxed set of reports edited by Colin Coulson-Thomas: *The*

Responsive Organisation: Re-engineering new patterns of work by Policy Publications (Tel: +44 (0) 171 240 3488; Fax: +44 (0) 171 240 2768), London, November 1995.

The COBRA methodology, developed to provide a framework for the re-engineering of supply chains through the enabling technologies of electronic commerce, has also been published along with nine detailed case studies as: *The Competitive Network* by Policy Publications (Tel: +44 (0) 171 240 3488; Fax: +44 (0) 171 240 2768), London, April 1996, a report on research by Peter Bartram, Colin Coulson-Thomas and Lee Tate.

Companies that would like to learn more about the COBRA project and share its findings are invited to contact the Project Leader (Prof. Colin Coulson-Thomas) at the COBRA Project Office, Rathgar House, 237 Baring Road, Grove Park, London SE12 0BE, England (Tel: +44 (0) 181 857 5907; Fax: +44 (0) 181 857 5947); or via the Faculty Office, Faculty of Management, University of Luton at Putteridge Bury, Hitchin Road, Luton, Bedfordshire LU2 8LE (Tel: + 44 (0) 1582 482555; Fax: +44 (0) 1582 482689).

BIBLIOGRAPHY

COBRA (1994), *Business restructuring and teleworking: Current practice.* (Report for the Commission of the European Communities), London: Adaptation.

COBRA (1994), *Business restructuring and teleworking: Issues, considerations and approaches.* (Methodology manual for the Commission of the European Communities), London: Adaptation.

COBRA (1994), *Business restructuring and teleworking: Selected cases.* (Report for the Commission of the European Communities), London: Adaptation.

COBRA (1994), *Business restructuring and teleworking: Future prospects.* (Report for the Commission of the European Communities), London: Adaptation.

COBRA (1995), Colin Coulson-Thomas (Executive Editor), *The Responsive Organisation: Re-engineering new patterns of work.* London: Policy Publications.

COBRA (1996), Peter Bartram, Colin Coulson-Thomas and Lee Tate, *The Competitive Network.* London: Policy Publications.

Commission of The European Communities (1993), Growth, competitiveness, employment: The challenges and ways forward into the 21st Century. White Paper. *Bulletin of the European Commission*, Supplement 6/93.

Coulson-Thomas, C. (1992), *Transforming the company: Bridging the gap between management myth and corporate reality.* London: Kogan Page.

Hall, G., Rosenthal, J. and Wade, J. (1993), How to make re-engineering really work. *Harvard Business Review*, November/December, pp. 119–131.

2

Re-engineering –
a Wonder Drug for the 90s?

Rohit Talwar

RE-ENGINEERING – IS THERE LIFE BEYOND THE HYPE?

Re-engineering has rapidly become the most fashionable and potentially most detested management concept of the 90s. Part of the reason for the dramatic growth in interest lies in the simplicity of the underlying idea. Re-engineering offers the promise of dramatic improvements in performance through streamlining the end-to-end processes by which the business creates and delivers value for its customers.

While some organisations have embraced re-engineering wholeheartedly, others have rejected it outright – often without any real understanding of what it is or how it can be made to work. Many have been put off by the excessive hype and dramatic claims of those seeking to sell re-engineering products and services.

Sadly, the hype and cycles of claim and counter-claim about re-engineering have obscured the issues that are actually of greatest importance. In this chapter my aim is to sidestep the hype and focus on providing the reader with an insight into the most critical issues and the management challenges they present.

The initial challenges for any organisation considering re-engineering are to understand the concept and gain a clear understanding of what it takes to achieve success. Armed with this knowledge the organisation must then make an honest assessment of whether it has, or can build, the managerial capability and commitment required to drive through such a fundamental and far-reaching programme of change.

To help the reader build the necessary understanding and make the required self assessment, this chapter addresses the following questions:

- What is re-engineering?
- What are the fundamental breakthroughs required to ensure the success?
- How are the opportunities being interpreted?
- What are the key steps in the re-engineering process?
- What role should technology play in the change process?
- What are the factors critical to the success of a re-engineering initiative?
- Is your organisation ready for re-engineering?

WHAT IS RE-ENGINEERING ?

Defining the concept

While there may be some debate about who originated the concept, the term 're-engineering' was first introduced into common business usage in 1990 in a seminal Harvard Business Review article: *Reengineering Work: Don't Automate Obliterate*[1]. The article's author was Michael Hammer, a former Computer Science professor at the Massachusetts Institute of Technology. Hammer then went on to develop the concept further in a book: *Reengineering the Corporation*[2], written jointly with James Champy. They provided the following definition:

> Reengineering is the fundamental rethinking and redesign of business processes to achieve dramatic improvements in critical, contemporary measures of performance, such as cost, quality, service, and speed.

Rethinking functions and processes

The implication of the Hammer and Champy definition is that we should be concentrating on processes rather than functions as the central focus for the design and management of business activity. For the purpose of this paper, a process is considered to be a *sequence of activities performed on one or more inputs to deliver an output to the customer of the process*. Typical examples might include fulfilling a customer order, issuing a new insurance policy and developing a new product. Functions are the task- or skill-based groupings around and into which most of us organise our activities, eg manufacturing, finance, sales and distribution.

The rationale behind re-engineering is that most organisations are not designed to support the actual work that they do – the execution of business processes to create and deliver goods and services to their customers. In most cases, the organisation's structure is defined before thinking about how the work will actually be performed. As a result, the steps in the execution of a process – such as processing an insurance claim – are usually divided up across several departments or functions within that structure.

Defining the challenges

In practice, while the customer is interested in the end-to-end or horizontal process, the organisation itself is often focused inwardly and on the vertical chains of command through which it manages its departments. Herein lies the first problem, to service the customer, work may have to flow across departmental divides. Each hand-off to another department introduces another potential source of delay in the process because the recipient department may be working to a different set of priorities. In such circumstances it is frequently the case that doing what is right for the customer is not necessarily what will satisfy your manager. As a result, on entering each new department the work goes into a queue awaiting processing according to its priorities.

A second critical problem which re-engineering seeks to address is the combination of lack of trust and limited training. In many cases, inspections, authorisations and sign-offs are introduced to 'prevent' those actually doing the work from making mistakes or defrauding the organisation. Again, the wait for approval can introduce extra delays.

Hence, a key challenge in re-engineering is one of empowerment, this implies giving staff:

- the training to perform a variety of roles within a process, thereby improving flexibility
- areas of responsibility to make decisions on behalf of the organisation without seeking managerial approval
- the authority to fulfil those responsibilities and a supportive environment which allows them to learn from mistakes.

However, while the headlines appear simple and attractive, the more closely we look at re-engineering, the more it becomes apparent that sustainable performance gains are unlikely to be brought about simply by redesigning the processes and telling people they are empowered. In each organisation the processes were designed by people, often in managerial positions, with a particular perspective or 'mindset' on how work should be done. It is that mindset that led them to design processes with the premise that people could not be trusted, to divide tasks across departmental boundaries, to introduce controls and inspections and to limit the flow of information to those on the front line.

Hence, I view the real challenge in re-engineering to be one of:

Changing mindset, attitude and behaviour to allow the fundamental rethinking and redesign of business activities, structures and working relationships in order to maximise added value and achieve radical and sustainable improvements in all aspects of business performance.

The re-engineering spectrum

A measure of the different way in which organisations have interpreted the concept of re-engineering lies in the range of ambition of those who are applying it (Fig. 2.1). The value of the spectrum is that it provides a guide to the degree of mindset change, typical scope, target gains and risk of each approach as described below:

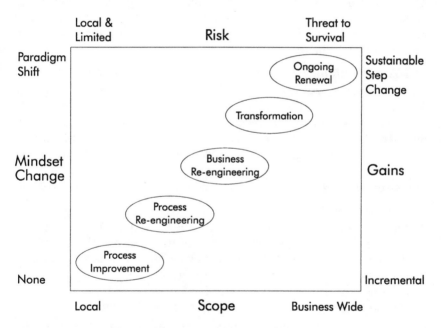

Fig. 2.1 The re-engineering spectrum

Process improvement

This approach is being adopted by a number of firms but is not re-engineering in the truest sense of the word. It usually entails improvement of that part of a process that falls within a particular function rather than of the entire end-to-end process (eg the financial appraisal task within a new product development process). As such the focus tends to be on improving the tasks that are done rather than eliminating the delays between each step. Typically the need for the process goes unchallenged and there is little critical appraisal of the overall process. Such initiatives can yield improvements of five to twenty per cent but rarely have a noticeable impact on overall business performance.

Process re-engineering

This is the approach adopted by the largest group doing what one would call 'true re-engineering'. This involves the fundamental rethinking and radical streamlining or total redesign of an end-to-end process and may start with the question 'should we be doing it all?' Such projects are usually targeted to deliver step change improvements of fifty per cent or more in critical measures of process performance such as cost, perceived quality and cycle time.

Process re-engineering should only be adopted if the desired improvements cannot be achieved using less painful and demanding approaches. The impact of successful initiatives can show through on the bottom line. However, if only one or two processes are redesigned then much of the business remains untouched and there will be only a marginal overall improvement in the organisation's performance.

Business re-engineering

This approach is typically adopted by firms that are seeking step change improvements across all of their processes. Hence, there is usually greater emphasis on appraisal and redesign of the entire business architecture. Such approaches usually demand significant top-level commitment and active involvement. Success will be demonstrable through step change improvements in both the performance of individual processes and of the business as a whole.

Transformation

A small but growing number of organisations are recognising that there is a need to 'reinvent the business'. Such firms start by asking why they exist and what they are trying to achieve. Only then do they go on to look at how they actually run their processes to achieve those goals.

A number of firms would claim to have undergone a successful transformation. The tests of a genuine transformation might include:

- Step change improvements against all critical measures/benchmarks of business performance.
- The perception amongst staff that the business is a dramatically better place to work than 3–5 years ago.
- A belief amongst customers, suppliers and other business partners that the organisation has become far easier and far better to work with and has helped them save time and cost.
- Organisation-wide clarity of purpose, direction, business architecture, capabilities and true mission, for example, Haagen-Dazs made the breakthrough when it realised that its mission was to sell pleasure not ice cream.

Ongoing renewal

Those that have completed successful transformations recognise that the process never actually stops. The techniques and newly shaped mindset have to become part of the organisation's DNA so that it can continue to refocus and reinvent itself as the world around it changes.

In practice, the majority of initiatives currently being labelled as re-engineering sit somewhere between process improvement and process re-engineering. There is no implicit criticism or praise associated with being at any point on the spectrum. The important thing it brings out is the need for honesty and clear communications between all involved. There is little point in the chief executive talking about transformation and expecting equivalent performance gains if those running and designing the initiative are actually focused on achieving more humble performance improvements. Similarly, there is little point attempting transformation if the techniques used are only ever likely to deliver more limited gains.

ACHIEVING THE PAYOFF – IDENTIFYING THE FUNDAMENTAL BREAKTHROUGHS

There has been much talk of the benefits and scale of potential returns on the re-engineering investment. However, while some have reaped rich rewards, for many of the organisations that have tried to apply it, re-engineering has failed to live up to its initial promise. The reason in many cases is that the latter have not made the necessary breakthroughs to new ways of thinking and working.

The experience of those that have realised dramatic gains suggests that there are six critical areas (Fig. 2.2) in particular in which attitudes and approaches need to be overturned completely. As can be seen from the outline given below, the emphasis is on forcing the organisation to tackle head-on many of the complexities and inefficiencies that have evolved over time and now act as a major hindrance to progress:

Process-based

The traditional hierarchical and inward-looking management philosophy has to be replaced by an obsessive commitment to adding value for customers. This forces us to look at the business from the outside in and to concentrate on the end-to-end management of the processes which serve those customers.

Fundamental rethink

Adopting a fundamental or zero-based approach to the redesign of key processes places the spotlight on three key issues:

START POINT >	BREAKTHROUGH >	OUTCOME >
• Function/Hierarchy driven organisations	PROCESS BASED	• Customer led • Added value focus • End to End management
• Layered complexity • Friction and Conflict	FUNDAMENTAL RETHINK	• Zero based • First principles redesign
• Incremental gains • Decreasing ROI	RADICAL IMPROVEMENT	• Step change • Sustainable
• Single focus improvements • Incoherent change	INTEGRATED CHANGE	• Balanced improvement • Viable solutions
• Command and control • Fear and confusion	PEOPLE CENTRED	• Empowerment and involvement • Business awareness
• Unwritten rules and constraints • Tied to history	MINDSET CHANGE	• Learning organisation • Forward looking

Fig. 2.2 Fundamental breakthroughs

1. The extent to which the current structure detracts from the creation and delivery of value by introducing complexity and delays.
2. The retarding effect that structure can have on any attempt to introduce change.
3. The unresolved cross-functional conflicts and tensions that create internal friction and divert energy away from serving the customer.

Radical improvement

All too often grand ambitions and radical options for change are gradually scaled down in the face of organisational politics and apparently immovable constraints. The resulting change may end up costing the same but delivering only a fraction of the intended benefits. Hence, the emphasis should be on achieving dramatic and sustainable leaps in performance. Re-engineering is not an appropriate solution if the gains can be achieved using an alternative approach.

Integrated change

When a major change initiative is added to the business agenda, we find that nothing is removed and the pressures on all involved increases. Furthermore, personal ambition can lead those at senior levels to launch competing initiatives or suggest delaying tactics that divert attention and resources and add to the confusion for those involved. Finally, these initiatives are often based around the functional focus of those who introduced them rather than taking the cross-functional perspective that best serves the customer.

Hence, the approach taken should attempt to deliver a balanced and holistic solution for which the relevant systems, people and training have been put in place. In this way we can help ensure the viability of the solution and the sustainability of the gains.

People centred

Despite the rhetoric about managers as coaches, empowerment, open cultures and support for innovation, the reality is that old-style managers, risk avoidance and fear still dominate the industrial scene. Furthermore, those in newly empowered cultures often lack the understanding of the business goals and the knowledge of its processes to be able to make decisions and take risks on behalf of the organisation.

Mindset change

The sixth and final breakthrough demands that we jettison much of the intellectual baggage and conditioning that binds us to the past. This requires us to build and communicate a shared understanding of the organisation's preferred future, create an environment and infrastructure that actively promotes learning and allows imagination — not conditioning — to guide our decisions.

HOW ARE THE OPPORTUNITIES BEING INTERPRETED?

Corporate anorexia or growth hormone?

The motivations for those considering re-engineering can be categorised into two broad groupings (Fig. 2.3). The majority of initiatives are motivated by a desire to cut costs – treating re-engineering as just the next wave of corporate anorexia. Obviously, enhanced customer service will always be a motivation, but the underlying cost concerns tend to dominate.

The problem in such cases is that the overriding concern for cost reduction force us to focus on historic cost information as our starting point. The risk is that we then create a redesigned process to meet the needs of yesterday rather than tomorrow. Furthermore, those at the top tend to be concerned solely with achieving the desired outcomes and have little commitment to the change process itself.

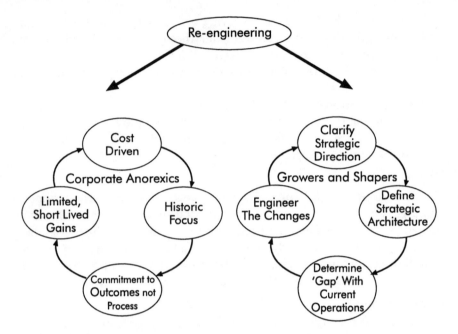

Fig. 2.3 *Interpreting the opportunities*

The champions trying to promote re-engineering are often forced to play down the pain and emphasise the gain in the hope that attitudes will soften – they rarely do. Indeed any failure to deliver dramatic quick wins can lead to a hardening of attitudes and an even narrower focus on the need for cost reduction.

The result of paying little attention to the change process and the so-called soft factors invariably results in a failure to realise the anticipated gains. Staff who do not understand the change and feel left out and undervalued are unlikely to be motivated to give their all to the organisation. The result is a downwards spiral of cost cutting programmes which deliver, at best, short lived gains and which serve to weaken still further the very heart and soul of the organisation.

The second, more optimistic, but currently less popular, motivation is that of rethinking the organisation and creating a platform from which to grow and shape future success. This normally involves a four stage process:

Clarify strategic direction

The aim here is to create a clear and widely communicated picture of our:

- Vision – how the world should feel for our stakeholders.
- Mission – how we will actually add value for those stakeholders.

- Goals – the desired scope, scale and speed of growth for our operations.
- Commercial proposition – the capabilities, resources, partnerships, alliances, products and services which will help us achieve success.
- Stakeholders – all those who believe they have in interest in how the business performs.
- Performance measures – the balanced scorecard of indicators through which we will measure progress and performance against stakeholder expectations.

Define strategic architecture

This involves creating the organisational blueprint (Fig. 2.4) or road map that sets out how we will achieve our strategic direction. The rationale is that, traditionally, we have started with an organisation's structure and then tried to map work to it. The architectural blueprint works to a different premise. The thinking here is that the infrastructure should actually be designed to enable the efficient working of the processes which allow us to exploit our distinctive capabilities in support of our strategy.

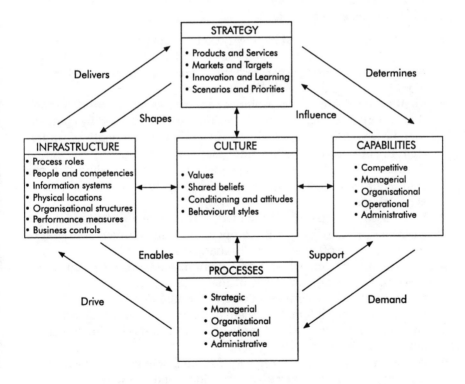

Fig. 2.4 *Defining strategic architecture*

Determine gap with current operations

Having mapped out the desired strategic architecture, we can then evaluate where we are now and assess the gap between the two.

Engineer the changes

After assessing the size of the gap we can then decide how best to close it and whether we will do it using a series of discrete steps or a big bang – 'total change' approach. The decision will again be based on the commitment and capability of those who will lead the change and the urgency with which it is required. Engineering the change for most companies is typically an iterative process which involves a series of discrete steps through which they rethink and reinvent the organisation.

Rethinking the organisation

Outlined below are the objectives for the three key elements of the 'total rethink' approach to re-engineering – strategy, processes and management.

Revisiting business strategy

The key challenges here are to:

- Ask the naive and challenging questions about why the business exists, what it is trying to achieve, whether we would pay for the activities that went on if we were the customer or owner, and how we would do things differently if starting again?
- Identify our distinctive capabilities/core competencies and determine their strength, the ease with which they can be replicated by competitors, how well they are exploited currently and the depth of understanding of those capabilities amongst the workforce.
- Examine where, how and why we add more or less value than our competitors and assess how this matches up to customer needs and expectations.
- Force a continuous and fundamental reassessment of product and customer profitability – with an open and results-driven appraisal of the value of the often emotionally charged subject of loss leaders.
- Go beyond the often bland and manipulable concept of customer surveys, and engage all levels of the organisation in regular face-to-face contact with customers – possibly through focus groups.
- Understand the different segmentations of customers that we serve and assess the priorities and trade-offs between service, functionality, quality and price for each segment.
- Assess the organisation's capacity for, and openness to, continuous learning, innovation and a diversity of ideas and opinions.

Redesigning business processes

The objectives and outcomes of any fundamental reappraisal of business processes should be to:

- Eliminate unnecessary tasks and reduce any delays introduced by multiple authorisations, inspections and hand-offs between departments.
- Ensure that process roles can be fulfilled by multiple staff and that staff are trained to perform multiple roles.
- Concentrate the responsibility for end-to-end tasks into single roles (eg case handlers in insurance) or small workgroups; automate the flows of work to minimise delays between processing stages where multiple participants are involved.
- Reduce the amount of paper handling and rekeying of data by promoting the use of electronic documents, by minimising the storage of paper copies of electronically generated documents and by encouraging electronic communications both internally and with customers and suppliers.
- Create a balanced set of process performance measures covering both external and internal needs eg quality, service levels, customer satisfaction, cycle time, throughput, resource efficiency, bottlenecks, error rates and costs.
- Build staff understanding of the business objectives, the end-to-end design and the critical performance measures for the processes they work on.
- Equip staff with the tools and techniques to allow them to take responsibility for the continuous review and refinement of the processes they work on.

Rethinking management approaches

Middle and junior management face potentially the greatest shift in roles and responsibilities in the re-engineered business. The challenges for them are to:

- Increase staffing flexibility by creating a multi-skilled workforce.
- Reduce duplication of effort and investment by forming stronger partnerships with customers and suppliers, sharing key information (eg point of sale data vs. sales forecasts), undertaking joint developments and entering into quick response networks which help eliminate multiple storage points in a supply chain, cut total inventory costs within the chain and reduce replenishment cycles.
- Improve cross-functional communications to speed up issue resolution and the development of new products and services.
- Give staff the freedom and authority to execute the responsibilities with which they have been empowered.

- Encourage the continuous challenging and elimination of non-value adding tasks, outsourcing those which are still required but which divert time and resources from critical business activities.
- Move from command and control models of managerial behaviour to one in which the prime responsibilities are to help staff make sense of the environment and the challenges they face.
- Encourage learning and the acquisition and exploitation of new knowledge by staff at all levels.

KEY STEPS IN THE RE-ENGINEERING PROCESS

There is a wide range of methodologies that seek to consolidate into a simple framework some or all of these ideas on what should happen in a re-engineering initiative. While some methods focus on the analysis and redesign tasks, others focus on the definition of strategy or the development of the underlying information systems. Given the wide variety of ways in which organisations are looking to apply re-engineering concepts, it is unlikely that one dominant or 'gold standard' approach will emerge.

The approach presented here (Fig. 2.5) seeks to strike a balance between strategy formulation, process redesign and the exploitation and management of the re-engineered business. The objectives for each step in the three main phases are:

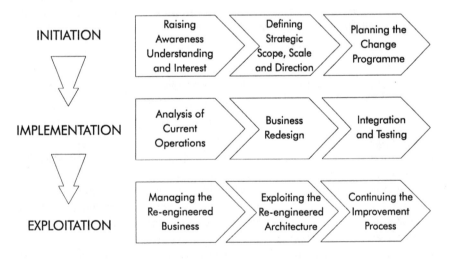

Fig. 2.5 *Stages in the re-engineering process*

Programme initiation

- Build the awareness of business processes, create an understanding of the concepts of re-engineering and generate an interest in the need for, and opportunities to achieve, sustainable performance improvement.
- Clarify the strategic direction and target architecture. Determine the strategic objectives for the exercise. Decide on the scale of change required and the number and scope of the candidate processes for re-engineering. Define the business requirements and performance objectives that the re-engineered processes will fulfil and select a programme owner and project team(s).
- Undertake the detailed planning of the change process.

Design and implementation

- Map, model and analyse the current process(es), capturing performance measures to help highlight the need for change and determine if immediate improvements can be made. Identify customer requirements and expectations from the process and (possibly) benchmark the process against best-of-breed organisations. In analysing a process it is important to distinguish between the flows of activity and control in the process and the ways in which data and documents are used in the process.
- Generate a range of options for redesigning the process that will each deliver significant performance improvements – typically using different configurations of process roles, work tasks and technology support. Develop an outline business case for each option.
- Test the options against key measures such as customer requirements, cost and quality objectives. Select the preferred option and develop the business case. Develop the redesigned business process(es), develop or enhance the underlying computer systems and plan the migration steps.
- Prototype, test and refine the redesign in a 'laboratory' setting, train the users and integrate the re-engineered processes into the live business environment, test them in operation and implement any immediate refinements.

Exploitation of the re-engineered business

- Provide ongoing support to the re-engineered operation, help managers and staff adjust to new roles, responsibilities and methods of working, monitor performance and initiate ongoing refinements.

- Ensure a continuous review of the opportunities to exploit the enhanced capabilities created through re-engineering.
- Maintain a balance between continuous incremental improvements and periodic fundamental changes in process design.

THE ROLE OF IT

The role of IT in re-engineering has undergone an interesting transformation over the past three years. At first the message was clear – re-engineer work through information technology. However, in the intervening period, there has been a major shift in emphasis towards business ownership of the initiative, with IT playing more of a supporting and enabling role.

Part of the reason for the shift is that – as with earlier attempts to promote IT for Competitive Advantage – the delivery has failed to live up to the promise. IT has been plagued by the same recurring problems of late delivery of over-specified, under-functional systems that cost far more than originally planned. To add insult to injury we have then paid IT staff far more than their peers in the rest of the business.

However, there are a number of examples of organisations that have made extensive and effective use of IT in their re-engineering initiatives. For example, many of the firms in the financial services industry that have successfully completed re-engineering projects started out by looking at how they could use IT to speed up and streamline business activity. These include:

Western Provident Association	–	Workflow, common customer databases
Birmingham Midshires	–	Document Image Processing and Workflow
National Vulcan	–	Laptop computers, customer database, standard forms
Cigna Health Insurance	–	Workgroup computing, common customer databases, Graphical User Interfaces.

Equally, there are a number of examples of organisations that used little or no new investment in IT to achieve their re-engineering goals. In such cases the aim is to:

- Take IT off the critical path.
- Make use of existing systems as far as possible.

- Use flexible front ends to provide the appearance of seamless common user access to a range of underlying systems.
- Only redevelop once the process has been redesigned and the new IT requirements, if any, are clear to all involved.

However, IT still retains a seductive charm. Many organisations still start their re-engineering projects by searching for appropriate technology – both to support the redesign phase and to execute the process once re-engineered.

The key technologies that one will see most frequently on re-engineering projects will include:

- Business and process modelling tools.
- Document image processing (DIP) and workflow.
- Electronic Data Interchange (EDI).
- Common customer databases – normally built around a relational model.
- Distributed systems and client server architectures.
- Knowledge-based systems to facilitate end user decision making.

One concern over the use of document image processing is that in many cases it is tackling the wrong problems. Over ninety-five per cent of the documents organisations work with have been generated electronically. Paradoxically by storing an image of the document as an electronic photograph we lose the ability to manipulate its contents.

ARE YOU READY FOR RE-ENGINEERING? – CRITICAL SUCCESS FACTORS

At the start of the chapter, I suggested that the critical decision was whether the organisation was ready for re-engineering. The subsequent discussion and the wealth of ideas and advice offered elsewhere in the book should help the reader draw up their own list of prerequisites or critical success factors. They can then assess whether they have or can build the necessary capability and leadership to make a success of it. The assessment of these factors will always be more of a subjective than objective exercise. While a number of people advocate the use of some form of scoring mechanism, the real value lies in the discussion and discovery process that those in leadership positions go through to determine their readiness for re-engineering. To help start that process I offer my own non-exhaustive checklist:

- *Leadership* – demonstrated through a combination of top level bravery in launching the initiative, defining bold ambitions and taking difficult and potentially unpopular decisions, sustaining commitment through the highs and lows of the project, being patient in allowing people to make mistakes, being open to criticism and getting actively involved.

■ *Direction* – if the re-engineering programme is not simply to create a better process for yesterday's needs it must be driven by a clear and consistent strategic focus and an evocative long-term vision.

■ *Motivation* – expressed in a passionate desire to change the status quo and challenge inappropriate structures and behaviours in order to create a totally customer focused organisation.

■ *Integration* – fundamental change demands that we address the entire strategic architecture and seek balanced improvements across all elements of it .

■ *Customers* – the organisation needs to engage in a continuous dialogue with customers to determine their requirements, priorities and trade-offs and to understand how best we can help them serve their customers.

■ *Participation* – we need a design for change that seeks to engage people at every level of the organisation and gain their active support and involvement – preferably in cross-functional teams.

■ *Ambition* – the goals for the change programme must be stretching – out of reach but not out of sight.

■ *Rethink* – re-engineering provides an opportunity to look at the organisation through a new lens. By challenging the prevailing mind-set we can help the organisation understand the need for change and unleash the skills, learning, creativity and innovation required to bring about radically new process designs.

■ *Support* – the process cannot and should not be led by external consultants but they can perform valuable roles such as design adviser, coach, facilitator, catalyst and devil's advocate.

■ *Communication* – the critical challenges here are to ensure that we test the interpretation of those to whom we communicate – both inside and outside the organisation – to surface and discuss residual concerns, fears and doubts and to maintain an open dialogue throughout the change process.

■ *Measurement* – the performance indicators used should assess both the change process itself and the resulting achievements against targets. The outcomes – positive and negative – need to be shared openly if the organisation is to learn and make progress.

■ *Technology* – information technology (IT) should be viewed as an enabler not the driver of change or the guardian of past practice. The challenge is to decide firstly what the organisation wants from the application of *IT in the business* and then determine how to manage *IT as a business* in order to achieve those objectives.

- *Passion* – a change of this scale needs to be seen as something more than business as usual – particularly by those not directly involved. The passion of those leading the change and their ability to enthuse others can help to generate and sustain momentum and support – particularly during the difficult stages.
- *Humanity* – the most critical assessment of the organisation's performance in managing any accompanying people changes will be made by its own staff. Any suspicion of heavy handedness or dishonesty will undoubtedly reflect in the morale and commitment of the workforce.

CONCLUSIONS

Re-engineering is a powerfully emotive topic and one which is still not well understood – despite all the hype and the proliferation of re-engineering projects. Re-engineering can do untold and lasting damage to the organisation when used rashly and indiscriminately as a blunt cost cutting tool. The climate of fear and the obsession with measurement that accompanies many so-called re-engineering projects can act to destroy the very lifeline to the future which we should actually be seeking to strengthen. This is because fear, accompanied by confusion over the organisation's goals, can act as powerful inhibitors on the key levers of progress – empowerment, team working, risk taking, innovation, learning and knowledge creation.

Where re-engineering is at its most powerful and effective is when it is used as a critical element in the fundamental rethinking and redesign of the business itself – not just its processes. Re-engineering offers us the opportunity to take an integrated view of the business and create a platform from which to grow and shape future business success.

The start point for success in re-engineering is a passionate commitment to serving the customer and to helping them achieve success. This commitment can then be reflected in the creation of distinctive capability, the design of the supporting processes and in the physical infrastructure which supports those processes. The result is that we can optimise performance across all aspects of the business and measure ourselves against the needs of multiple stakeholders.

Re-engineering forces on us the recognition that continued survival and success will be heavily dependent on our ability to unleash and tap the energy and potential of every member of the organisation. This in turn means that we have to ensure that everyone genuinely understands the business and that individuals are given the authority to make decisions and take action in line with business goals.

We have to acknowledge that allocating responsibility does not mean isolating blame. Rarely when things go wrong can we find one individual whose actions alone led to the error. Through collective responsibility we can build our ability to trust, to work in teams and to share knowledge and experience – commodities which are traditionally guarded jealously lest others should benefit at our expense.

In practice re-engineering can be both the catalyst for and a component of the type of holistic approach to change which is advocated throughout this book. However, in either case the issue is the same – we must ensure that the business achieves clarity on the fundamentals of what it is actually trying to achieve strategically. Clarity may not mean defining a ten-year pathway from which the organisation cannot deviate. It may mean deciding that the organisation will have no goals in the traditional sense and will simply pursue attractive opportunities as they arise. However, this is still a strategy and demands that we have an architecture which can respond rapidly and smoothly and that we recruit and develop people who are comfortable with – and capable of – working in such a fast and fluid environment.

Hence, whatever the longer-term goals may be, re-engineering should be seen as part of the process through which we ensure a strong alignment between strategic direction, business objectives, capabilities, processes, physical infrastructure and culture. Progress can then be measured through a balanced scorecard of performance measures which reflect critical aspects of business progress – external and internal, financial and non-financial.

Creating a new paradigm, changing the mindset, building trust, encouraging learning and empowerment are all ways in which we can shape the culture of the new organisation. To sit down and attempt to define that culture at the outset is pointless. The dynamic interplay between the elements of the architecture and the people themselves will help to shape the culture. Similarly, the intensity with which the change tasks are conducted – the extent to which people are immersed in or exposed to new ways of thinking and working – will help shape the culture. Ultimately though, the behaviour and language used by those at the top of the organisation will define the dominant culture. Herein lies the rub, the ultimate success or failure of re-engineering can be traced to similar roots as everything else we seek to do in the organisation, ie *how we behave* not *what we do*.

REFERENCES

1. Hammer, M. (1990), Re-engineering work – Don't automate obliterate. *Harvard Business Review*, July-August, pp 104–112.
2. Hammer, M. and Champy, J. (1993), *Re-engineering the corporation – A manifesto for business revolution*. London: Nicholas Brealey Publishing.

BIBLIOGRAPHY

Talwar, R. K. (1993), Business re-engineering – A strategy driven appraoch. *Long Range Planning, Vol 26–6*, December, pp 22–40.

Talwar, R. K. (1994), Managing change. *Imaging in Finance*, May, pp 9–11.

Talwar, R. K. (1994), *Re-engineering – the hope*. CCTA Conference Presentation, Brighton, March.

Talwar, R. K. (1994), *Strategic learning – The next competitive challenge*. IBC Conference Presentation, London, May.

NOTE

The application of the COBRA methodology and the technologies of electronic commerce to the re-engineering of supply chains is covered in: Peter Bartram, Colin Coulson-Thomas and Lee Tate (1996), *The Competitive Network*, London, Policy Publications.

3

Business Process Re-engineering – Contrasting what it is with what it is not

Clive Holtham

INTRODUCTION

It is argued here that BPR does have some core concepts that are valuable contributions to the evolution of management thought. However, these concepts are surrounded by subsidiary material that is either not novel, not necessary, or is even potentially antagonistic to the core concepts. BPR as evangelised may well be largely unremarkable or internally inconsistent. But this does not mean that all aspects of BPR should therefore be rejected. In looking to the future, there is in fact a need to correlate the core BPR concepts and other managerial concepts.

There are several recent articles that review BPR in some depth from theoretical perspectives (eg Grint, 1993; Earl and Khan, 1994). The aim here is to supplement these articles with a focus on some specific areas:

- The life-cycle of BPR as a managerial innovation
- BPR roots; the unrecognised debts
- BPR maps – needs, application and capability
- Process and task
- Process versus structure
- Definitely not BPR
- The key to BPR?
- A European perspective

The conventional definition of BPR

The text most widely used in business-oriented discussions of BPR is Hammer and Champy (1993) so this represents a well-known starting point. Their much-quoted definition of BPR is the one that will be assumed here, although acceptance of the definition does not necessarily imply acceptance of any other aspect of their text:

> the fundamental rethinking and radical redesign of business processes to achieve dramatic improvements in critical, contemporary measures of performance, such as cost, quality, service and speed.

LIFE CYCLE OF MANAGEMENT INNOVATIONS – WHITHER BPR?

This paper assumes that BPR as an evangelical movement has a strictly limited life (Lawrence, 1994). The history of any management innovation can be divided into five phases; the actual or predicted dates for BPR are shown in Table 3.1:

Table 3.1 *Five phases for BPR*

Stage	BPR
1. Initial research and conception.	to 1990
2. Conversion of academic concepts into consulting-oriented products for enthusiastic mass-market promotion and consumption.	1990–1993
3. Idea gains corporate momentum; negative experiences and conceptual problems begin to emerge.	1993–1995
4. Enthusiasts begin to run out of steam. Dramatic benefits fail to emerge consistently. New competitors emerge.	1995–1996
5. Falls into disrepute and disuse.	1996–1998

At the time of writing, Phase 3 is under way. Most of the major management consultancies and product vendors have already completed Phase 2 – rolling out either a *bona fide* product, or at least amending their sales and marketing material to refer to BPR. However, both consultancies and conference organisers already report a more discriminating audience for the BPR concept.

Explaining the success of BPR as concept – encapsulation

The great achievement of the evangelical advocates of BPR is not that they have invented something whose components are innovative. Not a single component of BPR is in any way innovative. Their first achievement is that they have coined a phrase which seems to strike a chord with managers across the world – what Grint (1993) describes as 'resonance'. The second achievement is that they have packaged and presented already existing concepts in a way that stimulates the interest of managers.

The great success of BPR is in creating a phrase, and related content, that encapsulates a number of important managerial themes. It is essentially a success of sales and marketing of existing managerial ideas, rather than contributing new ideas. There is an increasing trend to write-off BPR for this very reason, eg: 'We have known all this for 20 years' 'We should have been doing this anyway in the customer service process'.

Also, the fact that the great management evangelists of the 1980s – Peters and Waterman – used as case studies some companies that subsequently performed extremely badly – creates in the current climate an in-built resistance by some managers who are now particularly sceptical of fads.

Because of these reservations and although the term BPR has only a strictly limited life, its valuable features will only be sustained or even remembered if they are clearly understood, and if these are considered independently from the sales and promotion for evangelistic BPR.

BPR ROOTS

To identify some of the enduring features of BPR it is necessary to return to its roots. Since it is not made up of original components, the valuable features are also present in its roots.

There are essentially two forms of roots. The first are the deep roots, the underlying and for all practical purposes invisible ancestors of BPR. The second one, the shallow roots, clear and visible but of much more recent vintage.

Perhaps surprisingly, given Hammer and Champy's persistent negative references to him, there is little doubt that Frederick Taylor was an active proponent of radical change. He is unfairly caricatured as preoccupied with task optimisation. He was naturally concerned with the pressing managerial priorities at the turn of the century. Nevertheless, he was regarded as highly revolutionary in his day, and believed as strongly as any BPR consultant in the importance of processes breaking down traditional organisational structures. Scientific management is actually one of the deep roots of BPR.

But for a more direct lineage of BPR, reference can be made to the post-second world war management theorists. These can be divided into two separate groups. First, there was the quality movement, and in particular Duran. Second, there were the systems theorists, and a particularly relevant member of this group was Stafford Beer.

The unrecognised debt – breakthrough management

One of the major criticisms of the work of Hammer and Champy is their lack of apparent recognition of their historical antecedents. This criticism is much less valid of Davenport who includes a useful, if incomplete, review of antecedents. The basic concept of re-engineering was most visibly coined by Juran (1964). Although he used the term 'breakthrough' instead of 're-engineering', there is little doubt that his meaning is virtually the same. It is perhaps not surprising that an updated second edition of this neglected classic of management literature is reported to be imminent.

Juran summarises the task of management into two parts – control and breakthrough.

> Control means staying on course, adherence to standard, prevention of change... . We can become so pre-occupied with meeting targets that we fail to challenge the target itself.

> Breakthrough means change, a dynamic, decisive movement to new, higher levels of performance.

What is interesting about this is that Juran is concerned with the whole organisation, whether in the relatively steady state for which the control approach is valid, or whether radical change is needed via breakthrough management. One of the major weaknesses of BPR is its lack of a higher-level framework of relevance to most ongoing tasks. It is fascinating that the insights of Juran in this area have essentially been forgotten or ignored by later management writers.

It is also noteworthy that Juran's text did not make anywhere near the impact when it came out in the 1960s as might have been expected from its intrinsic worth. One of the reasons for this is that in the economic climate of that time, with full employment and the post-war economic growth still in train, there were not in general the same pre-occupations as found in the 1990s – of dealing with constraint and of survival. Juran's work on breakthrough was full of insight, but the potential audience did not see this as a central issue at that time.

The unrecognised debt – viable systems

At the same time as Juran was developing his breakthrough concept, there was a parallel set of work under way on systems thinking. It was initiated in pure science, particularly biology, but its commercial application arose out of some of the perceived pressures of managing major scientific projects, such as the US space programme, managing major infrastructure issues such as urban planning, and the conduct of war, most specifically by the USA in Vietnam.

In the words of the founder of general systems theory, Ludwig von Bertalanffy (1968):

> While in the past science tried to explain observable phenomena by reducing them to an interplay of elementary units investigated independently of each other, conceptions appear in contemporary science that are concerned with what is somewhat vaguely termed with 'wholeness', i.e. problems of organization, phenomena not dissolvable into local events, dynamic interactions manifested in the difference of behavior of parts.

This belief in wholeness was implicitly very critical of naive management theory based on purely hierarchical management principles (Senge, 1990).

In the UK, cybernetician Stafford Beer was particularly critical of the classical managerial hierarchies – he dismissed them as 'mechanisms for apportioning blame' (Beer, 1981). Through his Viable System Model (VSM) he was searching for a vehicle that would enable an holistic perspective of the organisation in its environment, that would recognise the needs for autonomy in operating units, and which would reconcile the inevitable tensions between central and front-line units.

Why the roots were passed over

So some of the real roots of BPR were well established by the end of the 1960s. Why then did it take more than 20 years for these ideas to re-surface in the mainstream perception of the practising manager? Several hypotheses can be put forward:

1. In the case of the systems approach, it never really became endorsed through widespread practical success. Indeed it became associated either with high profile perceived failures (see Lilienfeld, 1976) such as the application of systems thinking in the Department of Defense or urban management.
2. According to David Norton*, in the 1970s US businesses became increasingly functionalised, and in this climate there was simply no demand for systemic solutions that ran across functional boundaries.
3. The systems approaches were not presented in sufficiently simplistic terms. The packaging and presentation betrayed the underlying rigour of the approaches. Many managers perceived them as hard or demanding and preferred to search for more simplistic approaches such as those subsequently developed by Peters and Waterman (1982).

---

* Conversation with author, June 1994.

THE BPR MAPS – NEED, APPLICATION AND CAPABILITY

One of the weaknesses of BPR evangelists is that they are relatively silent on situations which are not BPR. In order to focus managerial thinking about BPR, we have found it useful to develop two grids or maps which set out some of the very basic considerations about the applicability of BPR to any given organisation and its processes. The first, Table 3.2, contrasts the need for BPR with whether BPR is actually being applied or not. An early question to ask at this point is what proportion of organisations will, at any one time, fall into the 'Need BPR' category.

WHY NOT?	OK	Need BPR
OK	DANGER	Don't Need BPR

Don't Apply BPR   Do Apply BPR

Figure 3.1 *Need and application*

A starting point for the need for BPR is to ask how often does any organisation need to undertake 'radical redesign of business processes to achieve dramatic improvements'. The straightforward answer is 'Not very often'. In business, as in economic and social life, it is simply not viable to have revolutions on a regular or continuous basis. It can be expected that there will be periods of radical change interspersed with periods of greater stability. It may well be that this stability is accompanied by intense self-criticism and aggressive continuous improvement programmes, but this is not the same as continuous revolution, and approaches other than BPR are needed for these periods.

As a rule of thumb, it is difficult to see how any individual organisation can fundamentally and radically redesign itself more than about once every five years, give or take a year. This is not least because the process of radical transformation can itself take two to three years from conception to full implementation. One can develop from this the idea that at any given time about twenty per cent of organisations, or processes within a given organisation, might be candidates for radical redesign.

The converse is that eighty per cent are not. They may be candidates for process redesign or for continuous improvement, but they are not candidates for BPR. At any one time, the majority of organisations do not need BPR, and particular attention therefore needs to be directed to the Don't Need/Do Apply quadrant. It is much quoted that fifty to seventy per cent of re-engineering projects fail to achieve the dramatic results intended. It can be surmised that a good proportion of these failures are actually organisations for whom BPR was an inappropriate approach in the first place.

One of the problems for BPR consultants, is that there may be marketing and business pressures to configure an organisation's problems into a BPR perspective. It also has to be said that there are many executives who are frustrated by the accidental accretion of non-value added activities in the organisation. Such executives are emotionally highly attracted to the idea of radical change, and of business revolution, to enable radical and rapid pruning of unnecessary activities.

Even if an organisation needs BPR, it may not be currently undertaking it (Do Need/Don't Apply). These organisations need to address the barriers to BPR, and more particularly whether they have any reasonable chance of overcoming those barriers. One of the most clear-cut and important barriers is the level of managerial capability, and this is the focus of the second map or grid. This contrasts the need for BPR with managerial capability.

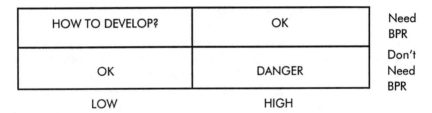

Figure 3.2 *Need and managerial capability*

Once again the Danger cell is present – carrying out BPR because the managerial capability exists rather than because it is appropriate.

The top left hand cell of Table 3.3 highlights a key issue for many organisations – Need BPR/Low Capability. In these circumstances there may be a temptation to use external resources to lead the BPR effort. External resources can be invaluable to support a BPR effort but they can never lead it.

PROCESS AND TASK

There is great confusion over what a process is. Different BPR advocates have different definitions, for example. Hammer and Champy define a process as:

> A collection of activities that takes one or more kinds of output and creates an input that is of value to the customer.

For Davenport (1993) it is:

> A specific ordering of work activities across time and space, with a beginning, an end, and clearly identified inputs and outputs: a structure for action.

While these definitions quite legitimately include non-task or non-functional orientated processes, in fact they also cover task and functionally-based processes as well. It seems that the definition of a process is defined at such an abstract level that the definition becomes almost meaningless, and hence the need to fall back on negative definitions – non-task or non-functional activities – instead. Many of the publicised examples of business processes that have been re-engineered are not very far from conventional departmental or functional redesign – when the verbiage and hype are stripped away.

PROCESS VERSUS STRUCTURE

Process can be contrasted with structure or function. A focus on process places relatively little, or no, emphasis on current organisational and functional structure. But it needs to be recognised that one of the alternatives to BPR is extensive structural change, and this latter is actually a more attractive option to many managers.

Most managers in business have had careers in organisations dominated by structural considerations. Many managers in the UK have educational and career backgrounds rooted in a specific profession such as finance, marketing or production.

They may well be familiar with developing and changing processes that are specific to their own professional area. But they will be much less familiar with across-business processes.

In reality managers are much more familiar with changing structure than they are with changing process. There are many businesses where organisational structures are changed frequently; such organisations can seem to be in an almost constant state of structural change.

There are always valid reasons for changing structure: changes in the marketplace, in the components of a business, in the individuals available, and responses to budget cuts. However, it needs to be understood that often structures are changed for quite different underlying reasons (even where some of the valid reasons are overtly put forward to justify the change).

There are two hidden reasons for structural change.

1. Changing the organisational structure sends an explicit message to the organisation that something will be different from now on. This could be regarded as part of the unfreezing process in organisational change. This can be described as 'symbolic structural change'.
2. More worrying is the type of change that is often associated with crisis. The organisation is under-performing. Costs are not under control. Sales are falling. The owners or directors decide 'something has to be done'. They will expect something to be done and – more critically – they will expect something to be seen to be done. The executives running the business (old or new) are now under pressure. Something has to be done, and done fast. They need to tackle something that can be tackled.

   Hence the popularity of structural change. It can actually be done. It can be seen to be done. It can be justified by valid reasons. It carries an element of symbolic change. It can be done fairly quickly.

But in reality there could be immense problems with this type of structural change, which could be described as 'can-do structural change'. Its focus is short-term. There can rarely, if ever, be any clear demonstration of the business benefits of the change, with the exception of cost reductions. But the cost reductions could well be achieved without structural change.

Can-do structural change, especially when carried out repeatedly, consumes vast amounts of human time and effort. It increases the insecurity of people in the organisation (sometimes this is an explicit objective). It focuses the business on internal administration, not external customer service.

It needs to be appreciated that *process change is actually competing with structural change*. On the surface, process change is considerably less attractive to many managers than Can-do structural change.

- Process change takes some time to implement.
- Process change is often almost invisible externally during the planning stages.
- Whereas structural change can be directly associated with, and credited to, senior executives, process change is the result of many people's effort and can more rarely give personal credit.

Now although the outcome of process change can be very radical, including radical effects on the organisational structure, at the time the process change is initiated the form of such structural changes cannot be precisely predicted.

In the current business environment, senior executives may only be in a particular post for two to three years. So the idea of embarking on process change with unpredictable outcomes, a relatively long gestation period, and no immediate credit to that executive, is not necessarily a comfortable one.

Too often the reluctance of senior executives to sponsor process change is interpreted in terms of inertia, fears about their own job, or active resistance to change. All these have some truth, but the underlying reluctance may be far more to do with how much credit executives will get, and how quickly they will get it.

Structure can be seen; process is difficult to see

There are a variety of reasons why an organisation needs a formal structure. Examples are: accountability, external and internal comprehensibility, resource allocation and providing a basis for remuneration.

A formal structure gives a degree of security to individuals. They know where they fit in. Above all an organisational structure can be embedded in a chart – it is physically visible. Names can be attached to function. It does not matter that the chart is only one representation of organisational reality, and not necessarily the most important one. By contrast, processes are much more amorphous, even though they too can be charted. It is difficult or impossible to show exactly where any given individual fits into a process chart, especially with multi-functional teams.

For those who have grown up in organisations dominated by structure, it is a huge psychological leap to move to a process orientation. It is still necessary to examine how to provide a degree of security in a process-driven organisation comparable with that in a structure-driven one.

DEFINITELY NOT BPR

Many of those who have joined the BPR bandwagon are advocating solutions where the term BPR is used in association with their product or service. Much of this is at best peripherally associated with BPR, and at worst has no logical connection to BPR at all. This can be described as 'definitely not BPR'.

Software re-engineering led change

The term 're-engineering' is an older term than 'business process re-engineering'. In the 1980s it was used particularly to describe the replacement of long-standing computer systems with more up-to-date hardware or software technologies. The terms 're-engineering' and 'software re-engineering' were commonly used, which directly related to the long-standing phrase 'software engineering' (Spurr, 1993).

This earlier use of the term software re-engineering should not have caused any problems when the concept of BPR was promulgated, but unfortunately it has. There has been some tendency for academics and consultants, predominantly with a computer science background, to use the terms BPR and software re-engineering almost interchangeably. The apparent logic underpinning this interchangeability is:

1. Software re-engineering is an important part of re-engineering computer systems.
2. Re-engineered computer systems are often an important part of BPR.
3. Therefore software re-engineering is often an important part of BPR (or even identical to it).

The fallibility of this logic is fairly clear. There is no dispute that re-engineering of computer systems is one of the elements required to implement BPR, sometimes representing a very significant element. But the confusion between software re-engineering and BPR is now so great in the quarters identified above that it is most straightforward to describe software re-engineering as: 'definitely not BPR'.

Technology-initiated change
Very few of the successful case studies in BPR have ever been initiated out of the new opportunities offered by IT (or technologies generally). Once again, this is not to say that BPR implementation will not draw on these technologies. However, the development of technologies such as workflow, groupware or document image processing have no *a priori* connection to the need to re-engineer business processes. Therefore they also fall into the category of: 'definitely not BPR'.

Tools-led change
There has been an explosion in computer-based tools to support BPR, plus considerable re-badging or re-positioning of existing tools so that they can be perceived to support BPR. Many such tools are invaluable in BPR implementation. However, they can play no part in the initiation of BPR and so they are: 'definitely not BPR'.

This harsh categorisation of 'definitely not BPR' is a direct response to exaggerated claims made for software re-engineering, for technology-initiated change and for tools-initiated change. Such exaggeration actually harms the genuine claims in support of specific aspects of BPR which can be made for all three approaches (Huckvale and Ould, 1993).

The relationship between IT and BPR
BPR does not absolutely require any use of IT at all. However, one of the distinctive features of BPR is the way that IT is almost invariably used to

'informate' in Zuboff's terminology – to reconstruct the nature of work. IT is a key feature of implementing BPR, but its revolutionary possibilities in reconstructing the nature of work has led to deep confusion amongst some IT practitioners and consultants.

Misconception – business process versus process in computer science

One of the greater misfortunes in the analysis of BPR is that the term 'process' has already been used to some degree in the fields of computer science and software engineering. There are, once again, academics and consultants in these fields who have, for example, developed methodologies and computer-based tools for 'analysing business processes'.

There are people in these fields who have latched on to the phrase BPR, with its clear link to strategic business success, and have re-positioned their methodologies to appear directly related to BPR.

This misconception may not always be deliberate, but it is unfortunate. It is certainly the case that such methodologies and tools can be useful in the process of implementing BPR. So too are interviews and meetings. It is as ridiculous to equate computer science-oriented methodologies and tools with BPR, as it is to suggest that interviews and meetings are also its equivalents.

The difficult and dominant issues of BPR are the strategic business issues, the need for revolution, people issues, business processes, and the capability of the organisation to go through a revolution. Methodologies and tools can be very important, but they are not of primary importance in the way some of the above issues tend to be. So it is particularly facile to suggest that they can by themselves be drivers of BPR.

Misconception – Business Process Redesign

In Venkatraman's model (1991), Business Process Redesign is one level of the revolutionary approach. It is a level that focuses more on the internal than network redesign or business reorientation. Again unfortunately, some IT-based advocates have used this term for the mere upgrading or replacing of existing computer systems.

Re-engineering the re-engineering process

Second-grade management consultants see BPR as a wonderful marketing opportunity – and some of them have been proved only too correct. The problem is not, of course, the second-grade consultant. It is the business unit managers who hire these consultants. It needs to be made crystal clear that business process re-engineering – if it is genuinely innovative – requires radical change to the consultancy process. If BPR on a business can lead to eighty per cent cost reductions, a reasonable suggestion must be that effective BPR consultancy should lead to eighty per cent reductions in consultancy costs (or four-hundred per cent better value from the same consultancy costs).

THE KEY TO BPR?

In having presented on the theme of BPR to many hundreds of practising managers in several countries, one is struck by the desire of at least a significant minority of these managers to discover the central core of BPR, the big idea, the specific key to unlock the process of business transformation in their organisation.

If it was possible to identify such a key, it would undoubtedly be the combination of:

◼ A weak or disastrous level of current performance.
◼ A charismatic, hard driving newly appointed chief executive, who can articulate the new vision, and then successfully set in train the whole range of practical implementation steps necessary.

The problem with this key is that relatively few organisations can either manoeuvre or accidentally develop this combination.

The majority of organisations are not actually sufferers from weak or disastrous performance levels. It may be, as external advisers like to emphasise in marketing their services, that weakness and disaster are only just around the corner. But it seems to be far more persuasive in most organisations if it has already happened, than if it is a future theoretical possibility.

There is then the question of the appointment of the new chief executive. The weak performance may well have precipitated the demise of the previous chief executive. But there is no guarantee that appointment of the new leader, with the personality characteristics listed above, will itself lead to the necessary changes being successfully implemented.

The new chief executive may well be able, over time, to force through a number of top-level changes in personnel to create a new or revamped top team that has the will and competence to secure the new vision. But equally, they may not be able to create quite the team needed, and overt or covert internal resistance can then thwart the radical changes necessary.

There is also an issue related to the style and personalities of the workforce generally. It is one thing to create a vision of a new, process-led, flexible and empowered workforce, but many of the existing workforce may be unhappy with such a vision. They may well prefer functionally-based, hierarchical, stable environments. Even organisations that have moved entirely to the process-led approach, will be the first to admit that:

1. They lost a number of staff at once who had no desire to be part of such an approach.

2. There is a significant minority, perhaps twenty to forty per cent of the workforce, who would strongly prefer to return to the traditional ways.

It is therefore ironic that some of the classic BPR case studies relate not to the re-engineering of existing businesses, but rather the creation of start-up organisations that embody a process approach. An early example was the Batterymarch fund management organisation; another was the Midland Bank subsidiary First Direct.

CONCLUSION – A EUROPEAN PERSPECTIVE

The concepts of business process design or business process re-engineering are essentially North American concepts. They may, or may not, be capable of being transplanted to European business. But it is advisable to begin from a perspective of scepticism and caution. It should not be automatically and (it has to be said) somewhat naively assumed that American management thought is relevant outside America; indeed there are even doubts about the extent to which the principles are valid within America itself.

One is often struck, when listening to American management speakers in Europe, how insensitive they are to the different history, culture and style found in Europe. As in the media and other areas, it is simply assumed that Europe is like America except most of the people speak different languages.

For example, in a German language article on BPR (Behrens and Groothuis, 1994), the head of Siemens, Heinrich von Pierer, commented:

> I don't feel completely comfortable with the radical theses of Mr. Hammer. Our employees are not neutrons, but people. That's why dialogue is important. [my translation]

There is not the space here to introduce the detailed content of a European approach to BPR. But on a preliminary view, it needs to be rooted in distinctive European managerial features:

1. Acceptance of the humanistic and holistic stream in European thought, in contrast to the more mechanistic and fragmented US approach.
2. Promotion of the concept of collaboration, between levels in the organisation, across organisations, between supplier and customer, and also across national boundaries.

The core elements of BPR have value beyond the evangelical North American approach, and BPR has value for Europe if it is set in a European context. However, it is essential that the subject is approached with a much greater awareness both of what BPR is, and is not.

BIBLIOGRAPHY

Beer, S. (1981), *The brain of the firm*. (2nd ed.). Chichester: Wiley.

Behrens, B. and Groothuis, U. (1994), *Vergeudung ist Sünde. WirtschaftsWoche*, 18th February, No 8, pp. 68–73.

Davenport, T. (1993), *Process Innovation: Reengineering work through information technology*. Boston: Harvard Business School Press.

Earl, M. and Khan, B. (1994), How new is business process redesign? *European Management Journal, Vol 12 No. 1*, March, pp.20–30.

Grint, K. (1993), *Reengineering history: An analysis of business process reengineering*. Templeton College, The Oxford Centre for Management Studies, Management Research Paper 93/20.

Hammer, M. and Champy, J. (1993), *Reengineering the corporation: A manifesto for business revolution*. London: Nicholas Brealey.

Huckvale, T. and Ould, M. (1993), Process modelling – Why, what and how. In K. Spurr *et al.* (Eds). *Software assistance for business re-engineering*. Chapter 6. Chichester: Wiley.

Juran, J.M. (1964), *Breakthrough management*. London: Macmillan.

Lawrence, A. (1994), BPR – Tool of controversy. *Computer Business Review*, March, pp.11–14.

Lilienfeld, R. (1976), *The rise of systems theory – An ideological analysis*. New York: Wiley-Interscience.

Peters, T. and Waterman, R. (1982), *In search of excellence*. Harper and Row.

Senge, P. (1990), *The fifth discipline*. New York: Doubleday.

Spurr, K. *et al.* (Eds). (1993), *Software assistance for business re-engineering*. Chichester: Wiley.

Venkatraman, N. (1991), IT-induced business reconfiguration. In M. Scott Morton, (Ed). *The corporation of the 1990s*. New York: Oxford University Press. pp.122–158.

Von Bertalanffy, L. (1968), *General systems theory*. New York: George Braziller.

4

Business Process Re-engineering – A German View

Karl A. Stroetmann, Matthias Maier and Walter Schertler

WHAT IS BUSINESS PROCESS RE-ENGINEERING?

Business Process Re-engineering (BPR) has recently become the most widely discussed approach to change-management. 'New' issues raised by BPR are:

- Its fiction of starting a business from scratch.
- Organising business along processes neglecting traditional departmental barriers.
- Its intense and innovative conceptual use of modern information technology (IT).
- Its strong focus on customers.

As a re-engineer puts it: 'It is time to stop paving the cow paths. Instead of embedding outdated processes in silicon and software, we should obliterate them and start over. We should "re-engineer" our businesses: use the power of modern information technology to radically redesign our business processes in order to achieve dramatic improvements in their performance' (Hammer, 1990, p. 104).

BPR has to be regarded as being *not one product* but as a product mix. Consulting firms welcome this seemingly new approach as it offers the opportunity of packing together well-established tools with only slight alterations. BPR might be the long-awaited consulting-product that is able to integrate a variety of approaches like TQM, Kanban, Simultaneous Engineering or Timebased Competition. Some consultants equate it with Lean Management. This is also a reason for the rapid adoption of this approach not only in the US but also in Europe. There are consultants who argue that radical approaches like BPR 'tend to come into vogue during periods of economic recession' (Rigby, 1993, p. 25) and disappear from stage in times of economic recovery. With regained prosperity, more stable organisational structures associated with some slack might be more appropriate, or even necessary, to serve market demand.

Following Rigby, a re-engineering package normally consists of four major components:

1. A fundamental rethinking of process organisation with the aim of drastically improving productivity and cycle times.
2. A reorganisation of organisational structure aiming at breaking functional hierarchies into cross-functional (horizontal) teams.
3. Implementation of a new state-of-the-art information system, providing information to the places where it is really needed.
4. Once again – a strong focus on the company´s customers.

BPR EXPERIENCE IN GERMANY

Soon after its German introduction Hammer and Champy´s (1993) book on BPR became a best-seller in management literature. The discussion was to a great extent accelerated by the publication of several articles in the business press. Each of the articles centred around the activities of a certain consulting firm – and all the articles were enthusiastic about the concept. Naturally, because of the concept´s origin, American consulting firms were the first to make the concept popular. But until now empirical information on the mode and intermediate success of implementation has been scarce. It will be a pioneer task for COBRA to investigate these issues in a European context.

Some big German companies claim to have already started the re-engineering of their processes. The business press has reported activities of the following German corporations: BASF Magnetics, Bosch-Siemens Hausgeräte, Asea Brown Boveri, BMW, Hewlett Packard, Freudenberg, Webasto, and Birkel Sonnen Bassermann. It is likely that in some cases BPR has been applied without using this buzzword. The German consultancy Diebold reports of having already realised several BPR-projects with firms in the small to medium-sized enterprise (SME) category. Clients were Fresenius AG, Wegmann & Co, Grammer AG, and Stadtwerke Wuppertal.

As the concept of BPR has only recently received attention in Germany, results of scientific research are not yet available. Reports in the business press proved to be insufficient to provide an overview of BPR practice. For this reason it was necessary to gather information through telephone interviews with consulting firms and research institutions.

The concept has rapidly been adopted by consultancies operating in the Germanophone countries. As far as the subsidiaries of the big American consultancies like McKinsey, Boston Consulting Group, Gemini, Arthur D. Little are concerned, the original concept has not been altered. German consultants have adapted the American concept; Diebold claims to have developed its own concept of process re-engineering ('Geschäftsprozeßoptimierung', GPO) already in the late 1980s. Since then, Diebold reports, a great number of projects applying BPR have been realised. It is not unlikely that American and German firms might have discovered, in parallel, the weaknesses of the functional organisation structure and have independently developed an approach for process reorganisation. But the experience of this consultancy seems not to be the rule.

As BPR can be interpreted as a package of already existing consulting products, it is likely that many firms can now argue that they have always done consulting in this way. As already said, the key issue of BPR is implementation – but empirical information on this point has been very weak up to now. As all the consultants interviewed in this survey have underlined, the concept of BPR is broad and abstract enough to be applied to almost every kind of business regardless of industry, size – or national culture.

Recently the German consultancy Droege & Comp. (among the top 20) conducted a study of BPR practice in Europe, US, and Japan. On the basis of the results of a standardised questionnaire they found out that only four per cent of European companies have realised a process approach.

THE GERMAN SOCIO-ECONOMIC FRAMEWORK AND BPR

Implementation of BPR in German companies has to take into account structural elements of the specific socio-economic system. In certain aspects relevant to business transformation, German socio-economic realities are distinctively shaped by specifically German institutions. The model of labour-management co-operation ('Mitbestimmung'), the unique system of vocational training of the work force ('Duales System der Berufsausbildung') and the great economic importance of small and medium-sized companies ('Mittelstand') are to be referred to in this context.

Labour-management co-operation
Strong unions are often heavily involved in decision-making at all corporate levels. The practice of 'Mitbestimmung' (co-determination) at various company levels usually goes beyond the formal requirements of legal regulations. The institutional framework incorporated in 'Mitbestimmung'

is also used by the participants to solve daily conflicts and smooth labour relations. Ideological issues play no important role in this context. Issues discussed are usually of a very practical nature.

All in all there is a broad consensus that co-determination implies a longer start-up phase for restructuring projects, as worker representatives have relatively far-reaching rights. But implementation is generally faster and more efficient compared with other European countries.

Wever and Allen argue, that:

> Joint labor-management institutions make up a remarkable machine for producing consensus, which helps German companies adapt to change (...) By allowing the German system to define external challenges in terms acceptable to *all* the stakeholders, such institutions make it easier for interest groups to agree on strategies for change.

As change programmes like BPR rely on the participation of the workforce, their willingness is of crucial importance. Hence Germany probably has an advantage in this respect.

Qualificational structure of the workforce

Traditionally the German workforce is internationally regarded as having superior skills. The reason for this lies in the unique system of vocational training that involves parallel learning at school and in a company. This means that young people are being confronted with working life and being socialised early with corporate German patterns of work practice, communication and participation in decision-making. Enriched and enlarged jobs as an outcome of BPR make the availability of a skilled and motivated workforce a *conditio sine qua non* for successful implementation.

Small and medium-sized enterprises

The picture of Germany's SMEs is fragmented. There exists a group of very competitive enterprises many of whom are world market leaders in their particular fields. A survey in the March/April (1992) issue of *Harvard Business Review* written by Hermann Simon (professor of business administration at the University of Mainz) identified this group of 'midsize giants'. He attributed their superior performance and continued growth to their ability to integrate customer and technological orientations.

But, as interviews with SME-experts show, the typical SME does not necessarily perform that well. They have several specific problems, eg capital raising and – as they are still often family-owned – the search for an entrepreneurial successor. With the founder of the business handing leadership to the younger generation of family members or management staff recruited outside, inherited styles and techniques of management are questioned. Not infrequently, as an adviser to several SMEs pointed out, this leads to deep activities of organisational restructuring. Naturally BPR is one of its options, the consultant added.

But management problems are in general not regarded to be a specific weakness of SMEs. Many of them are regarded as already being lean and process-driven. One could argue they have had to be lean, having neither the means nor the necessity to build up huge bureaucracies to manage fragmented business processes.

As re-engineering projects that take two years have to be regarded as being fast, and because the costs associated with re-engineering processes are not at all negligible, BPR will – with present methodologies – be a way to go only for the biggest of the SMEs.

NEW CHALLENGES FOR BPR IN GERMANY

In the Bibliography at the end of this chapter, all articles that cover issues of 'the German way to manage' end with a question mark in their titles. As the literature referred to comes from inside and outside the country, one might ask whether Germany's competitive advantage is still alive. Actually this is the tenor of today's discussion. Evidence on this point is clearly fragmented. Germany's high cost of labour and its tightly knit net of regulations becomes a definite weakness if it cannot be leveraged by strengths – or competitive advantages – in other respects.

The following major weak points of German businesses, and of the economy as a whole, are the focus of a broad discussion inside and outside the country.

Lack of customer orientation
German product quality is traditionally regarded to be high. What is often missing is the right product at the right price. The term 'over-engineering' applies perfectly to the outputs of several German industries. This holds true as well where flexible and fast responses to customer needs are asked for. The 'not invented here' syndrome is not uncommon. BPR seems to be perfectly suited to rectify this defect.

Departmental barriers
A rigid division of tasks and responsibilities between departments is regarded by some consultants as being the greatest obstacle for a new competitiveness of German companies. BPR clearly is a means for overcoming this. Implementation of process organisation means that habits give way to new structures.

Resistance to change
Although the German workforce is well educated and trained – there are still problems. For example, there is a certain resistance to new forms of work organisation and in particular less striving for technical innovations. Public acceptance of innovative techniques is not as advanced as it often is in the US. German consultants state that the majority of failures

in BPR are due to these resistances. So Change Management becomes a hot issue.

As expected, in general the strongest resistance to change comes from middle-management and not from the lower-level employees. The reason is that employees gain a lot of responsibility, they become responsible for outcomes and hence are now accountable for their own performance. Middle managers on the other hand fear they have a lot to lose.

Perhaps its drive for basic change is the strongest asset for the future application of BPR in Germany. By building completely new organisational structures, the problems of other change-approaches can be avoided. The participation of employees through existing structures cannot play the same role as in TQM and other bottom-up approaches.

OUTLOOK

Theorists argue that management as a social activity has to be analysed as being shaped by its socio-economic environment. This is a position typically held by European researchers. The other position – admittedly idealised – is the thesis of culture-free management, which is largely advocated by American management thinkers.

Interviews with consulting firms in Germany and an analysis of their concepts indeed reflect these two positions. Whereas the representatives of the American consultancies obviously adhere to the culture-free thesis, their colleagues at firms of German origin showed at least more ambivalence concerning this issue. The latter were in general more willing to discuss the cultural content of their consulting concepts and tools. As far as the successful application of BPR in a German context is concerned this will be a most important issue.

BIBLIOGRAPHY

Davenport, T. (1994), Reengineering in the United States. *Focus on Change Management*, 1, pp.1–2.

Davenport, T. and Nohria, N. (1994), Case management and the integration of labor. *Sloan Management Review*, 4, pp.11–23.

Fischer, F-W. (1994), Industriestandort Deutschland – Krise oder Chance durch das Arbeitsrecht. *Betriebs-Berater*, 4, pp.278–281.

Gatermann, M. and Krogh, H. (1993), Kurzer Prozeß. *Manager Magazin*, 12, pp.177–213.

Hammer, M. (1990), Reengineering work: Don't automate, obliterate. *Harvard Business Review*, July-August, pp.104–112.

Hammer, M. and Champy, J. (1993), *Reengineering the corporation: A manifesto for business revolution*. London: Nicholas Brealey.

Lorenz, C. (1993), Sculptors in jelly. *Financial Times*, 28 July.

Maier, F. (1993), Revolution der Prozesse. *Top Business*, December, pp.46–54.

Randall, R. (1993), The reengineer – Interview with Michael Hammer. *Planning Review*, May-June, pp.18–21.

Rigby, D. (1993), The secret history of process reengineering. *Planning Review*, March-April, pp.24–27.

Schmitz, W. (1994), Siemens will Produktivität im Quantensprung verbessern. *Handelsblatt, 11./12. 2.*

Schneider, M. (1994) Methoden-Puzzle. *Manager Magazin, 2*, pp.120–127.

Simon, H. (1992), Lessons from Germany's midsize giants. *Harvard Business Review*, March-April, pp.115–123.

Skinner, C. (1994), Does reengineering equal success? *Focus on Change Management 1*, pp.3–6.

Wächter, H. (1992), German co-determination – an outdated model? In *Researchgroup International Business in Europe: Transnational Business in Europe – Economic and Social Perspectives*. Tilburg. pp.258–264.

Wächter, H. (1992), Gibt es ein spezifisch deutsches Management? *Management Revue, 4*, pp.327–336.

Wever, K. and Allen, C. (1992), Is Germany a model for managers? *Harvard Business Review*, September-October, pp.36–43.

5

Initiating and Preparing for Re-engineering

Colin J Coulson-Thomas

Re-engineering, especially of the 'obliterating' variety, can be disruptive, painful and risky. It should not be undertaken lightly. Those who are carpet-bombed with corporate drives and initiatives can feel numb rather than liberated, and may become defensive rather than creative.

Before jumping in, an organisation needs to clarify its motives, decide how much change is required and establish the scope of what it is trying to do. For example, is it engaged in re-engineering one or more processes, or wholescale corporate transformation? Should customers and supply chain partners be involved? Do we need to put a torch to the past in order to face the future?

If re-engineering is to have a human face some core values may need to be agreed, and ground rules concerning the involvement and treatment of people established. Not only are employees key stakeholders, but in the longer term, it is difficult to sustain high levels of customer satisfaction with a dissatisfied team.

Too often people are victims rather than beneficiaries of change. How many re-engineering exercises are driven by a desire to take pressure off people, to make their working lives more rewarding, or to help them work or learn in new ways? There is an imbalance which the COBRA initiative is seeking to address.

In this chapter, we will examine the opportunity for BPR, establishing goals, where to begin, methodologies, the BPR process and the various stages of a representative approach. We will examine some practical issues, such as outcomes, the length of a BPR project, some areas of caution, and success factors. We will then turn to transformation strategy and the first two stages of the COBRA methodology: 1. Establishing an Organisation's Approach to BPR and Goal Setting; 2. Opportunity Seeking. The remaining COBRA steps will be examined in the next chapter on implementing BPR.

THE OPPORTUNITY

There are alternative models of organisations and ways of working and learning that can be much more rewarding for those involved. Where these do not involve repetitive processes, a process-centred (BPR) approach might not be appropriate. However, evidence suggests that inherited bureaucratic forms of organisation have a need to focus on processes and re-engineering (Coulson-Thomas, 1992b):

- In general, due to a desire for continuity and predictability, organisations tend to take too much for granted. In particular, they do not regularly question or redefine the value they are seeking to create and what actually represents value for customers.
- Few organisations are able to identify, let alone understand, the key cross-functional processes that add the value that is sought by their customers. In most organisations no one has end-to-end responsibility for them.
- Although greater use is being made of multi-functional project groups and teams, the departmental form of organisation persists. Most IT and training continues to be departmental, and hence makes a minimal contribution to improving the effectiveness of cross-functional processes.
- New approaches and techniques have been developed by world-class organisations that are resulting in substantial improvements in management performance. However, most companies cling to traditional approaches that have been shown to be wanting. In some organisations managerial productivity is actually falling as managers struggle to cope with extra responsibilities resulting from headcount reduction, and little is done to equip them to work in new ways.
- Despite a massive investment in teamwork training, too many teams are struggling to be effective rather than delivering outputs. Their objectives are often not expressed in clear, measurable output terms, while only rarely are the necessary empowerments and supporting technology in place.

In some sectors, when cases or transactions are broadly similar, there is advantage in the definition and support of repetitive processes (Bartram, 1992). They should never be assumed, but they can provide a welcome framework within which many people may prefer to operate. Repetition can also provide scope for movement along a learning curve.

Establishing goals

We saw in Chapter 1 that the motivations, or drivers, for considering or embracing re-engineering can be both extremely varied and either negative or positive. In itself, re-engineering is a neutral instrument. Our goals and purposes circumscribe and largely determine its impacts and outcomes.

Much restructuring and many destructive exercises are now being undertaken in the name of BPR. Michael Hammer and James Champy (1993, p. 48) point out that:

> Reengineering is not restructuring or downsizing. These are just fancy terms for reducing capacity to meet current, lower demand. . . . Reengineering also is not the same as reorganising, delayering, or flattening an organisation, although reengineering may, in fact, produce a flatter organisation.

A BPR exercise might be crucial or irrelevant, and welcomed or feared, depending on the goals set. Objectives range from the modest to the ambitious. With hindsight they can also sometimes turn out to be wrong. A focus on cost cutting could lead to a descending spiral of retrenchment. An emphasis on building capability might lead via an ascending spiral to longer term competitiveness.

The focus of re-engineering could be to review and radically change:

1. One or more business processes;
2. A total organisation;
3. How business is done within a particular marketplace;
4. A community;
5. A whole society.

Individual BPR initiatives can be relatively self-contained or may form part of an overall business excellence drive or transformation strategy.

Attacking individual processes will not of itself transform a total organisation. For this an holistic approach is required. BPR should encourage creative thinking about different ways of achieving corporate goals and objectives, rather than be used to avoid wholescale change.

The goal of an enterprise-wide corporate transformation could be a world-class capability that:

1. Delivers value and benchmark levels of satisfaction to customers, employees and business partners;
2. Differentiates in the marketplace;
3. Can support ambitious learning, business development and commercial objectives.

The BPR review process, and subsequent implementation and operation, should invigorate the people and teams concerned, and provide them with enhanced development opportunities.

WHERE TO BEGIN?

Assuming a focus on repetitive processes is required, should one begin by tackling management, support or business processes? While either management or support processes are being reviewed, today's business may die. However, ignoring them can result in an unfocused, uncoordinated company without direction – or the right activities with the wrong support. As a consequence, BPR may be applied to what is not strategically important.

Because of the risks involved, decisions on whether or not to initiate BPR, what form it should take, and where to begin are often taken in the boardroom. However, most boards have little if any experience of either process ownership or corporate transformation. Hence their individual members may need to be equipped with new skills and supported by new management processes that begin and end in the boardroom (Coulson-Thomas, 1993a and b). New models of organisation can also benefit from new forms of corporate governance.

Assuming that at some point it is decided to tackle individual business processes, the next question is: Which processes? Criteria to consider might include the vision, goals and values of the organisation, its priorities vis-à-vis customers and other stakeholders, the tackling of obstacles and bottlenecks, or distance from best-in-class as revealed by benchmarking.

To a pragmatist, considerations such as ease of implementation, time to deliver, and the opportunity to build confidence and senior management interest through early and tangible success may loom large. The sophisticate might use multiple and weighted criteria that reflect the contemporary context and current concerns.

The best form of long-term insurance against failure or irrelevance, and protection against errors of judgement or perception, is to build learning loops into processes and create a learning community. A BPR programme could pay particular attention to learning and learning processes (see Fig. 5.1). Many who talk about 'the learning organisation' fail to identify the processes that enable an enterprise to match its vision, goals and capability to the changing requirements of customers and other stakeholders.

Methodologies

Preparation for BPR includes consideration of what approaches, methodologies, tools and techniques to adopt. A wide range of each are available

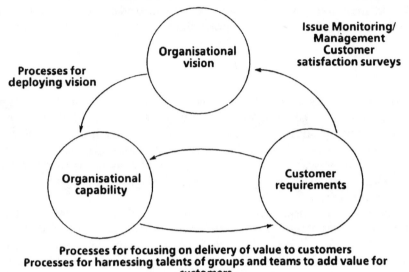

Processes for focusing on delivery of value to customers
Processes for harnessing talents of groups and teams to add value for
customers
Processes for continuous learning and improvement

Source: Colin Coulson-Thomas, *Transforming the Company*, 1992

Fig. 5.1 *Organisational Learning*

from a diversity of suppliers. (Derek Miers examines the different categories of tools that can be used to support BPR in Chapter 8.)

There are almost as many BPR approaches and methodologies as there
are active consultants in the field. Both should be chosen with care.
Which, if any, of the available alternatives are relevant, or even desirable,
will depend on the situation and circumstances. For many consultants,
BPR has represented a gravy train, and it has been used by some IT
vendors as a slicker way of selling systems.

Various combinations of previously existing methodologies and tools
have been brought together and repositioned under the BPR umbrella.
Certain approaches to re-engineering are little more than process
improvement, system re-design, or productivity tools re-named to capitalise on the BPR bandwagon. TQM and activity value analysis have
been used in the context of BPR although they have in the past been
associated with incremental rather than radical change.

Innovations have occurred independently of BPR where people have
asked bold, first principles questions prior to becoming aware of BPR
methodologies. The roots of many transformation or restructuring
success stories pre-date the more recent growth of interest in the BPR

combination of approaches. Increasingly, the term 're-engineering' is becoming synonymous with change, whether or not BPR methodologies are used.

What is available?

Most major firms of consultants have their own particular approach to BPR, as do some companies and other organisations. Which of these are relevant, or even desirable, will depend on the situation and circumstances.

Methodologies can be arranged along a spectrum according to the degree of change that is sought (see, for example, Chapters 1 and 2).

A re-engineering exercise could use techniques such as environmental scanning, modelling and visioning that might not be considered by a simplification team. On the other hand, benchmarking, problem-solving techniques, and a range of statistical and process analysis tools could be used in both re-engineering and simplification contexts.

'Corporate transformation' is more demanding still. It involves the re-design or transformation of the whole organisation, its values, structure, how it works and learns, and the attitudes and expectations of its people. Corporate transformation could use a wide range of approaches (including BPR) to move, for example, from a traditional to a network form of organisation.

Many practitioners who use the rhetoric of process re-engineering are actually engaged in process simplification. Bread-and-butter, relatively low risk approaches to simplification, can generate considerable short-term benefits. However, will they be enough if survival demands fundamental change?

Full-scale re-engineering has the potential to transform an organisation, but the risks of failure and of doing great harm are correspondingly greater. Which route is adopted, and when, may be constrained by the creativity and imagination of the BPR team. The timescale to achieve fundamental change may also extend beyond the lifetime of the change requirement.

Although different methodologies can appear very similar, the uses to which they are put can vary greatly, depending on the motivations for initiating BPR and how the task is approached. Much of what is termed re-engineering operates within an existing framework of attitudes and assumptions, and does not radically challenge them (see Chapter 1). To the purist, BPR is about revolution rather than evolution, fundamental change not incremental improvement.

Maintaining a sense of balance

When considering methodologies a sense of balance needs to be maintained. Advocates of methodologies stress how a shared framework can quickly enable people from different parts of a business to work together. However, there is a danger that common tools can ride roughshod over cultural differences and create identikit clones. Too detailed and extensive a methodology can also result in people going automatic. The importance of questioning, sensitivity and feel cannot be over-stressed.

Approaches, methodologies, techniques and tools are a means to an end, and should not be allowed to become an end in themselves. The purpose of BPR is to achieve a radical improvement in performance, not to provide experts with an excuse to plough methodically through endless checklists.

Whereas some resist methodologies and view them as inhibitors of original thought, others argue that it is difficult for people to co-operate without a common language and shared understanding of the steps involved. Much will depend on the calibre of the BPR team. Are they open-minded and courageous? Do they challenge? Do they have a tolerance for uncertainty and diversity, an overview perspective, and a desire to learn?

Those who go to the essence of what needs to be done to generate value and build relevant capability, and who keep it simple, tend to be the most successful. Considerable success in process simplification can result from using such basic questions as: Would a customer pay for this? or, Would I do this if it were my business?

A BPR methodology is only as strong as its weakest link. The boxes labelled 'visioning', 're-design' or 'blue skies thinking' tend to be the most suspect, especially when little guidance is given. Simply telling people to go out, be creative and think up some alternative options is sometimes just as effective.

What is generally important is approach and attitude rather than methodology *per se*. Thus one group might plod through the various stages of a methodology with little imagination or enthusiasm, while another could use the same framework to harness and channel creativity and commitment. Also, the unexpected tends to occur, and both sensitivity and flexibility are required.

A restless community of seeking, challenging people for whom aspiring to match or beat the best becomes a way of life would not need to consider BPR as a separate exercise. Its approaches and attitudes would represent aspects of normal business.

THE BPR PROCESS

A BPR review process might pass through goal setting, opportunity seeking, modelling, analysis, design, implementation and monitoring phases, and should be tailored to the situation and context. It could involve the assessment of internal and external requirements; the use of benchmarking, environmental scanning, modelling, visioning, design and planning tools; and the analysis of the interaction of people, work processes, information and technology.

Among BPR practitioners, there are differences of opinion over the order in which BPR steps should be undertaken. Thus:

1. Some believe that alternative options should not be contemplated until the existing processes have been documented and understood. In the light of this grounding, an alternative model can then be developed and implemented.
2. Others argue passionately that examining 'what is' can condition people and limit their creativity. Better to ignore what exists until imaginative thinking has led to a new model. Then is the time to examine 'what is' in order to develop a programme to migrate from a current situation to a desired future state of affairs.

Which option is adopted can depend on the nature and extent of the gap between where an organisation is and where it would like to be; ie on the degree of change that is required. For example:

■ If there is a wide gap, and what exists is unlikely to provide a sufficient base for doing what is necessary, it is better to start afresh. Then having designed an alternative, one can always go back to see if some existing elements could feature in a new solution.
■ However, if there is a narrow gap, and it is thought that what exists has considerable potential for development, priority may be given to the analysis of 'what is' in order to identify opportunities for improvement.

BPR can appear disruptive to a complacent organisation. It is often a sense of crisis that gives rise to the requirement for more than incremental adaptation. The nature of the business environment can also have a significant impact on which approach is adopted. Thus:

■ If an initial environmental scan and situation analysis suggests that existing practice, however much changed, is unlikely to provide a launch pad for the radical improvements that are sought, the more unfettered approach (2) above might be preferable.
■ In a more stable and risk-averse context where there is a desire not to waste past investments in infrastructure, and where people sense there is much potential that has not been fully exploited, approach (1) above that leverages an existing capability may be preferred.

The live COBRA case study situations in which questions relating to new patterns of work have been posed, suggest approach (1) is more likely to be adopted in simplification exercises, while approach (2), although less common, should be recommended if there is a genuine desire to break free from the past and adopt a re-engineering approach.

A representative approach

Once the need for radical action is agreed, what should happen next? There is no right or wrong sequence of BPR steps, so the following summary of an approach (that of Adaptation Ltd) developed and used by the author is given only for the purposes of illustrating certain points:

1. If an organisation is new to BPR, some event or situation needs to give rise to the requirement. BPR should be front-ended by a strategic review process that includes issue monitoring and management, SWOT and competitor analysis to ensure that re-engineering supports strategic business development objectives.

2. A useful initial step could be to appoint a sponsor (preferably a key member of the board) and assemble an initial BPR team. At this stage, the group selected needs to be capable of acting as a catalyst and securing commitment to an agreed course of action. Hence it could be at a higher level than the group which might later be assembled to tackle an individual process.

3. With the help of the sponsor and initial team, an assessment needs to be undertaken of the organisation's will and capability to undertake BPR. There is little point initiating BPR activity without first checking that the organisation has the commitment and has, or has access to, the necessary skills successfully to undertake it. The team should be led by someone at senior management and preferably director-level who has been given responsibility for pulling together a BPR approach and strategy for consideration by the board. In many organisations, a board-level steering group is appointed to act as an ongoing link with the BPR project team or teams.

4. At the level of the total organisation, BPR goals, objectives and specific targets will need to be set. The BPR team should be given both demanding goals and the authority to proceed. At this goal-setting stage, a decision should be taken of whether to tackle an individual process or aim at wholescale corporate transformation.

5. Once a BPR strategy has been agreed, a core BPR team needs to be established of those who can actually make it happen. The composition of the team will reflect the agreed strategy, eg whether the chosen route is one of improvement, re-engineering, or a wider corporate transformation.

6. Assuming a decision to focus on a particular area of opportunity or process, and where a problem or bottleneck process does not suggest itself as an obvious candidate for BPR, the next step is to seek out opportunities for radical action, eg select an area for innovation or an

initial process to re-engineer. Attention should be focused where the potential for achieving a significant impact on business objectives and performance, within an acceptable timescale, is the greatest.

7. A portfolio of projects, some of an incremental change nature, others aiming at more fundamental change, could now be established. A separate BPR action team would normally be formed to tackle each of the re-engineering exercises. The initial BPR team could by now have evolved into a steering group with a brief to coordinate and support the various initiatives underway.

8. Rather than be pre-occupied with what is, a BPR action team should be encouraged systematically to seek out alternative ways of undertaking the subject of their review. The enquiry should be free and wide ranging.

9. An action team in a customer-led organisation might at this point spend some time questioning who the customer really is, and the extent to which customer requirements are actually understood. What represents value to the customer from the customer's perspective? What other forms of relationship with the customer could be developed? The answer to questions such as these might be something which does not, but could, exist.

10. In a policy-led organisation, a team should go back to basics and re-examine the reasons for policies and the nature of policy objectives. Are existing activities dealing with symptoms or underlying causes? At this stage, insight and clear thinking are required. If activities being re-engineered do not represent the heart of a problem, improving a cosmetic may distract people from taking necessary action where it is most needed.

11. Environmental scanning can lead to unfamiliar and novel options being encountered, perhaps in unrelated fields. The aim should be to obtain a feel for the limits of what is possible.

12. Once the BPR action team's thinking has become bold and challenging, it may be time to establish a vision for the area that is being examined. This could take the form of a model of operation quite different from that which currently exists.

13. In order to design a new model or approach, it may be advisable to agree some design principles. These should not be drawn so tightly as to prematurely close off promising lines of enquiry.

14. Once the broad scoping of what is desirable has occurred, the next step is to examine the extent to which it can be achieved. This involves looking at such factors as different ways of learning or performing the work, available technologies, a range of people issues, and alternative ways in which people, processes, information and technology can be brought together. Particular attention should be

paid to innovations and levers that could unlock breakthrough levels of performance.

15. The first principles stage of a BPR review should not be rushed, even though others may encourage the team to curtail airy-fairy thinking in order to proceed. However, once the major building blocks of a new approach appear to have been identified, the project can move on to a more detailed design phase.

16. Situations, circumstances, people, requirements and priorities are ever changing. At this point, if not earlier, thought should be given to how learning and refinement might be incorporated into the new approach. Measures ensuring that the solution remains appropriate and current must be built-in to prevent it from having a limited shelf-life.

17. Up until this point, BPR activity has been largely cerebral, namely modelling and analysis, with just enough design work to establish the technical feasibility of an emerging solution. Most organisations will now require some form of 'business' or project proposal with an economic case for moving ahead.

18. Assuming that a compelling argument can be made for progressing, more detailed design work, and implementation planning, can now be commissioned. From this point the cost and impact of a BPR exercise can increase quite significantly.

19. In the case of a complex process, the project plan could provide for implementation in phases. Interim milestones could be established to focus effort on one part of a process, or one sub-process, at a time. In a dynamic environment the emphasis should be on rapid development. If implementation takes too long, either people may lose interest or a solution may be overtaken by events.

20. Where the risk of failure is high, and there are existing and ongoing services to deliver, it is usually advisable to test a new approach on a pilot basis.

21. Assuming a successful pilot, the full programme can then be rolled out, and its subsequent operation monitored, to enable refinements to be introduced, or changes made as appropriate.

22. At a suitable point after implementation (eg when the potential is being fully realised) an organisation should review what it has learned from a particular BPR exercise and ensure that the lessons are shared.

23. If BPR is regarded as a one-off exercise, then over time the new approach may become set in concrete. All processes should be reviewed on a periodic cycle which should be built into the process itself. Thus BPR should become an aspect of normal operation. It should not be regarded as something different that is done by some people, who are BPR specialists, to others.

There is no right or wrong sequence of BPR steps, and the above summary description of the Adaptation Ltd approach is for illustration only. (The COBRA approach is considered later in this and the next chapter, while other approaches in this book include those of Rohit Talwar in Chapter 2 and ESRC in Chapter 9.) Whether or not the BPR team should move on from one stage to the next will depend on whether this is thought to be justified, and further time and additional analysis would result in a materially better solution.

As an exercise progresses along the lines described, the composition of a BPR team should be periodically reviewed and the people of the organisation should be updated on progress and next steps. Periodic risk assessments should also be undertaken so that the risks involved in continuing can be compared with the expected benefits.

BPR can be built into an organisation's policy-making process. One policy-making stream could determine priorities from issue monitoring exercises, customer satisfaction surveys, and competitor and market analyses. A second implementation stream could review how the key priorities can be achieved. For example, benchmarking could be used to identify gaps that probably cannot be bridged by incremental steps alone.

Thinking application

To understand what is distinct about BPR, compare the above broad phases with the more precise steps of a typical improvement or simplification methodology. When identifying process owners, defining and documenting a process, defining and agreeing customer requirements and so on, some creative thinking is of course required. However, many exercises tend to become a matter of filling in the boxes as one ploughs through the methodology manual.

Given a detailed process improvement or simplification methodology, the steady plodder can emerge with acceptable levels of performance improvement. However, effective re-engineering requires a very different type of person. One of the challenges of BPR is to find people who can push innovation and creativity to the limit without stepping over the boundary of what is practical.

Pragmatic decisions still have to be made. For example, should a complex process be created to handle all the various forms of a transaction that are likely to arise, or should the transactions be screened into different categories, each of which might be handled by a distinct and simpler process, or a separate sub-process?

Once a particular BPR exercise has reached what appears to be an end point, it should be remembered that situations, circumstances, people, requirements and priorities are ever changing. Hence the importance of

building continuous learning, renewal and further periodic first principles reviews into the re-engineered process. Particular attention should
be devoted to assembling the combination of processes (Fig. 5.1) that
enable an organisation continually to match its capability and corporate
vision to changing customer requirements.

BPR OUTCOMES

Although its advocates claim that BPR is concerned with long-term
(rather than short-term) impacts, the competitive advantage yielded by
some applications has proved very short-lived. BPR solutions can be
copied. Me-too exercises mean that soon everyone is responding in hours
rather than days. Having created more demanding customers and made
life tougher for all suppliers, the pioneer is then faced with the What
now? question.

The outcomes and benefits of BPR can be viewed in absolute and relative terms:

■ In absolute terms, an improvement over what was experienced prior
   to a BPR exercise ought to be maintained. However, over time the
   level of improvement may settle down to a lower level as people
   become accustomed to a new pattern of working and the initial buzz
   or challenge of a different way of operating wears off. Regression can
   also occur.

■ In relative terms (ie in comparison with other organisations), the level
   of performance achieved as a result of a BPR exercise can, over time,
   fall below best-practice. Hence, it may be advisable at periodic inter-
   vals to consider further re-engineering activities.

The best guarantee of high levels of both absolute and relative performance is eternal vigilance, and a commitment to seeking out, learning
from and striving to improve on best-practice on an international basis.

Outcomes that develop people and give them space and thinking
time, and which support new ways of working and learning, can often
yield longer lasting benefits than those concerned with speed and cost
reduction.

The length of a project

The length of a BPR project will depend on the nature of the process
being re-designed and its context. For the re-design of an individual
process in a large organisation, a period of 18 months to complete an
implementation is not unusual. A project involving a sub-process or part
of a process should be completed more quickly than one involving a
whole process, while corporate transformation could take several years.

Some processes are relatively self-contained, others may impact on a number of other processes. Where an organisation is made up of a complex network of overlapping and inter-dependent processes one would expect projects to require more time to complete.

More radical changes need not take longer to achieve. A first principles review could involve a relatively short burst of creative thought. Achieving more modest results might require time-consuming analysis and documentation of 'what is' for improvements to be made.

Some BPR exercises are prolonged by a desire to take every relevant factor into account. It is generally possible to speed them up, eg by concentrating on those areas which appear to have the greatest impact on customers and which consume the greatest amount of resources. One could aim to get it roughly right – based on the most significant factors. Further elaboration can then be undertaken until the incremental benefits are no longer worth the extra effort involved.

Areas of caution

There is a growing gulf between the rhetoric and the practice of BPR. Pure BPR is rare, while simplification exercises abound. People are getting bogged down with incremental improvements to 'what is', rather than thinking creatively about what ought to be.

Creativity, or the lack of it, is the Achilles heel of many approaches to BPR. Although the re-design step in most re-engineering methodologies demands a degree of flair and imagination, people generally find it very difficult to think creatively. The methodologies themselves often provide little help beyond suggesting the use of tools such as brainstorming.

The focus of too many BPR exercises is internal, ie on the organisation and its processes, rather than on what represents value for the external customer. The initiative stops at the boundary of the organisation and does not embrace the supply chain – suppliers, customers and business partners. Also, one can sometimes attend a BPR 'event', or even a series of BPR team meetings, without hearing the word 'customer' mentioned once.

Many approaches to BPR are also insufficiently tailored to the situation, circumstances and context. Standard approaches to BPR and quality can provide a common language, but, as pointed out earlier, they can also destroy diversity. Global companies that introduce new approaches tend to find they travel better in some parts of the world than in others (Coulson-Thomas, 1992a).

Approaches to BPR are often mechanical and crude rather than creative and sensitive. There is excessive focus on the hard and quantifiable, such as document flows and supporting technology. Insufficient attention is devoted to the softer people issues because these are perceived as difficult or intangible. BPR is being 'done' to too many people who are not themselves sufficiently actively involved, motivated or empowered.

Why, given the mixed experience and risks involved, should anyone be interested in BPR? A cynic might answer: 'because nothing else has worked', or 'because it is good business for consultants'. Some people just want to be seen to be doing something. Others wish to join a bandwagon, or being desperate for results, become victims of peddlers of hype and simplistic solutions.

Success factors

Successful re-engineering requires a number of complementary factors, including a desire to change, the courage to search for ambitious outcomes, the active participation at each phase of the people of the process, and top management commitment. The latter is sometimes lacking because many of those wishing to undertake fundamental transformations are insecure.

The creative use of IT can transform a marketplace and IT has become inextricably linked with BPR. At the same time, radical improvements of performance have resulted from simplifying IT, or even the virtual elimination of IT. One operation was transformed by the introduction of a card index system. Instead of relating only to VDU screens and sending electronic mail messages to each other that get lost among electronic junk mail, people started sitting around a table, talking, and resolving customer problems there and then as a cross-functional group.

BPR is too important to be left to IT specialists and anaemic consultants who methodically plod through standard checklists. The critical implementation issues and barriers tend to concern attitudes, beliefs and behaviour. Interpersonal communication and involvement are usually the limiting factors rather than the capability of technology.

An approach to BPR should be adopted that is compatible with the local corporate culture. For example, where such values as continuity, predictability, fairness and equality are deeply entrenched, and change, innovation and efficiency are alien, the context may be more suited to incremental change, or process improvement and simplification, rather than more radical BPR.

Many re-engineering projects are doomed to fail from the moment they are initiated because vital pieces of the jig-saw puzzle are missing. Well-thought-out programmes, even a variety of distinct initiatives that in themselves are worthy, may not be enough. To make a significant impact on an end-to-end process, let alone a total organisation, an holistic approach is likely to be required, comprised of a wide range of elements.

Perhaps the most important success requirement is to assemble the combination of change elements to make it happen in the particular situation and circumstances (Coulson-Thomas, 1992b). No two contexts are likely to be the same, and the key elements needed can vary greatly between them.

Transformation strategy

So what advice should be given to the busy CEO? A first step is to face up to the question: do you really want to turn your world upside down and radically transform your organisation? The half-hearted should look elsewhere.

To develop an effective strategy for corporate re-engineering, and before agreeing transformation vision, goals, values and objectives, it is necessary to assess and understand: (1) the challenge and the risks; and (2) stakeholder expectations. People need to be pressed as to whether they want, or need, radical change with all the risks inherent in BPR initiatives.

The next step is to relate the elements of a programme to what is necessary to tackle the hindrances, obstacles and barriers. If dramatic breakthroughs in performance are to occur, these must be identified and overcome.

Clear roles and responsibilities, and the vital few priorities, can ensure that resources are applied where they are likely to have the greatest impact. The review process should address any gaps and deficiencies. An action programme of recommendations should detail the next steps to be taken, any missing elements, and the tools and techniques that could be used to overcome implementation barriers.

Successful transformation depends critically on the selection, combination and application of relevant change elements at each stage of the change process. It is generally easier to get the strategy right than to manage the consequences of getting it wrong.

COBRA METHODOLOGY

It is not easy to build responsive, sensitive and caring forms of organisations in an unthinking and short-term oriented environment. If organisations and societies are to reap the full benefits of BPR, attitudes and behaviours will need to change.

The COBRA (1994–96) project has developed a six stage BPR methodology (Fig. 5.2) which is designed to complement other approaches in order to ensure that due attention is paid to issues relating to new ways of working and the re-engineering of supply chains.

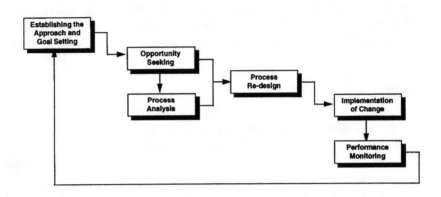

© Commission of the European Communities, 1994

Fig. 5.2 *COBRA methodology*

The first two stages of the COBRA (1994–96) methodology are examined below in relation to initiating and preparing for BPR, while the remaining four stages are examined in the next chapter which is concerned with implementing BPR. (The material summarised in this and the next chapter relates to BPR in general rather than new ways of working in particular.)

As pointed out in Chapter 1, organisations are not machines to be re-engineered by taking pieces out, changing them and putting them back, but communities of people with feelings. Punch them in the face and they bleed. Too many management teams are feeding like vultures on the hopes and dreams of their people. Some heart needs to be put into BPR.

Establishing an organisation's approach to BPR

Let us now examine in more detail the planning stages of the approach to re-engineering suggested by the COBRA team in its methodology manual (COBRA, 1994–96): (1) Establishing an organisation's approach to BPR and goal setting; and (2) Opportunity seeking (or selecting which process to re-engineer when the exercise is concerned with an individual process).

Establishing an organisation's approach to BPR and goal setting (see Fig. 5.3 for an overview) effectively sets the corporate direction and strategy for BPR. An assessment needs to be made of the situation and circumstances, and of the context within which an organisation operates, in order to determine how much change is required, the scope of a BPR exercise, what form it should take and where it should start. For example:

© Commission of the European Communities, 1994

Fig. 5.3 *Establishing the approach and goal setting*

■ Should the focus be on the re-engineering of an individual and existing process, the holistic transformation of the total organisation, or on creating a new area of activity?

■ Should an attempt be made to transform the nature of the marketplace within which the organisation operates?

To answer questions such as these, a company might need to undertake issue monitoring and management, or opportunity and competitor analysis, better to understand the business environment and identify the extent of the gap between actual and desired capability and performance.

Outputs at this stage should include both a change vision, agreed parameters for the scale, scope and nature of what needs to be done, and a shared understanding of the risks involved. An agreed BPR strategy or approach to BPR should be consistent with, and supportive of, overall business vision and strategy.

Senior management commitment to appropriate, and if need be radical, action should have been secured, and, given a variety of stakeholder interests and concerns, priorities for action should have been agreed. Those undertaking a BPR exercise need to be confident of senior management support, and will need to have a sense of corporate priorities in order to handle any trade-offs and critical choices that might emerge.

While the practitioner focuses on the management of the individual BPR project, a board's perspective and concern is more likely to be the contribution of BPR to the wider transformation of an organisation.

As part of the review process, the purpose, values and beliefs of the organisation should be re-examined in the light of the changing interests and perspectives of stakeholders. There are some critical issues to address, for example, what is the rationale of the organisation, and the nature of the value it is seeking to create? What actually represents value to customers and other stakeholders (particularly shareholders and employees)?

Many BPR initiatives are undertaken in isolation, rather than as part of an overall transformation strategy. Any programme that emerges must be consistent with an organisation's overall vision, values, goals and objectives – and the interests of its stakeholders. Suppliers, customers and business partners should be involved in the review process.

The practicalities of goal setting

An organisation should carefully consider the imperatives for change and assess the likely costs and benefits against other priorities. BPR should not be assumed. Fundamental change can be both risky and may involve high short-term costs. It could make considerable claims on scarce management resources at a time when other pressing issues demand attention. Alternatives and their implications should be considered before one particular approach is adopted.

The re-design of one or more processes might be but one option to be considered. Improvement or simplification, wholescale transformation, or even creating a new organisation from scratch could be more appropriate in certain circumstances. Key questions to address are: Does the organisation need to undergo a total transformation? Would this be too risky? Is the change required tactical or strategic? Does the organisation face a crisis? Does it have the will, commitment and capability to bring about fundamental change?

Where deficiencies of a modest kind exist across a great many areas, an organisation may opt for a broad range of process simplification or improvement initiatives. If much more serious deficiencies are found in a few areas, then the more radical treatment of re-engineering may be adopted. With re-engineering it will be necessary to be more selective, as most organisations are only able to handle a small number of radical transformations at any one time.

To judge whether or not an organisation has the capability to make a step change, a review may need to be undertaken of corporate strengths and weaknesses (eg financial, cultural, operational and regulatory constraints) in relation to the degree of change that is sought. What existing skills, know-how, reputation, or capability could be better exploited? Not every organisation will have the base to support what is needed to achieve a revolutionary impact within their market sector or create a new business opportunity.

When a BPR initiative is launched, its relationship with other corporate programmes such as TQM should be made clear. In many organisations people are confused about the relationship between BPR and TQM. The two can complement each other, as when a re-engineered solution is continually reviewed and refined to ensure that it does not become out of date.

Specific BPR objectives could be set for improvements in management and business processes at the level of the organisation as a whole, a part of an organisation, individual processes or particular sub-processes. So far as BPR is concerned, demanding objectives often prove easier to achieve than more modest ones, as they encourage the radical thinking that is more likely to lead to breakthroughs in performance.

From time to time, an organisation's approach to BPR should be re-visited and reviewed. For example: Have stakeholder expectations changed? Does the organisation's approach to BPR meet its clients' needs and corporate objectives, represent best-practice, and match its corporate culture? Is the emphasis in BPR assignments slipping back to simplification and incremental improvement, and away from fundamental transformation? Action may be needed to re-capture the original BPR drive and vision.

IDENTIFYING THE OPPORTUNITY

Having established an approach, the next stage is Opportunity Seeking (see Fig. 5.4 for an overview), ie to identify areas where there is scope for fundamental and strategic change, opportunities for achieving radical breakthroughs in performance and sustainable competitive advantage. The most significant opportunities and processes, from the point of view of impact on the customer and the achievement of business objectives need to be assessed and prioritised, and one (or more) greenfield opportunities or process(es) selected as the focus of a re-engineering exercise.

The major levers, spring-boards and opportunities, including key current processes need to be identified, and some assessment made of the impact of each on the achievement of the organisation's goals and objectives (eg what impact do, or could, they have on customer and shareholder value?).

Outputs at this stage could include: (1) a list of areas of opportunity (eg where there appear to be levers, gaps, or spring-boards) that would allow more than incremental changes to be achieved; and (2) an agreed set of re-engineering targets and priorities, along with agreed and measurable objectives in terms of what would represent a successful outcome. The targets could take the form of benchmark levels of performance, while the priorities could take the form of areas of new capability (including processes) and activity that need to be created, and/or existing processes that need to be re-engineered.

Issues Related to New Ways of Working

• Clear Definition of What Represents Value to Customers.

• Extent and Balance of Change Between Management and Business Processes.

• Core Team's Familiarity with Existing Business Processes as a Block to Creative Thinking.

Customers' and Competitors' Ways of Working

Existing Organisational Structure

Unfreeze

Change Requirements

Management Desire / Need For Change

Outputs of BPR Stage

• Re-engineering Opportunities Identified.

• Core Team Selected.

• Change Priorities Agreed.

Fig. 5.4   *Opportunity seeking*

Criteria need to be established to enable the identified opportunities and/or processes to be ranked in order of priority for re-engineering. For example, what risks are inherent in both the nature of the opportunity and the organisation's ability to tackle it? Priority could be given to creating the capability and processes to exploit a major opportunity, or to the potential for introducing elements of a learning organisation.

An action programme will be required for each selected priority for action. A different change strategy may also be required for each priority. One should only progress to the next BPR stage when a change strategy has been agreed and an appropriate team has been brought together to undertake the work. The aim should be to secure sustainable competitive advantage by clearly differentiating from the alternatives available. The genuine innovator strives to offer something which is unique.

Many corporate restructurings have little, if any, impact on the core processes that actually deliver value to the end customer. It is important that a customer eye view or perspective on the organisation is adopted, as it may look very different from the viewpoint of an external user or partner.

For changes to have a noticeable impact on an end customer, a BPR exercise must be focused on what represents value to the end customer (ie it should work from outside in). If value is not understood from a customer perspective, the team may select the wrong process to re-engineer. Where it is understood, a search can be more purposive, ie the team can positively and creatively look out for the levers and opportunities of making the greatest impact.

The practicalities of opportunity seeking

If BPR is to be applied, a process should be repetitive. BPR may not be advisable where a high proportion of activities are of a one-off nature. Key questions to consider are: Would a standard process improve or inhibit creativity? Does each challenge require a unique process?

A group should not contrive to create a process where one does not, or should not, exist. The following questions could be used to help identify the existence of a process: Who are the customers? What are the outputs? What activities produce these outputs? What decisions are taken? What inputs are required? Who supplies these inputs? Who is involved? How long does it take? Where satisfactory answers to such questions are not possible, what is being observed could well be a number of *ad hoc* events rather than a formal process.

Processes should not be assumed to have a continuing relevance just because they exist. All should be challenged: What value do they add in relation to their cost? How frequently are they used? Could they become a distinctive source of enduring advantage, that would be difficult to copy and which could be further refined and developed?

Which process is selected will depend on the relative weighting attached to the various factors that are taken into account. Errors of judgement can be made. Thus an organisation may begin with a complex process that has the most direct impact on the customer, when starting elsewhere would result in an easier exercise within a shorter timescale, which might thus deliver tangible benefits earlier and enable confidence and experience to be built up prior to a more demanding exercise.

People who find it difficult to make choices tend to be among those who are keen at this stage to undertake detailed process mapping. Attempting to build an elaborate process model of an organisation at this point can represent a time-consuming distraction.

A sense of what is deliverable is essential, and of for how long people can be expected to retain their enthusiasm and commitment in the absence of visible successes. An organisation that is opportunist might seek temporary advantages, while one that is committed longer term to being a player in a market may need to seek more fundamental and lasting changes.

Some organisations attempt to do too much too quickly (eg it may be risky for a large organisation to attempt to change simultaneously more than two or three major processes). Other organisations are excessively cautious, perhaps because senior management is not confident about their collective commitment or ability to overcome various implementation barriers.

Playing it safe, for example by opting for an area in which implementation is thought to be relatively easy, can distract an organisation from opportunities to make more significant impacts. Radical change demands a willingness to be bold.

An assessment needs to be made of how willing different groups are to challenge assumptions and undertake a radical change. Do they feel under pressure (eg is there a perceived crisis?) or is there a strong desire for change? How strong and committed are the actual and likely advocates and opponents of change?

To encourage creative thinking at this stage, some work may need to be done to raise ambitions, break down prejudices and other perceptual barriers, challenge assumptions, unfreeze attitudes, and encourage free and creative thinking. Benchmarking could be undertaken to open people up to quite different ways of doing things and very different levels of performance.

REFERENCES

Bartram, P. (1992), *Business re-engineering – The use of process redesign and IT to transform corporate performance*. London: Business Intelligence.

Coulson-Thomas, C. (1992a), *Creating the global company: Successful internationalisation*. London: McGraw Hill Europe.

Coulson-Thomas, C. (1992b), *Transforming the company: Bridging the gap between management myth and corporate reality*. London: Kogan Page.

Coulson-Thomas, C. (1993a), *Creating excellence in the boardroom*. London: McGraw Hill Europe.

Coulson-Thomas, C. (1993b), *Developing directors: Building an effective boardroom team*. London: McGraw Hill Europe.

COBRA (1994), *Business restructuring and teleworking: Issues, considerations and approaches*. (Methodology Manual for the Commission of the European Communities) London: Adaptation.

COBRA (1995), Colin Coulson-Thomas (Executive Editor), *The Responsive Organisation: Re-engineering new patterns of work*. London: Policy Publications.

COBRA (1996), Peter Bartram, Colin Coulson-Thomas and Lee Tate, *The Competitive Network*, London: Policy Publications.

Hammer, M. and Champy, J. (1993), *Reengineering the corporation: A manifesto for business revolution*. London: Nicholas Brealey Publishing.

6

Implementing Re-engineering

Colin J Coulson-Thomas

Today's demanding and dynamic business environment confronts organisations with a variety of challenges and opportunities. For many of them, more than incremental change may be required, ie revolution rather than evolution is sought. People are increasingly turning to radical, or blue skies, approaches such as re-engineering, whether of particular processes, of their total organisation, or of a whole market-place.

Many management teams are seeking a step change in response times and in the extent to which they can access and develop relevant resources and empowered people, and deliver value. The issue is not so much the desire for fundamental change, but whether it can be achieved.

In Chapter 5 we examined initiating and preparing for BPR and introduced the first two stages of the COBRA (1994–96) approach. In this chapter, we will examine the remaining COBRA stages from a BPR perspective, namely Process analysis, Process re-design, Implementation of change, and Performance monitoring.

But first, some general points about the implementation of BPR. We will look at some warning signs, the prospects for BPR, the pitfalls and dangers, some public sector issues and implementation success factors. We will then turn to the BPR team, the skills they need, how methodologies and consultants should be used, and the role of IT.

IMPLEMENTATION: AN OVERVIEW

Warning signs

Despite the desire and opportunity for radical change, and the '10×' improvements in productivity or response times chalked up by well-publicised case studies, a degree of caution is required. While time and cost are being taken out, only a few transformation, re-engineering, or quality programmes are resulting in significant changes of attitudes or behaviour.

There is a huge gulf between the rhetoric of BPR and the reality of its application. Quite simply, many BPR exercises are failing to deliver. Why is this? Is it because of a failure of leadership, a lack of an holistic perspective, a reluctance to address reality, intolerance of diversity, mechanical and unthinking application of BPR tools and methodologies, or a failure to identify and tackle obstacles and barriers? Often all these failings are present. In Chapters 1 and 5 it was pointed out that people are getting bogged down with incremental improvements to 'what is', rather than thinking creatively about what ought to be.

Prospects

Let us review the evidence assembled by COBRA to assess the prospects for BPR. It suggests that the implementation of BPR, and hence the results of much effort, activity and anguish are likely to continue to disappoint:

- BPR goals and objectives are generally either too modest or inappropriate. It is being too rarely used to secure longer term advantages. For example, the emphasis is typically on short-term cost, 'headcount' and time saving rather than the introduction of new ways of working and learning that would better secure sustained competitive advantage. A high long-term cost in terms of loss of morale and trust is often paid for short-term improvements in response times.
- Significant and positive changes of attitude and behaviour are unlikely to occur while crucial change elements are missing and emphasis is placed on squeezing more out of people. Key and complementary change elements do not feature in some BPR methodologies.
- Commitment is often at a superficial level. People go along with BPR because it appears to be the 'in thing', but they have not really had the time to think it through and are not convinced that it is different in kind from other attempts at change.
- Many BPR initiatives are undertaken in isolation, rather than as part of an overall transformation vision. Transformation or re-engineering goals and strategy are generally not clear or shared, while very often the resources and capability required for implementation have not been assembled.
- It is difficult for organisations without vision to use a vision-led approach such as BPR. Most organisations lack a compelling rationale for existing, clear corporate direction, a distinctive vision, shared goals

and objectives, an effective strategy, or a policy deployment process. Hence BPR is blind.

■ We saw in Chapter 5 that approaches to BPR tend to be insufficiently tailored to the particular situation, circumstances and context, and they are often procedural rather than creative.

■ Involvement is lacking in many BPR exercises, while empowerment is largely rhetoric. Like many recent concepts, they are employed before those who lead organisations have thought through their full implications.

■ Many companies are not as open as they could be about the real driver of BPR. Often it is downsizing or headcount reduction in order to reduce the cost base rather than value to customers. When people catch on, trust is lost.

■ Those undertaking BPR have a tendency to focus internally, on the processes being re-engineered, as if they have an existence and rationale of their own, and to lose sight of the external customer. Ultimately all value is generated by the external customer.

■ Excessive amounts of time are devoted to documenting and understanding current organisations rather than thinking about alternative models. Trivial, or time-consuming exercises are taking an age to demonstrate benefits. In certain cases, the day of action is postponed indefinitely while complex process models are developed that resemble plates of spaghetti.

■ In some organisations, the relationship between BPR and other programmes such as TQM or downsizing is not clear. Rivalries develop and different initiatives can undercut each other's effectiveness.

■ In particular, attempts to transform organisations can lead to a new division of labour between specialist and self-contained groups. Thus IT takes responsibility for BPR, while elsewhere, perhaps in personnel, another group is examining new ways of working. Typically, the two groups work in isolation, with neither achieving their full potential.

■ Voices of caution are still drowned out by the growing number of suppliers of consultancy and other services that are using the full range of communications opportunities and techniques to push and promote the benefits of BPR. Health warnings are rare.

Against this background, it is not surprising that many senior managements doubt the ability of their colleagues to bring about fundamental changes of attitudes, values, approach and perspective within an acceptable timescale. Their resulting caution is then taken as evidence of a lack of top management commitment.

It is not anticipated that the success rate of BPR projects will improve. Any positive learning effects are likely to be more than balanced by the negative effects of so-called BPR approaches and methodologies offered by ever more marginal suppliers. In the larger firms of consultants, the product is becoming a commodity and is passing from the hands of early, thinking, pioneers into those of the typical assignment-fodder consultant.

Potential pitfalls

While BPR has resulted in a greater focus on the paths through the organisation that deliver value to customers, it has not always led to an equivalent level of concern about management processes. These are used to control and monitor the activities and outcomes of business processes. Inadequate management processes have resulted in well intentioned and competent BPR teams being given inadequate and inappropriate goals and objectives.

Improved business processes from the perspective of the customer could create problems for other stakeholders where management processes are unchanged. Management and business processes should be compatible and mutually supportive. Some companies approach their management and business processes differently, while others attempt to bring them together within the framework of an overall process model of how an organisation should operate.

In a particular context, there may be practical problems to address. For example, are there repeatable processes? In many fast moving contexts, each path through the organisation in response to an individual problem or opportunity may be unique. Establishing, documenting and supporting particular paths may create a new set of inflexibilities.

It not unusual for BPR to replace case by case thinking with a selection from options presented by a software package. In the drive for speed of response the thinking that could result in some tailoring is perceived as a luxury. Over time, insight, sensitivity and flexibility is replaced by the automatic, predictable and programmed. BPR thus enslaves rather than liberates, and reduces rather than increases options.

There comes a point when trying to cope with every eventuality results in a process becoming too elaborate and complex. The solution of categorisation and putting cases through sub-processes may not work if common features are difficult to determine.

Undertaking self-contained BPR exercises at the level of the individual process can actually reduce the prospects of wider transformation. As a consequence of making an existing form of organisation more effective, the impetus and desire for an overall transformation may be reduced.

Care also needs to be taken to ensure that a BPR initiative is compatible with other corporate programmes. For example:

■ An empowerment drive could encourage and trust people to be flexible and catholic in how they work, while a parallel BPR initiative seeks to define and document particular ways of approaching certain tasks.

■ Hiving-off or market testing can result in the carving up of an organisation into a collection of contractual agreements of varying timescales with the result that, in effect, there is no longer an organisational whole to re-engineer or transform.

When implementing BPR, one should expect particular concerns to arise in certain quarters. For example, it is so easy to lose control. Thus internal auditors would be negligent if they did not raise the question of what financial and other controls would apply following the empowerment of self-organised teams.

BPR creates new opportunities for white-collar fraud and can be hard on the naive. Hence new ways need to be found to achieve financial and other disciplines, and monitor performance in the context of the loser forms of network organisations that are emerging.

Few organisations exist in isolation. A group that is willing to change, for example, by adopting a new technology or pattern of working, may find that its enthusiasm for innovation is not shared by the other business units and organisations with which it has to deal. Similarly, old systems may have to be maintained in order to receive inputs from other elements of a supply chain or related processes.

An organisation may be tempted to select more than one, perhaps several processes, for a re-engineering exercise. Experience suggests that very often tackling more than two or three critical processes simultaneously can overload an organisation's ability to cope with change.

Public sector issues

Within particular sectors there may be further potential pitfalls. For example, although in some parts of the public sector considerable innovation is occurring, elsewhere there may be a reluctance to take risks. Annual budgeting can be an inhibitor when a BPR exercise may last over a year. At a senior level, giving priority to immediate issues such as responses to Parliamentary questions can distract from the longer term review of underlying processes. Account will also need to be taken of *ultra vires* and public accountability considerations, and constraints on diversification.

BPR is most appropriate when: (1) the statutory basis or rationale of a service specifies the outcomes that are to be sought, but allows an organisation considerable freedom to determine how these might be achieved; and (2) cases are not too dissimilar, ie there is scope for a repeatable process.

BPR should not be allowed to become a substitute for creative thinking about alternative ways of achieving policy outcomes. For example, BPR could be used within a health service to examine whether certain forms of treatment could be delivered more cost-effectively. However, a wider policy review might suggest that a greater impact on various indicators could be achieved by switching resources from acute health care to preventive measures.

Departmentalism within the public sector can hinder the adoption of a cross-functional approach. When specialist units are contracted out, care has to be taken to ensure that new organisational barriers are not placed across wider processes. The tendency towards fragmentation of larger departments into a collection of distinct units of varying status, and each with its own objectives, may complicate the task of coordination.

Initiatives of the Citizen's Charter variety could provide a reason for introducing BPR into certain areas of the public sector. What can responsibly be promised must depend on how confident an organisation is about its ability to deliver. Understanding the combination and sequence of activities that delivers value to an end customer may increase the willingness of a management team to commit.

Processism

While a 'focus upon process' can be healthy, an excessive preoccupation can turn into an obsession. BPR can lead to 'processism', a belief that all one needs to do is 'get the processes right' and the 'right' outcomes will emerge. This can be a dangerous view if it leads to a lack of concern with the quality of what flows along the processes. Judgements and decisions still have to be made. Inadequate implementation has saved many organisations from the full consequences of errors of judgement on the part of those who lead them. BPR can also lead to processes taking priority over those they should serve. Outstanding processes become an end in themselves, people becoming mere operators who perform certain activities at particular stages. If need be, individuals are sacrificed in the interest of the efficiency of the whole.

SUCCESS FACTORS

In Chapter 5 we examined some success factors that relate to preparing for BPR. Re-engineering, as opposed to incremental improvement, requires a willingness to be bold. To get the full benefit of BPR, an organisation must be prepared to ask fundamental questions. Those involved need to be capable of challenging assumptions, and senior management must support and actively seek radical change.

The success of the implementation of transformation can be assessed by the extent to which: (1) the potential and capabilities of individuals and teams are harnessed; and (2) corporate capability and commitment are applied to those activities that deliver value to customers and achieve business objectives (Coulson-Thomas, 1992). My own experience of BPR projects suggests:

1. The BPR vision must be stretching and shared, the purpose of change communicated, and employee involvement and commitment secured. No amount of technique can save people from a lack of purpose, direction, shared vision and focus.
2. The full potential of the many means we have of transforming organisations is unlikely to be achieved until those running them become more imaginative. In many cases, people need to re-think the rationale, purpose and values of their organisations.
3. One should not assume, either that directors are competent or that boards are effective (Coulson-Thomas, 1993). Corporate transformation is a new challenge for many boards and their individual members may need to be equipped with new skills and supported by new management processes that begin and end in the boardroom.
4. Organisations are communities of people with feelings and sensitivities. In view of the attitudinal and behavioural changes that are likely to be required, particular attention should be paid to internal communication, involvement and other people issues. Some of these are considered by Hamid Aghassi in Chapter 12 and Edna Murphy in Chapter 13.
5. Where consultants are used, a company should ensure visible client ownership of a review. BPR should be headed by an internal person, and appropriate local staff included within the review team.
6. Given the total process scope of BPR reviews, the demanding goals which ought to be set, and the fundamental nature of the issues and choices which may emerge, sustained and intense involvement of appropriate members of a senior management team is usually needed.
7. To ensure buy-in, commitment and effective implementation, the review process has to be seen to be authoritative and comprehensive. The divisions and functions effected and the people of the process should be actively involved.
8. Major corporate challenges tend to be cross-functional or multi-functional in their impact. Those whose interests are threatened by cross-functionalism may resist or undermine it. A fundamental question is the extent to which experts in various functional fields are barriers to, or facilitators of, change.
9. Whether an organisation reaps the full benefits of BPR can depend on the extent to which people are equipped to assume new roles and work in new ways with new technology. In some BPR exercises large

sums are spent on IT investments to create a potential which does not become a reality because of inadequate expenditure on training.

10. Particular attention should be devoted to learning and learning processes. Standard approaches to BPR often drive out diversity, while induction into their use often destroys the desire to learn.

11. Success requires the effective management of fundamental change. This largely concerns feelings, attitudes, values, behaviours, commitments, and personal qualities such as being open-minded. Techniques, methodologies and supporting IT are only elements of what needs to be done.

12. In general, people are too wedded to what is. The existing organisation should not be used as a point of departure, when it is inappropriate compared with alternative models that are available.

13. Those who go to the essence of what needs to be done to generate value and build relevant capability, and who keep it simple, tend to be the most successful. Clear thinking, foresight and an ability to identify what is important is required, especially where many processes impact on each other.

14. Mutual trust, especially between senior management and change teams is critically important. The blather and hype of much corporate communication emphasise the gulf between words and actions, and spread disappointment and despair. Many managers end up feeling betrayed and conned.

15. Facilitated sessions can ensure the active participation of the people of the process at each phase. Workshops can be arranged to introduce the necessary corporate transformation or process review, improvement and re-engineering tools and approaches.

An holistic approach is required. The building blocks might include a distinctive and compelling vision, shared goals and values, clear and measurable objectives, policy deployment, demonstrable top management commitment, role model behaviour, a focus on the customer, employee involvement and empowerment, and supportive reward and remuneration (Coulson-Thomas, 1992).

THE BPR TEAM

A BPR team needs to be authoritative and should command the support of colleagues. Team members should be secure personalities, who are able to think outside of the square while always attentive to impacts on end customers. There does appear to be a shortage of those with the breadth of view and other qualities required for BPR implementation. If a key process is the subject of BPR, close and intimate senior management involvement will be needed. The exercise should have its champion at board level.

A process owner should be nominated. An ideal owner shares the vision, goals, values and objectives of the organisation, understands the significance of the particular process, is committed to radical change, and has both the available time and the authority to act. The individual's personal qualities should be an inspiration to the BPR team.

The size of the BPR team will depend on the context. There is often a trade-off between ensuring that important interests are represented and achieving a group that is manageable.

All members of the team should be committed to fundamental change. Those who do not share the vision and commitment of others can seriously impede progress. Within the team there should also be mutual respect. Sufficient diversity should be included within a team to encourage questioning and debate. Groups made up entirely of people with similar backgrounds and experience are unlikely to be as creative as those whose membership is more varied.

A BPR exercise needs to be project managed. Where the owner of a key process is a senior and busy person within an organisation, a separate project manager or coordinator may be required.

The need for other roles within the team will depend on the nature and context of the exercise and the extent to which there are other specialist resources that can be accessed as required. It sometimes helps if one or more individuals have a specific brief to act as facilitators.

Re-engineering skills

The main skills required by members of a BPR team are as follows:

- An ability to think holistically about a total process and to always keep in mind impacts on end customers. TQM encourages people to think of those representing the next step in a process as internal customers. However, the ultimate test of the quality of a service is its effect on end customers.
- A willingness to think creatively and to challenge fundamental assumptions. Imagination is also required. What at first sight might appear implausible could turn out to be the germ of an eventual solution.
- Open-mindedness and the courage to venture into the unknown. True pioneers often find that there are few, if any, role models for them to learn from.
- A secure personality, a tolerance for differences and uncertainties, and a willingness to assume personal and collective accountability and responsibility. A BPR team is no place for an insecure, risk-averse individual who prefers to hide behind a role that is not in the spotlight.

- A natural desire to build bridges between functional departments and other groups.

Those to avoid are people who rush to judgement and who think in black and white terms. Some individuals have such a wide range of fixed views that they find it difficult to think creatively.

Heavily professionalised areas can present particular problems for BPR. Many professionals think in terms of inputs and charging for time spent rather than solutions or delivered outputs. They may also view problems and issues from a specifically functional rather than an holistic or corporate perspective.

In order to broaden the pool of people capable of undertaking BPR exercises, organisations face considerable pressures to define methodologies and build ever more detailed diagnostics. Care has to be taken to ensure these do not de-skill as a result of encouraging people to slavishly follow them rather than think creatively about the fundamental issues involved. BPR is going well when people are building creative alternatives rather than filling in checklists.

The use of methodologies

We saw in the last chapter that techniques, approaches, methodologies and tools are a means to an end, and should not be allowed to become an end in themselves. Opinions concerning their value differ:

- Some resist methodologies and view them as inhibitors of original thought about a particular context, encouraging people to behave as though programmed.
- Others argue that it is difficult for people to work together without a shared understanding of the steps involved. A common language can help both internal and external communication.

The nature of a methodology will also influence its use. The more detailed and prescriptive a methodology, the greater the danger that it will be slavishly followed. The results of testing reactions in COBRA case studies suggest that a re-engineering methodology should be positioned as an aide to creative thought, and be less prescriptive and more open than those used in simplification exercises. It should aim to be a guide (and the shorter the better if it is to be used) to the main issues and considerations to be taken into account, rather than an exhaustive treatment of every eventuality.

In the COBRA (1994–96) methodology, the level of detail in elements relating to new patterns of work aims to match that in the more general BPR methodologies alongside which it may be used, eg in case an excess of detail biases a solution for or against, say, teleworking.

People should not feel compelled to use particular tools and techniques. They should dip selectively, as appropriate, into a toolkit and use whatever is thought to be of value in the context of the exercise in which they are engaged.

Tools selected need to be appropriate for both the task and the level at which one is working. A heavy investment in the technology to support certain tools can sometimes result in people searching for opportunities to use them.

Much will depend on the context. Thus in structured environments, it may be advantageous to use methodologies, while in more fluid situations it may be advisable to put the emphasis on the recruitment of bright and creative people.

Sensitive implementation

A BPR group should avoid the temptation to rush through a list of questions in order to demonstrate that an assignment is progressing. The BPR team should be the first to understand the distinction between activity and outcomes. On occasion, it can be advantageous to delay in order to reach the root causes.

Processes and activities can have informal as well as ostensible purposes. An apparently meaningless ritual could provide a rare opportunity for people to get together. Perhaps such informal activities should be formalised.

People are prone to exaggerate the contribution of their own activities to group vision, mission, goals, values, objectives and priorities. Protective shells build up around activities that people in organisations enjoy, regardless of their relevance.

Consultancy support

Consultants should be chosen with care. Their professional backgrounds may prevent them from adopting an holistic overview. It is essential to avoid standard and packaged methodologies that do not reflect the unique features of a particular context and approaches that are over-elaborate and still incomplete, should be avoided.

The external assistance that is required will depend on the scale and complexity of the BPR exercise to be undertaken and the calibre and availability of in-house staff. The following considerations should be borne in mind:

■ Where BPR is expected to become a continuing feature of organisational life, an internal capability will need to be built up. When selecting and using consultants every effort should be made to ensure that the transfer of know-how occurs.

- How important is it that quick results are achieved? Where an organisation is new to BPR, external support may enable tangible outcomes to be achieved more quickly than might otherwise be the case.
- Every organisation is unique. Preference should be given to those external suppliers who focus on what the organisation is trying to achieve. Suppliers to avoid are those looking for an opportunity to apply a standard methodology irrespective of local circumstances.
- Those working on the processes being re-engineered should be fully involved. An external supplier may be so keen to complete a project to budget and time, that inadequate consultation results in implementation problems that should have been foreseen.
- Control and initiative should not be lost or abdicated to an external supplier.

The right consultant can be a valuable ally and useful resource. An external supplier could act as a catalyst in pushing a group to adopt more radical approaches than might otherwise be the case. Also, where people have a tendency to introversion, and cannot see the wood for the trees, an external partner can introduce both objectivity and perspective.

THE ROLE OF IT

Within the origins of the concept of BPR (Scott Morton, 1990) and, to a lesser extent, process improvement (Davenport, 1993) there lies both a concern with the effectiveness of past applications of IT and an awareness of its potential, when properly used, to break the mould and support new forms of relationships and new ways of working.

IT (eg EDI links) can be a key element of the re-engineering solution, while IT tools (eg process modelling) could be used to support the actual work of re-engineering. While IT can be a key enabler of radical transformation, it may not play such a role in every BPR exercise. A radical breakthrough could result from putting people first and freeing them from constraints imposed by IT. IT is sometimes the problem rather than the solution.

Many past investments in IT have set an existing departmental organisation in concrete, rather than support those key cross-functional and inter-organisational processes that add value for customers. BPR provides opportunities to: (1) facilitate network relationships with customers, suppliers and business partners; (2) support new patterns of group and distance working, and (3) enable and facilitate new approaches to learning. IT that is relevant to these opportunities is of particular value (see Chapter 11 for one view of the contribution of networks technology).

It would be helpful if a greater distinction were made between BPR, IT itself, IT that might be used to support a re-engineered process, and IT that is used to facilitate the BPR process. Some organisations become so drawn in to heavy and protracted IT investment, and so exposed to the risk of non-delivery, that the IT tail ends up wagging the corporate dog.

It is not always the case that investments in new technology have to be made to reap the fruits of BPR. Radical improvements can and do result from reducing the level of investment in IT. A degree of pragmatism is required.

Documents, whether in electronic or physical form, are the lifeblood of most processes, and IT that can support the creation, communication and sharing of documents can be more relevant to BPR than traditional data-processing.

The application of BPR often results in fewer people working in relative isolation on specialist/narrow tasks, and more people working collaboratively and sharing a broader range of responsibilities. Hence the relevance of IT (eg groupware) that can support collaborative group working.

Given the emphasis in BPR on linking related people and activities, solutions should be as open as possible to multi-vendor involvement and likely future developments.

Solutions should also be as simple as possible. Past investments in IT should be regarded as sunk costs. They should not be allowed to constrain the future just because they cost a great deal of time and money to develop. Decisions on the way ahead should be taken on the basis of incremental costs and revenues. BPR should be undertaken ahead of further or new investment in IT.

In many market sectors greater international collaboration is required. For example, in a European context, many public sector organisations can expect to work more closely with their equivalents in other states. Hence the value of technology that can overcome barriers of national standards and culture, as well as barriers of function, location and organisation in the creation of Euro-networks.

If IT is to play its part as an enabler of fundamental change, an organisation's IT department must be up to the challenge. The capability of the existing team should not be taken for granted. How willing are they to ask fundamental questions? Do they have the drive and people skills to make it happen?

PROCESSES: UNDERTAKING ANALYSIS AND RE-DESIGN

We considered how to initiate and prepare for BPR in the last chapter. Let us now examine in more detail the implementation stages (3–6) of the approach to re-engineering suggested by the COBRA team in its method-ology manual (COBRA, 1994–96): (3) The Analysis of an existing process; (4) Process re-design; (5) Implementation of the re-design; and (6) Performance monitoring. (see Fig. 5.2 in Chapter 5)

The purist, for whom re-engineering represents blue-skies thinking, the greenfield approach, or the clean slate, might object to stage (3) as an unnecessary distraction from creativity and innovation. However, the step is found in many BPR methodologies, and the purpose of the COBRA manual is to complement approaches in actual use (in order, in the manual, to flag those questions that relate particularly to the intro-duction of a new pattern of work such as teleworking).

The Analysis of an existing process

The purpose of the process analysis stage (see Fig. 6.1 for an overview) is to provide an overview understanding of where the organisation is in terms of the process under review. This requires an understanding of the main features of an existing process 'as it is', its performance in terms of the objectives of the BPR exercise, and the extent to which elements of it might feature in a final solution (ie would the team be justified in under-taking the lengthy task of re-designing the process or should it start again?).

If at any point it becomes apparent that building on or leveraging an existing base is unlikely to result in a step change in performance the team should pause and consider whether it would be much more productive to start again with a blank sheet of paper, free from the constraints of 'what is'. In such a case, the team should move to the next phase (process re-design) and design a new process from scratch.

Work done at this stage could include documentation of the main features of the existing process to enable them to be better understood,

© Commission of the European Communities, 1994

Fig. 6.1 *Process Analysis*

and to establish the basis on which changes are to be introduced. The aim should be to assemble a quick overview that will allow a judgement to be made about how much of what exists could become part of a solution that would deliver radical improvements in performance. If elements of what exists are thought to be usable, then more detailed process mapping could occur at the re-design stage.

If the results of an overview analysis or benchmarking suggests that what exists falls a long way short of best-practice, or what is needed to differentiate and secure clear competitive advantage in the marketplace, the BPR team may wish to skip this next stage (the analysis of an existing process) and jump straight to the process re-design stage. The process analysis stage may also be omitted if it is decided to seek an innovative greenfield solution.

An organisation could undertake this and the next stage in parallel, ie separating the assessment of where it is from the determination of where it ought to be. Thus one activity would not bias the other. Comparing the results of the two exercises could then enable gaps and action areas to be identified.

The practicalities of process analysis

A common mistake is to undertake an analysis at an inappropriate level of detail (eg too little, or too much). In many exercises, and at both the analysis and re-design stages, people fail to distinguish between the process and its supporting systems. As they may be relatively well documented, the latter sometimes exert an undue influence.

Those who set out to document their existing processes often find that it turns out to be a time-consuming and protracted exercise. Analyses should not be undertaken for their own sake, but to enable processes to be understood, and this understanding to be communicated and shared.

A disadvantage of flow charts is that they can encourage too early a focus on the handling of documents at the expense of overview questions about whether or not certain roles add value. Exercises can become so engrossed in the details that the purpose of a process and its impacts on the end customer become overlooked.

On occasion, devoting an excessive amount of time to understanding and documenting existing practices becomes a form of avoidance behaviour, a means of postponing what is perceived as the harder work of devising alternatives. While elaborate process models are built, other people in the organisation may begin to lose interest and commitment due to the lack of apparent progress.

The emphasis should be on what people actually do and how they interact. It often quickly becomes apparent that many individuals are just passing on requests for information or authorisation without adding much of value. Where certain activities can yield informal benefits apart from their ostensible purposes certain of their aspects could be formalised. Thus alternative arrangements might need to be made for people to get together to share experiences and discuss issues of common interest.

On occasion, the outputs at this stage can enable some quick wins to be identified, areas in which tangible improvements can be made quickly and at low cost, without prejudicing the timetable to achieve more dramatic gains. An analysis of 'what is' may reveal other adequate opportunities to achieve desired performance targets. These could be improvement or simplification actions and initiatives that mean a more demanding and risky re-engineering exercise need not be undertaken.

Process Re-design

The opportunity phase will have identified areas in which innovations and breakthroughs could occur, and some levers and possibilities for dramatic or step changes. The purpose of the process re-design stage (see Fig. 6.2 for an overview) is to produce a vision of where the organisation would like to be in respect of the area or process under review.

A preferred model of a re-designed process is the eventual output. However, it may be advisable to demand a number of alternative re-design options, each worked up in the form of a role activity diagram, as an intermediate step.

Where the solution is a new or re-designed process, this should be defined and scoped in terms of its critical elements, and an implementation plan developed for turning the envisaged solution into an operational reality. The plan should cover resource requirements and include communications activity.

© Commission of the European Communities, 1994

Fig. 6.2 *Process Re-design*

Where the step to be taken is a fundamental one, and likely to be both risky and demanding of time and other resources, some form of business justification or cost-benefit analysis may be required before a decision to proceed is taken.

Work undertaken at this stage could include modelling and design activity to generate various solution options from which one can be selected for implementation. This will involve:

1. Development of a vision and design principles for the area or process being examined, based on original thought and the results of environmental scanning and monitoring.
2. Looking creatively at the inter-action between people, processes, information, understanding and supporting technology. This is to develop innovative ways in which these elements can be brought together to achieve breakthrough levels of performance improvement.

The review team should be given the responsibility, authority, and time to be creative, and be held accountable for the quality of the options and designs they generate and, subsequently, for implementation. They may need to throw away early solutions and start again a number of times before they sense 'this is it'. Fear of criticism or ridicule can dampen creativity.

The design process is likely to be iterative, as different options are generated and assessed, and further refinements are examined to assess whether their benefits will outweigh the incremental costs and time of implementation. It should be remembered that performance can be improved both by creating or seizing opportunities, and by tackling the root causes of significant obstacles and barriers.

The practicalities of process re-design

The re-design process should be vision-led (ie it should focus on the future, not how better to deliver today's needs and requirements). The goals are large and should have longer term impacts. A vision-led approach to re-engineering can be difficult to implement in an organisation that itself lacks a clear and compelling vision.

It is generally advisable to start with the value the organisation is seeking to create. The team undertaking the re-design should include at least one representative of the customer, while all team members should aim to view the issues and situations they encounter from the perspective of the customer.

An organisation that fails to undertake adequate environmental scanning may remain unaware of some achievable options. Ignorance of what is possible may result in a less radical solution being adopted that fails to achieve the desired impact.

An area or process vision should match an organisation's overall vision. The objectives established for each BPR exercise should collectively enable the organisation to achieve its corporate goals and objectives.

Clear and demanding performance targets are required, and these should relate to what represents value for end customers and the stakeholders of an organisation. In the absence of such targets, the BPR team may lack a sense of direction when deciding which aspects of improvement to focus on (ie should throughput time take priority, or do other factors become more significant once a minimum level of performance improvement has been achieved).

Setting ambitious goals and objectives may force the team to look beyond the more obvious sources of improvements. These easy wins are the areas that are also most likely to be targeted by competitors.

Where it is thought that an existing process could provide a stepping-stone to a new design, or make a significant contribution, it may now be necessary to analyse it in greater detail than has hitherto been the case.

Where improvement rather than transformation is sought, non-value added steps and those that deliver little benefit in relation to the costs or delays imposed will suggest themselves as candidates for elimination.

An excess of complexity should be avoided. Fundamental improvements have been achieved by groups asking such basic questions as: What if any value does it add?, Would it be used if we charged for it? The simpler the representation of the available options (eg high-level role activity diagrams), the easier it will be to communicate them and ensure they are properly discussed.

People have a tendency to drown in the details of 'what is' and become bogged down with incremental improvements at the expense of thinking creatively about wider issues and alternatives. Should the focus become internal, (ie on the organisation and its processes), and overlook what represents value for the external customer, an external partner might introduce both objectivity and perspective. Where people exhibit a tendency towards introversion, an external catalyst can sometimes encourage a group to come up with more radical approaches than might otherwise be the case.

Pressuring some groups to deliver so that the work of implementation might proceed can significantly reduce the chance of a revolutionary outcome emerging. A group may require time to break free from the constraints of experience, while another team may become more daring in stages. At the same time, a group should not be allowed to go off the boil, or to sleep.

To avoid getting drawn too early into an excess of detail, or into blind alleys, a BPR team could aim to get it roughly right by developing a solution based on the most significant factors. Further investigation can then be undertaken, and additional aspects considered, until the apparent incremental benefits are clearly not worth the extra effort involved.

The composition of a re-design team can have an important bearing on the ease with which its recommendations are accepted. In the interest of 'do-ability', those active in the area concerned should be included in the re-design group. This is especially important in the case of experts and knowledge workers.

Implementation of the re-design

The purpose of the implementation of change stage (see Fig. 6.3 for an overview) is to turn the radical change vision into a reality and achieve a sustainable advantage in the delivery of value to stakeholders. This includes tackling the attitudinal and behavioural issues, measuring and monitoring outcomes, and ensuring that a resulting solution incorporates the means of further learning and refinement.

The output sought is a re-engineered process operated by a group of people who have been properly equipped (eg in terms of attitudes, training, and supporting systems) to achieve the full potential of the chosen solution.

Interim outputs could consist of prototypes or demonstrators to test a concept. Final outputs could take the form of the achievement of the benefits or outcomes that were originally established (eg leaping so far ahead of the competition as to establish a new benchmark standard according to critical criteria). In the case of a fundamental change, the work of consolidation and embedding may continue until it is thought

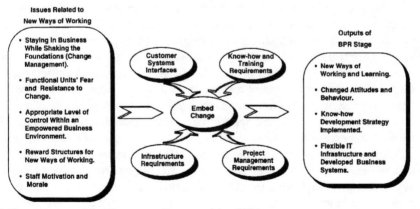

© Commission of the European Communities, 1994

Fig. 6.3 *Implementation of change*

that attitudes and behaviours have changed sufficiently to prevent regression from occurring.

The precise nature of the work done (eg the contribution of technology) will depend on the nature of the changes that are sought. The more revolutionary the changes, the more advisable it will be to assess and refine a proposed solution by means of a field test of the concept, a prototype of the selected design, and a pilot trial of a first cut of the delivered package.

The systems and business architecture of the organisation may need to be re-designed to support the re-designed process. The more radical the change, the more likely it is that new enabling technology will be required, and that IT might itself be the key to unlocking the potential of a new model of operation.

The practicalities of re-design

People issues tend to be the key determinants of success. Are they informed, involved, empowered, committed and effectively led throughout the BPR exercise, and especially during the implementation phase? Are they equipped, in terms of training, to do what is expected of them?

Earlier approaches to training have been departmental, and applied to activities that may or may not be significant from a customer point of view. As a consequence of BPR, training can be focused on those sequences and combinations of activities that deliver value to customers and achieve organisational objectives.

The approach to implementation needs to be matched to both the nature of the work being undertaken and to those involved. An empowered and self-managed workgroup may handle the same tasks very differently from a group of people who tend to work alone under the supervision of a coordinating manager.

A balance has to be struck between monitoring and control. An excess of prescription should be avoided. Loss of motivation and contribution will occur if highly skilled, value adding staff are expected to distort their working preferences to meet new process requirements.

Judgement is needed to distinguish between a negative reluctance to implement certain aspects of a solution and the positive search for ways of improving or coping with genuine problems that emerge.

In the case of knowledge workers and professionals, sufficient flexibility should be built in to allow individuals to vary a process to take account of particular circumstances. Successful solutions are often distinguished by the ease with which they can handle exceptions and variations. Some systems allow so much freedom of action, that their main use is to monitor what is going on.

Many activities are not as repetitive as people assume when they start to re-design a process. Anticipating and planning for every eventuality may be an almost impossible task. Where considerable diversity occurs, it may be advisable to build whatever best supports the attitudes and behaviours which will result in those concerned adopting the right course of action depending on the circumstances. The acid test of implementation is whether the required changes of attitude and behaviour have occurred.

Performance monitoring

Last but not least is the performance monitoring stage (see Fig. 6.4 for an overview) which assesses the extent to which attitudinal, behavioural and performance changes have occurred and initial goals and objectives are being achieved.

Depending on the outcomes, this stage could lead to a completion of the BPR circle with a return to stage (1) and a re-assessment of an organisation's approach and goal setting (see Fig. 5.3 in Chapter 5). The original goals and objectives may have changed during the course of implementation, while developments in the business environment or the situation and circumstances of the company may suggest a new approach is necessary.

Implementation should not be allowed to introduce new sources of inflexibility. To consolidate gains, and ensure a new approach is fully implemented, there may be a temptation to embed it in operating manuals and to create various controls. However, in the interest of flexibility, people should be encouraged to criticise and question.

Learning should be incorporated into the re-design and implementation stages as it is felt that (1) learning should be built into a solution rather than tagged on to the end; and (2) implementation cannot be said to have happened until means of monitoring, learning, refinement, and continuous improvement are both established and practised. The

© Commission of the European Communities, 1994

Fig. 6.4 *Performance monitoring*

purposes of this stage are to ensure these are occurring and to identify areas where further change (including BPR) may be necessary. Implementation cannot be said to be complete until the outcomes of the exercise have been monitored and measured, satisfactory levels of performance are achieved, and further learning and improvement occurs. The loop should also be closed by returning to those measures (eg customer satisfaction surveys and benchmarking) the results of which originally gave rise to the requirement for change. An organisation that does not progress along a learning curve may find itself overtaken by a competitor that copies its innovations.

The implementation should be monitored until it is clear that the organisation is fully exploiting the potential and opportunity that has been created. The work of review, learning and refinement should continue as benchmark status is maintained where it has been achieved, and extended to further areas.

BIBLIOGRAPHY

COBRA (1994), *Business restructuring and teleworking: Issues, considerations and approaches.* (Methodology Manual for the Commission of the European Communities). London: Adaptation.

COBRA (1995), Colin Coulson-Thomas (Executive Editor), *The Responsive Organisation: Re-engineering new patterns of work.* London: Policy Publications.

COBRA (1996), Peter Bartram, Colin Coulson-Thomas and Lee Tate, *The Competitive Network,* London: Policy Publications.

Coulson-Thomas, C. (1992), *Transforming the company: Bridging the gap between management myth and corporate reality.* London: Kogan Page.

Coulson-Thomas, C. (1993), *Creating excellence in the boardroom, and developing directors: Building an effective boardroom team.* London: McGraw Hill Europe.

Davenport, T. H. (1993), *Process innovation: Reengineering work through information technology.* Boston: Harvard Business School Press.

Scott Morton, M. S. (1990), *The corporation of the 1990s: Information technology and organisational transformation.* New York and Oxford: Oxford University Press.

7

Implications of Business Process Re-engineering for the Management of Telework

Simon Robinson

INTRODUCTION

The expansion of telework over the decades since this idea of remote work using information technology first arose has been constrained, less by a lack of availability of appropriate technology, than by problems perceived in organising and managing telework. Managers expect problems in managing staff who are not in front of them. This partially explains the widespread inertia expressed by management when faced with the question as to whether they are interested in introducing telework in their organisation (Huws, Korte, Robinson, 1990). As a recent survey by empirica shows, these attitudes have been changing, with managers generally much more aware of the need to introduce new modes of working and much more interested in telework (empirica, forthcoming).

Over the years, and in most cases independently of any consideration of telework, managers have slowly responded to exhortations to move away from direct supervision towards management of the results of work. This is a technique which has always been seen as a prerequisite for effective management of remote staff.

A number of other currents of change have significantly affected management practice in ways relevant to telework. Examples include Total Quality Management, the emphasis over the last decade on process speed, time to market, increased parallel operation and just-in-time coordination. As organisations restructure under these influences, new requirements are placed on the process of management generally, and on the management of telework in particular.

One of the key influences on organisational structure and management practice in the recent past has been business process re-engineering. This chapter sets out to summarise the BPR approach, based on extensive references to the 1993 publication by Hammer and Champy (H&C). It will draw out the implications for change in the functions of management generally, and of the management of telework in particular. The chapter is based on a contribution by the author to work on telework management in PRACTICE, sister project to COBRA in the European Commission Telework Initiative (Wierda, Overmars & Partners, 1994).

BPR IN SUMMARY

The idea behind business process re-engineering is radical: not just to change, but to reinvent the corporation. 'Business re-engineering means starting all over . . . from scratch [it] can't be carried out in small and cautious steps [but is] an all-or-nothing proposition that produces dramatically impressive results' (H&C). The idea is not to look for cost, speed or quality savings in current operations but to question why operations exist, why what is being done is done at all.

Defining a process as 'a set of activities that, taken together, produce a result of value to a customer' the key lies in 'value to the customer'. The process orientation sees the structure of the organisation as secondary, and will tend to result in networked rather than hierarchical and functionally streamlined organisations.

Re-engineering is driven by crisis, caused by the shift in power from suppliers to customers, itself a result of increasing competition. Another factor is the increasing pace of change, which is both a response to competitive pressure and results from exogenous factors such as technological development.

Profitability in future will lie in ensuring an organisation learns rapidly and in a way responsive to customer needs. According to Hammer, the problem is not one of lazy workers or poor managers, but that the design of organisations – as pyramids – is out of date. Pyramidal structures were designed for an assembly line approach to process design, for breaking processes into simple repetitive steps. This used to allow short training periods, for supervisors to ensure consistent performance, and to enable budgets to be easily monitored, but now makes coordination complicated and increases middle management.

Order-fulfilment is a good example because it is common to most economic sectors and is a process in which fragmentation is often clearly visible. Order-fulfilment starts when a customer places an order and ends when goods are delivered. The process typically – before re-engineering – involves a dozen or so steps performed by different people in different departments. The BPR approach challenges the need for and the appropriateness of this kind of process segmentation. The following list of advantages and disadvantages of fragmenting processes into specialised steps summarises the arguments:

+ low training requirements for process participants
+ clear task responsibility
+ everyone is accountable
− no one person is responsible
− many hand-offs make the process error-prone
− queues, batches and wait times halt progress at every hand-off
− no customer service element at all
− no-one can tell a customer when the order will arrive
− no flexibility to respond to special requests
− the order might as well be lost till it comes out the end.

There are a number of further problems with process fragmentation and functionally structured organisations. Tasks in a process are often split across functional departments and levels in a hierarchy. Also, a pyramidal structure encourages people to look inwards and upwards. Their attention is on what their boss wants or how to get on in their department, rather than outwards, towards ways of satisfying customers. Furthermore, innovation is stifled by the need to sell a new idea up the hierarchy.

For the topic at hand, telework management, it is of particular significance how traditional organisations inflate management overhead. In traditional organisations there is a need for managers to monitor work. They have to ensure that inputs match outputs along the process, ensure that shoddy work at one point does not lead to problems downstream, and conversely that downstream slips are not blamed unjustly on poor previous work. Forcing the organisation to work against the intrinsic interests of those doing the work means adding overhead jobs. These include expediters and chasers to accelerate work, auditors and controllers to check on effectiveness, and supervisors to ensure everyone does the right thing on a day-to-day basis. Questioning this aspect of old-style organisations makes BPR of particular significance to telework management.

Re-engineering begins by – in imagination at least – starting from scratch, asking 'If I were re-creating this company today, given what I know and given current technology, what would it look like?' A more formal statement is that: 'Re-engineering . . . is the fundamental rethinking and radical redesign of business processes to achieve dramatic improvements in critical, contemporary measures of performance, such as cost, quality, service, and speed' (H&C).

The BPR author's description of how re-engineering is done and when and by whom is not of great significance to the aims of this paper. The point to be made here is that the re-engineering paradigm is being adopted by an increasing number of corporations, and the new management practice which ensues will apply to telework. This is best seen in some of the commonalities between re-engineering initiatives picked out by Hammer and Champy from their case studies. The next section summarises each of these commonalities, and draws out implications for telework management in each case.

COMMONALITIES IN SUCCESSFUL BPR

Several jobs combined
This aspect of the re-engineered process is also referred to as 'horizontal compression', because, where possible, a drawn-out and fragmented process is reduced to being the job of a single person: a 'case worker' or potentially a 'case teleworker'.

The benefits of horizontal compression are particularly significant to telework. Putting the whole job in the hands of the teleworker removes any handing on of work to others. In traditional structures, this hand-on imposes a significant communication overhead on teleworking arrangements. For a case teleworker, there is also no need to check for the quality of intermediate work since there is no intermediate product: the teleworker does the whole job. The teleworker is responsible for the process output, which is, by definition, something the customer wants.

Workers make decisions
Where the teleworker is adequately motivated to take up full process responsibility and work towards satisfying customers, telework management can concentrate on giving empowerment and encouragement to innovate and improve.

This leads to a reduction in the number of occasions when a (tele)worker has to obtain approval from further up the hierarchy: 'vertical' compression. Taking the right decisions becomes part of getting the job done properly. BPR encourages moving decision-making into the real work, as part of the overall job to do, and away from the domain of specialist managers. The up-front jobs are expanded to include monitoring and control activity. As a consequence, teleworkers must be hired with – or must be trained in – the knowledge to evaluate alternatives correctly, and to cope with exceptions.

The work-load of telework management is reduced by the fact that teleworkers in re-engineered processes are given the means of taking decisions themselves, and have been given the training to help them evaluate decision outcomes. At the same time, vertical compression means reducing the level of formal interaction between teleworker and manager, removing a communication burden from both sides of the teleworking relationship.

Steps performed in natural order

BPR experts note that many processes have been found to contain tasks which wait for each other unnecessarily, and point out that enforcing precedence or sequentiality unnecessarily slows work down. A need for sequential performance of work can be removed by introducing the simultaneous access abilities of information technology for many documents used in a process. This is preferable to making participants in the process wait for their turn to access a paper document or file.

Removing the inefficiency of unnecessary serialisation in current processes has no discernible direct effects that are particularly relevant to telework management. However, the reduction achieved in throughput times may well relieve a need for progress monitoring and chasing activity.

Processes in multiple forms

This feature of re-engineered processes refers to the fact that the mass-production logic of handling everything in a standard way has become obsolete. The mass markets which mass-production served have disappeared. Instead, multiple versions of a process are designed to deal with the range of complexity of cases to be dealt with, and to match the qualifications and experience needed in each case. Easy cases are automated, difficult ones dealt with by one or a number of specialists, and a class of intermediate difficulty is given to generalist case teleworkers.

The critical triage step, in which the decision is taken as to who gets a particular case, is relevant to telework management only if it cannot be automated. If the criteria on which the decision is made can be embedded in software, and the information about the case is available, then the automation of triage means there is no impact on telework or its management.

In other cases the situation may be significantly more complex. Here solutions include those in which a case teleworker may make a preliminary decision as to whether to take on a case themselves, or whether it is a more complex one, which must be passed on to specialists. The load on telework management depends on the sophistication of software support for achieving effective triage in co-operation.

Work is performed where it makes sense

On the face of it, this feature seems to be the essence of telework. However, rather than the home or central office being the places where it makes sense to work, what is meant by Hammer and Champy is the need to reconsider the division of labour between departments or even organisations. The 'where' is considered less in a geographic, more in an organisational sense. However, the examples they give do suggest some impact on telework management. For instance, moving purchasing decisions and processes to the customer of the purchasing process – the person or group who wants to buy whatever it is for their own work – means that teleworkers who may make purchases must also have access to the software supporting the purchasing process.

Another example is to get the customers to contribute to the maintenance of products. Providing diagnosis over the telephone and maintaining the supply of spare parts at the customer site, changes the content of customer service occupations. These occupations are currently strongly represented in telework. Such changes reduce somewhat the premium of working away from the employer's office and closer to the organisation's customers. The impacts on telework management are clearly numerous but difficult to generalise.

Checks and controls are reduced

The simple BPR position is that checks and controls are non-value-adding work and should be minimised. However, Hammer and Champy recognise that controls may have a valuable function without being able to say that the value they have is 'added' in any way. They stipulate that in re-engineered organisations, controls should only be used 'to the extent that they make economic sense'.

Disregarding the confusion evident here, the more specific proposals made for changing control procedures are very relevant to management practice. These go in the direction of aggregate or deferred controls, towards explicitly tolerating modest abuse for a limited time in order to reduce the cost control. Older systems tried to be water-tight, for instance to make any unauthorised purchase impossible by checking every order for signature and for authorisation to order goods of a given type and value. In these cases, the cost of the checking often exceeds the cost of goods being purchased. Alternatives, for instance use of a credit card, can limit without preventing abuse and at a lower cost. Another example is insurance practice whereby instead of estimating the cost of repair for every accident, an approved list of body-shops is periodically and inexpensively reviewed against statistical evidence of each shop's estimation and charging practice.

The effect on telework management depends on the case at hand. However, the trend is towards a reduction in the need for day-to-day or even minute-to-minute interaction between management and teleworker to monitor progress or quality.

Reconciliation is minimised

This feature concerns two documents that have to be matched, such as an invoice and delivery note, and the problems and further work caused if they do not. Eliminating this reconciliation work is a strategic objective of re-engineering.

There are certain operations without any clear relevance to telework management. These include removal of invoicing from a supply chain, continuous stock replenishment models and permitting suppliers direct access to their client manufacturers' production schedules to reduce the matching and reconciliation workload. However, it is worth considering the impact of the underlying principle – reducing work arising at external points of contact – on telework and its management.

The conclusion must be that the mode of communication with teleworkers should not require any reconciliation work. This requires, as assumed here, that teleworkers work with the organisation in an employment-like situation. They are within the sphere of control of their employer and do not need any contractual documentation to be passed between them in paper form on a day-to-day basis. There should be no (paper) orders and invoices in teleworking relationships. However, they are still typical of most supplier-client relationships, and cause the reconciliation work that re-engineers recommend being removed.

A case manager: A single point of contact

The need for a single point of contact with a process customer is best realised by organising processes to be carried out from start to finish by an individual case teleworker. The role of a case manager is introduced by Hammer and Champy to cope with environments where this is not possible, where processes are too complex or dispersed even to integrate into the work of a small case team. The case manager is to buffer the customer from process complexity 'as if he or she were responsible for performing the entire process, even though that is really not the case' (H&C).

Where the case manager is the teleworker, the case telemanager will require access to all the information systems the process participants use. It should be noted that the case manager's need to question and seek further assistance from each process participant will restrict teleworkers in their choice of working time.

Hybrid centralisation/decentralisation operations

This feature points directly at the increasing advantages telework can offer. The message is that information technology can and should be used to reap economies of scale and the unified control of centralisation. Simultaneously, IT allows widespread autonomous operation. Where field sales representatives use laptops with portable modems, this empowers them with access to central information and allows them to generate quotes immediately. This also improves organisational control over pricing and conditions by incorporating centrally programmed software checks. Quoting prices or delivery conditions that the organisation cannot meet are thereby avoided.

RE-ENGINEERED PROCESSES

When processes are re-engineered, jobs evolve. Narrow and task-oriented jobs become multi-dimensional; a 'do-as-you-are-told' mode is now 'make-your-own-decisions'; meeting the needs of the boss is replaced by meeting the needs of the customers. Assembly-line work disappears, taking functional departments with it, and managers move from supervision to coaching as new incentive systems are introduced.

These three sentences summarise the features of re-engineered processes, each of which is described below, together with the effect each can be seen to have on the functions of telework management.

Work units change: Functional departments to process teams

BPR signals the demise of functional departments and the rise of teams. This feature is of course only relevant where it is not possible to have one person, the case teleworker, perform the whole process. Often, the requirement is for people with different skills to work together in a team. These teams may be permanent, as for the repetitive day-to-day workloads of insurance-claim processing. They may be more short-lived, eg for product development. And a team's members may belong to more than one team at once.

The implication for managing telework is that many of the problems of handing-off work between different people or departments remain where a case teleworker cannot do the whole process and team members must agree on who does what when.

Hierarchical methods of ensuring each team member pulls their weight are avoided by putting teams together physically, in one room if need be. This co-location policy is, on the face of it, anathema to telework. However, examined more closely, co-location is used to reduce the threshold of interaction between team members. More information passes voluntarily among members of the team. This facilitation of communication is seen as essential to supporting the self-management feature of teams, and could be supported by technically mediated communications instead of co-location. Some work on specifying requirements and testing communications systems which might meet this need despite distance between team members has been done by empirica and Integrata (Anderer 1992) among others.

Jobs change: Simple tasks to the multi-dimensional

Compared to the narrow specialist work of yesterday, the re-engineering view is of a process team worker who must be familiar with – and use – a broader range of skills and must think of a far bigger picture.

This point impacts on training requirements for telework rather than management functions as such. However, there are some lessons to be learned from typical instances. For example, software systems can be used to move purchasing out of a specialist purchasing department into the hands of those wanting the purchased goods. Desk-top publishing systems enable engineers, who have the information, rather than specialist publishers, who have to be given it, to produce marketing brochures. The lesson is that the employees concerned, and teleworkers in particular, need access to this software and data if they are to be included in the re-engineered process.

Jobs in re-engineered processes are portrayed as being more satisfying. This derives from the greater sense of completion, closure and accomplishment of a whole job, process or a sub-process. One 'that by definition produces a result that somebody cares about' (H&C). This encourages thinking more like an entrepreneur and a focus on customers and their satisfaction. The jobs provide for more growth and learning. As competence grows, so the job grows to match. The increase in value-adding content also allows for better compensation. But they are complex jobs for smart people, not simple tasks for simple people. Fewer unskilled jobs are to be found in a re-engineered environment.

Roles change: Controlled to empowered

Re-engineered companies do not want people to follow rules but to make their own, to exercise judgement to do the right thing. There should be no supervisory activity to disturb ongoing work. Process teams are to be self-directing, and having the necessary education, training and skills is not enough. Being self-starting, self-disciplined and motivated to do what it takes to please a customer are also essential.

Achieving these objectives relieves telework management of the need to develop extensive systems of rules, to communicate these to teleworkers and ensure their compliance. It remains an open point as to what proportion of the workforce will adopt the necessary self-discipline and other characteristics required of employees in future. However, just as they are needed in employees of the re-engineered corporation, these qualities have been essential for teleworkers. What in the past was an exceptional requirement becomes the norm for all employees.

As these changes take hold, telework management functions become less different from management functions applicable to the remainder of the workforce.

Hammer and Champy explain that training is for the 'how' of a particular job whereas it is education that is needed to understand the 'why'. They assert that after processes have been re-engineered, it is education that is needed to enable employees to continue doing the job, even as the 'how' changes. A further consequence is that employees must continue education throughout their working life.

Encouraging personal development and ongoing education is a new, or at least more important task for telework management in a re-engineered corporation.

Measurement changes: Activity to results

Pointing out that, traditionally, people are paid for their time, Hammer and Champy argue this must be replaced by rewards linked to achievements of value to the employing organisation. In the re-engineered corporation, compensation assumptions move away from paying people for job rank, seniority, number of subordinates, just for showing up, or because a year has passed.

Payment by results has often been argued as one of the preconditions for introducing telework, so that this aspect of re-engineered corporations serves to lower the threshold to telework. In terms of management generally, one of the tasks in payment by results is to define the value to the employing organisation of the various products of work. Then the production of these intermediate products has to be monitored and linked to payment systems. Here lies considerable difficulty, and not only for management of telework. These difficulties are illustrated by the problem of assigning a dollar value to something as intangible and distant from the customer as the verification of information in an insurance application form.

The argument for re-engineering is that jobs should be so designed that intermediate products no longer have to be evaluated. Instead, the responsibility – and rewarding – of the individual is linked directly to results of value to customers. This removes much of the work assessment and monitoring which payment by results otherwise entails, and eases the job of telework management.

Advancement criteria change: Performance to ability

This feature represents related changes in both reward and career systems. Arguing that it is a bonus payment, not promotion, which is the reward appropriate for a job well done, BPR moves promotions out of the reward system, neutralising them as a mere change of job.

Concerns expressed by teleworkers in traditional organisations, that because of being out of sight they were out of mind and therefore passed over for promotion, would not apply in re-engineered organisations. However, the point raises the more general issue as to how jobs in the organisation are to be filled by candidates from within, including tele-workers, and what role managers have in this process.

It seems that continuous assessment and monitoring of results is unnecessary in the situation where employees know what is to be done, can do it and are motivated to do it. However, ongoing assessment at the more general level of identifying qualities applicable to jobs not currently being done would be useful in re-engineered environments. The alternative is to introduce explicit assessment when a vacancy is to be filled. The advantage of a pro-active human resource management, which identifies potential independently of whether an individual applies for a given post, would be lost.

Values change: Protective to productive

Shifting the prevalent attitudes in the organisation, eg from powerless-ness to empowerment, or from working for the organisation to working for the organisation's customers, is part of the drive of BPR and one that must be extended to teleworkers. Other obsolete values to be changed include measuring importance by the number of direct reports, that coming to work on time means most of the job is done, and that one's own job contributes little to the success or failure of the organisation.

Changed attitudes will recognise that: customers pay all the salaries; showing up is no accomplishment; problem ownership is accepted by stopping the buck; you are personally dependent on the success or fail-ure of the whole team; and that there is a need to cope with an unknown tomorrow.

Hammer and Champy insist that reward practices must reinforce the value system. At Xerox, a major portion of a manager's salary is accord-ingly based on measures of customer satisfaction. The value change should be backed up by management systems and senior management adherence demonstrated, not just professed.

Given that this kind of value change can be effected, many of the preconditions for effective telework are achieved, reducing or eliminat-ing the management role of supervisor and controller, as seen next.

Managers change: Supervisors to coaches

Integrating a process into a team removes the need for a manager to supervise, monitor, control and check work as it moves from one task performer to the next. Either teams do it themselves, or the team consists of one individual only. Supervisory and coordination activity, and design and allocation work by a manager is redundant in re-engineered systems. A business process team needs a coach, a facilitator, an enabler to help solve problems. The coach must be close to, but not in, the action, and able to develop subordinates' skills.

This is a change of great significance for managing telework. Instead of providing channels of communication for monitoring and control, channels for recognising problems and providing facilities are needed, and for coaching and skill improvement.

For teleworker management, too, the lesson is to be learned that promoting people into management roles because they are good at their present job is not to be recommended. Management is a profession in itself, and not one in which a good team player is necessarily effective.

Structures change: Hierarchical to flat

Decisions and interdepartmental issues that used to require manager meetings are now resolved within teams. Organisational structure, whether functional departments or strategic business units, consumes a lot of energy through its effect on lines of communication and determination of decision-making hierarchies. After re-engineering, structure is not such an issue. People communicate with whoever they need and take decisions themselves. Organisational charts are irrelevant, the organisation is a bunch of co-equal people doing work.

There are no direct implications in this reduced importance of structure for managing telework. However, the implication is that fewer managers are needed in a re-engineered organisation. Each manager can supervise only about seven, but a typical manager can be expected to coach up to thirty. The impact on telework management is that modes of communication for all management functions have to take account of this ratio. If there is a communication overhead in dealing with teleworkers rather than on-site workers, this will negatively affect the ratio of employees to managers.

Executives change: Scorekeeper to leader

The prophets of BPR point out that traditional executives are divorced from operations and their perspective is primarily financial. More modern, flatter organisations move senior executives closer to customers and to those doing value-adding work. Executives have to change their role to leaders who can reinforce values by word and deed. They are responsible for ensuring that processes are designed in such a way that workers can do the job required. And that they are motivated by the company's performance measurement and compensation systems to do it.

For managing teleworkers, the lesson is again that the executive role now includes more coaching than monitoring. However, the element of leadership introduced here means that sufficient opportunities must exists for an executive to communicate this leadership to teleworkers. Ensuring the regular presence of teleworkers at premises where the executive is also present will provide some opportunities, but these must be planned. Many important occasions for leadership arise unpredictably, in particular where leadership is demonstrated by taking on problems and challenges immediately and acting in line with the values to be propagated.

For this to be visible to teleworkers, the bandwidth for non-intentional communication must be increased. For example, by providing a non-intrusive communication media currently being prototyped at Bellcore or Xerox PARC. This allows teleworkers access to informal communication of activities much as happens around the coffee pot in a traditional office. An alternative is that the executive must take on an additional workload of explicit communication. If this has to be to the extent of giving blow-by-blow accounts of events in the office and their own response to them, then much of the communication overhead of telework management returns, which BPR promises to reduce.

SUMMARY

The implications of business process re-engineering for telework management can be summarised as follows:

- Horizontal compression of whole processes into the job of a single case-teleworker weakens or removes any requirement on telework managers for ongoing monitoring of results.
- Vertical compression, moving decision-making down the hierarchy, means that the front-line teleworker rarely has to refer to the manager for authorisation and further relieves telework managers.
- Accelerating processes by removing unnecessary sequentiality constraints reduces the overhead for chasing late orders etc.
- Burdening front-line teleworkers with the decision as to whether a given case of work is simple enough for them to handle alone may increase management overhead unless adequate software support for these decisions is provided.
- Moving work 'to where it makes most sense' generally brings with it an increased sophistication of telework jobs, and a reduction of the need for coordination by telework management.
- Introducing statistical rather than continuous monitoring and checking can greatly reduce some of the problems found in traditional telework management.
- Supporting team self-management in telework, ie without team co-location, means careful consideration of communication support between team-members: support must have very low threshold and disturbance, at best better than communication opportunities in co-location.
- Multi-dimensional telework jobs requires careful management at its introduction rather than day-to-day, and raises the skill requirements of both teleworkers and their managers.

- Empowerment and the responsibility devolvement it implies relieves management of much control work, and makes management of telework less different from management of on-site staff.
- Encouraging and arranging for life-long education of the teleworkforce is a growing challenge not only in telework management.
- Removing the need for reconciliation of documents originating from different domains (of consistency control) and avoiding any need for such reconciliation between teleworker and employer can greatly reduce overhead work and its management.
- Where teleworkers are case managers and provide a point-of-contact to their employer's customers, this may limit the freedom of self-selection of working time, which is in many cases a major motivator to take up telework.
- Centralising automated control while increasing decentralised autonomy increases the viability of teleworking and relieves telework management of another burden.
- Moving the basis of compensation from activity or time to results, potentially gives rise to the management task of intermediate outcome evaluation and associated negotiation. The simultaneous integration across the length of a process removes this overhead again.
- Identifying candidates for a change of post should be decoupled from performance monitoring, using techniques such as assessment centres for both teleworkers and other candidates, including external applicants.
- Introducing re-engineered values significantly reduces a need for motivating or driving activity by telework managers.
- Telework managers are not automatically to be recruited from good team performers, but rather to be chosen for their coaching and enabling skills.
- In an organisation structured as 'a bunch of co-equals just doing work', coaching ratios of over one to twenty will be common, with a consequential decrease in the number of telework managers, but raising issues of providing communication channels between coach and a large teleworker team.

In conclusion, management functions in a re-engineered working environment are less extensive on most counts than in traditional organisations. The management role is more nearly equal between on-site and teleworking staff, but requirements for sophisticated communication and decision support are significantly greater.

BIBLIOGRAPHY

Anderer, G. (1992), Telearbeit: Empirische Erfahrungen und Einstz neuer Kommunikationsmedien am Beispiel Bildtelefon. In: *empirica: Management Issues in Telework and Mobile Working*, Conference Proceedings, 2–3 November, Bonn.

Hammer, M. and Champy, J. (1993), *Re-engineering the corporation*. New York: Harper Collins.

Huws, U., Korte, W. B. and Robinson, S. (1980), *Telework: Towards the elusive office*. Chichester: Wiley.

Wierda, Overmars & Partners. (1994) *PRACTICE – Code of practice for telework in Europe*. den Haag / Brussels.

NOTE

The COBRA methodology for integrating BPR and teleworking, along with 21 case studies, are available as: Colin Coulson-Thomas (Executive Editor) (1995), *The Responsive Organisation: Re-engineering new patterns of work*, London, Policy Publications.

8

Use Of Tools and Technology Within A BPR Initiative

Derek Miers

INTRODUCTION

There are as many definitions of Business Process Re-engineering (BPR) as there are consulting companies selling services. For the purposes of examining the use of technology we (Enix Ltd) find a useful definition of BPR is: *the constant search for, and implementation of, radical new approaches to business practice leading to step change improvements in productivity and customer service.*

The term BPR describes the transformation from functional to process oriented methods. The aim is to achieve streamlined activity chains that support corporate objectives and goals. An operation complicated by the patch-and-mend tactics of the past resulted in vastly complex administration systems.

Experience suggests that technology represents just one facet of a re-engineering initiative and will not, in itself, bring about sustainable improvements. The essential set of tools for a BPR initiative are a stack of blank paper, pens and a team of people from within the business with enquiring and creative minds.

The use of technology is relevant in two major areas of the BPR initiative. First, computerised modelling tools might be used to help in the analysis and communication of business processes. Second, computer systems which automate and assist in the support and management of the re-engineered business. It is useful to subdivide further these two bands as shown in Fig. 8.1.

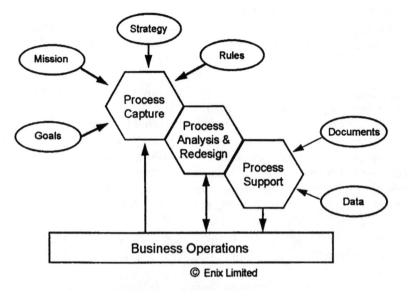

© Enix Limited

Fig. 8.1 *Broad phases of a BPR initiative*

Note that documents and data only become important in the implementation phase (Process Support).

We are currently aware of only one or two tools specifically supporting the envisioning of a re-engineered business (represented by the strategy, goals and mission bubbles). Many more products are being used to map and model business processes. Some of those tools provide additional mechanisms to support the analysis and re-design phases of activity.

One of the reasons why the above definition of BPR is more accurate than many is that it captures the constant change imperative for which ancillary systems must provide support. There is no such thing as a finished system. Most process support environments (typified by Workflow products) do little more than automate repetitive procedures and are relatively inaccessible to change (ie they require expert support from IT specialists).

PROCESS CAPTURE, ANALYSIS AND RE-DESIGN

No matter how sophisticated the tools used, their real value lies in the extent to which they can stimulate and support communication about the changes to be made. Hence, it is helpful to identify the different types of communication in which we might engage during a project. The three most commonly required forms of communication are those among the members of the team undertaking the study, between the team and the business, and between the business and its partners (customers and suppliers). The need for effective communication is particularly important where the team and the business are geographically or logically spread.

It is important to emphasise the need to communicate to every level of the business throughout the initiative. For example, business units and process owners must be able to understand what they are responsible for and maintain relevant business models as they evolve over time. Employees in turn need regular communications to convince them of the necessity for change, to gain their commitment and confidence and to maintain their enthusiasm during difficult stages of the project. Through regular, effective communication, the study team can help reduce the resistance to change and ease staff through the transition. Communication helps staff members understand the purpose of a process, where they fit into it, and how the process contributes to company goals.

Unless the use of enterprise modelling tools is moved into the business (rather than the IT department), experience shows that change will overtake the models before they deliver any significant benefit. A number of developments are underway to build modelling tools that executives and non-expert computer users can use to capture and communicate their vision and insights into the re-engineered enterprise.

One of the problems facing vendors and users alike is that there are no universally agreed terms or design rules that can be applied to business processes. As a result, different vendors interpret processes in very different ways. Some see a process as the entire sequence of tasks required to satisfy a customer requirement. Other definitions include a step within a particular procedure, activities with defined inputs and outputs leading to an increase in value. There is a spectrum of interpretations lying between these extremes. It is worth noting that a process need not necessarily have a hierarchical structure as some products and methods imply.

Our preference for a definition of the word process is based around the idea of a number of roles collaborating and interacting to achieve some goal. This approach aids in communication during process capture and analysis. Additionally, almost all work management systems operate on the concept of transferring the responsibility for action between the internal roles defined for a process.

Business Models

To aid communication we build *descriptive models* that attempt to represent the business 'as is' or 'as desired'. Such models are typically a combination of diagrams, text and performance measures. Hence in the case of a business process they might represent the roles within a process and the flow of activity between them. These models may have been built using some form of automated process-modelling tool which in turn may support the simulated running of the process as described. More recently, methods of communication have emerged that create a richer, more detailed representation of the process than was achievable with traditional flow diagrams.

A good process definition should exhibit a number of properties – namely it should concentrate on the essentials of the process, reflecting the real world yet handling the complexity of the process. The model should be intuitively understandable and accessible to the uninitiated.

In all cases we must always keep in mind the purpose of the model. Experience suggests that those models that are most useful in BPR allow us to represent the relationship between things of interest rather than necessarily being constrained to following the chain of inputs and outputs of each activity.

The enterprise business model that is developed should typically be composed of a number of process definitions containing the goals, business rules, actions, roles and interactions of the business.

Modelling tools should be capable of capturing the high-level processes and the context of the business within its market place. An example of a high-level process might be to maintain financial stability of the business. Other aspects that we need to model include the management processes (top to bottom within the organisation) and the operational processes (spanning functions and usually involving customers and/or suppliers). An example of a management process might be to ensure that all staff are appraised twice a year. An operational process could be sales order processing, spanning the sales, warehousing, production and financial divisions of the organisation.

Business models must reflect the natural language of the enterprise. This is essential to managing change as users must see the business concepts they work with clearly reflected. With this in mind, the key to building competent business models is in the abstraction of the problem domain.

We believe that for business modelling tools to be effective they must allow the user to relate actions and processes to the roles within the process. These roles may be either internal or external to the organisation. Modelling products must also provide a framework for capturing and analysing the key process measures.

Diagramming techniques

The right diagram, like a picture, speaks a thousand words. Diagrams underpin the description, analysis and communication of ideas. They normally form the core of the models that we use to describe the processes of the business whether capturing the current 'as is', considering the various 're-design options', or presenting the 'to be implemented' versions. Diagrams act as a focus for BPR team members to work around, communicating with each other and often the business as a whole. Sometimes referred to as a process map, diagrams are an essential element in the visualisation of the process and provide a basis on which to maintain process measures.

Diagrams need to present a great deal of information. To be understandable intuitively the diagram must convey several dimensions at once – examples of a dimension would be the order of activities, flow type, role responsibility, role interactions, location, quality checks and decision points. The individuals building up the models are often constrained by the diagram metaphors with which they are familiar.

Flow Diagrams
When using diagrams to support the definition of processes people normally choose the flow diagram. Although this diagramming style may be familiar it is not particularly useful except to convey the order of activities. It is not uncommon for a process map based on a flow diagram to cover several walls when printed out, for example, the sales process for the North American division of a major chemicals company was over 20 metres long. Given the size of these diagrams people usually find it very difficult to decide whether or not this is a good process based on just a process map.

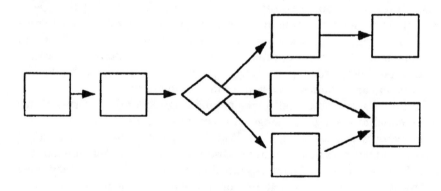

Fig. 8.2 *A typical flow diagram*

Users tend to annotate flow diagrams with role information in order to convey more meaning (effectively adding another dimension to the diagram). This is achieved either by highlighting activities with different colours, by segmenting the diagram with 'swim lanes' to show where the activities cross role boundaries, or by placing a role icon on the diagram beside the activity and using an arrow connector to join it to the activity.

It is possible to prove virtually anything with a flow diagram – even that the unsuspecting reader might be expected to travel back in time.

IDEF0 Diagrams
IDEF0 also represents the elements of the process with boxes and arrows. The boxes represent the activities or functions of the system, the arrows represent the information or products necessary to carry out the activities (the inputs and outputs of the activity). Mechanisms are the things used to perform the activity – a machine or human resource. Controls represent the information that influence the way in which the activity is performed. The combination of activities with ICOMs (Inputs, Controls, Outputs and Mechanisms) form a highly rigorous method of describing systems of any sort. Both the analysts expected to undertake the modelling and the individuals within the business require significant training in the techniques for meaningful models to be built and communicated.

Although this technique is widely used by consultants (because of the rigorous approach) we believe that this approach should not be used in the early stages of a BPR initiative. When modelling the existing business processes the use of existing data and documents should be specifically excluded from the model as the inputs and outputs of activities are, by definition, the things used to co-ordinate the process. If these items are included as a central part of the model it becomes far more difficult to break down links with the past when seeking re-design options. The use of data and documents are important implementation details but should not be considered relevant until that phase.

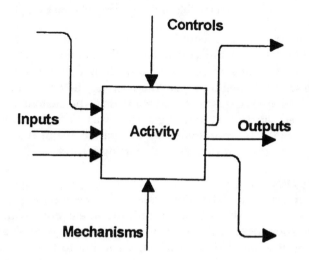

Fig. 8.3 *Essentials of an IDEF0 diagram.*

ActionWorkflow Diagrams
One method that concentrates on modelling roles and their interactions is the ActionWorkflow diagramming method, developed by Dr Fernando Flores and Dr Terrry Winograd (Professor of Computer Science at Stanford). The technique followed on from research undertaken by Dr Flores into linguistics and the network of commitments that people make with one another. The things people talk about are represented within an elliptical loop.

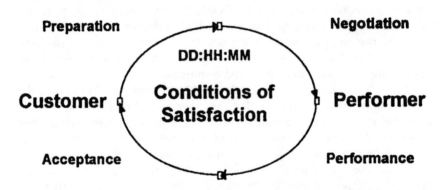

Fig. 8.4 *The ActionWorkflow loop*

Each quadrant within the loop represents one of the four phases of activity in any human interaction. The role of the 'customer' (either internal or external), is always shown on the left and the role of the 'performer' is on the right.

Every business process could be defined with several of the ActionWorkflow loops connected to each other, moving through all four phases of activity. For example, when modelling the sale of a product or service, the salesman might prepare the sale, negotiate the terms with the customer, delegate the despatch and shipment. The customer would not have expressed satisfaction until the invoice was paid. Each one of these interactions might be represented as a separate ActionWorkflow loop connected to the main process definition using arrows.

Role Activity Diagrams
Another method of modelling processes is to observe the process from the point of view of the roles capturing the interactions within a Role Activity Diagram (RAD). Roles carry out actions (activities) and make decisions about what to do and when, according to the business rules. Roles may carry out activities in parallel, interacting with each other to progress the work and achieve the goals of the process. Actions may

involve the use and production of information or documents (the implementation details).

With two minutes of instruction the concepts are easily understood on the shop floor or in the board room. Individuals quickly identify the actions that are normally their responsibility leading to the rapid identification of variations between the perceived method of operation and reality. Roles that do not add value quickly become apparent – usually where actions involve passing information or instructions from one party to another (a hand off). In most cases the modelling process leads to the immediate identification of re-design options.

RADs support process modelling at any level of abstraction – the interaction between functions and customers/suppliers or the detail of a sub-procedure. We can even examine the way computer systems communicate with each other and the business. In the example shown,

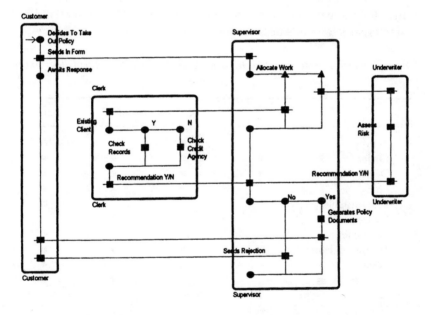

Fig. 8.5 *A RAD showing part of an insurance process*

Understanding RADs: The diagram should be read from top to bottom with the triggering action being where the customer decides to apply for the policy. The only real actions in the process are those for the Underwriter (in assessing the risk), the clerk who either checks existing payment records or contacts an external credit agency. The supervisor takes the final decision and either sends a standard rejection letter or generates the desired policy. The waiting time of the customer could be an attribute of the state represented with the circle.

the methods used by the underwriter to assess the risk are not shown on the diagram as they are not deemed to be important within this model.

In our opinion the RAD diagramming technique is the most powerful method of representing the degrees of freedom or limits of empowerment offered to workers within the business. Where the individual actor fulfilling the role is empowered to act under their own volition, the model could show a black box for the action which in itself may be a whole sub-process where the worker decides how best to undertake the work.

The above diagram does not show those features of the process deemed to be unimportant for the model – we have not shown the role of the mail room or the computer system which might be used to support the process. Neither does the model force us to stipulate the mechanisms used to support the process (data and documents).

Table 8.1 summarises the support of these four diagramming techniques for the various dimensions we have outlined as potential display characteristics for a business model.

Table 8.1 *Comparison of Flow/IDEF0/RAD/ActionWorkflow Loop diagramming techniques*

	Flow	RAD	IDEF	Action
Activity	■	■	■	■
Order	■	■	■	■
Decisions	■	■	■	■
Roles	–	■	–	■
Responsibility for Decisions	–	■	–	■
Interactions	–	■	–	■
Triggering Events	–	■	■	■
Goals	–	■	–	■
Business Rules	?	■	■	?
Source/Sink Data	?	–	■	–
Movement of Data	■	?	■	?

In our opinion the ActionWorkflow diagram is not as good at representing the process from the point of view of a role compared with a Role Activity Diagram.

Modelling tools generally support flow diagramming methods although several commonly used products support IDEF0. Surprisingly, only one or two products provide mechanisms for identifying roles within the diagramming interface with most providing an editing screen to add role information.

Measures

Business modelling tools should support the user in capturing process measures. Process measures are an integral part of the modelling exercise and are important for later analysis phases. Examples of measures include cost, capital employed, overall cycle time, elapsed time (of the activity), value added content and quality.

The measures which are of interest will be influenced by the overall aim of the BPR initiative and the issues being addressed. For instance, in a pharmaceuticals company, if the aim of the initiative were to reduce the time to market for new drugs then one of the measures associated with the model might include the number of days taken to produce the first submission to the regulatory authorities after the last document was received from researchers.

Process measures are often 'local' in the sense that they have a meaning only inside the context of the business. For instance, the definition of a quality measure would differ greatly between an insurance company and a steel works.

Tools should support a number of format types:

■ Numbers, dates, text strings, costs and time.
■ A simple list of values – where the user of the tool is presented with the allowable list of potential values and must choose only one.
■ A multiple list of values – where the user is presented with the list and may choose any number of values (eg for skills or specialisations required in a role).

The definition and explanation of these measures should be stored within the tool. To a varying extent, products provide facilities to support the user definition and attribution of process measures. In several cases tools include fixed Activity Based Costing suites, but these products do not usually provide any capability for the user to define further local process measures.

There is a requirement in some modelling exercises to store a different set of process measures for different parts of the business. By this we mean the same process model might be applicable to a number of functional or geographic units. Each one of these functions might have differing process measures which must be taken into account when analysing and simulating the process. There are, apparently, no tools supporting this requirement at present.

Some tools allow the user to derive variables based on calculations of other variables within the model. For example, the total cost of an activity can be defined as the unit cost multiplied by transactions – the number of times the activity takes place. Also, in the case of hierarchical models containing number variables, the values of an individual object can be inherited from its children, either as totals or averages.

Analysis and re-design

The emphasis of the analysis phase is to understand exactly where and how effort is currently applied and where the problems lie. The re-design stage then involves taking these new-found insights, combining them with other inputs such as benchmarking results and target performance levels to generate options for re-design.

Both activities can take many forms, involving varying degrees of computer support. It is the humans involved in the analysis and re-design phases and the insights they can provide that are of greatest importance to the BPR initiative – tools can not generally replace this element. There is at least one product attempting to provide 'expert system' support to the identification of re-design options.

Peer group review

This is the first of four levels of process analysis. The large majority of all workable re-design options will be thrown up by the specialists from the business working within the BPR study team. The team must be representative of the business functions involved and have the visible support of senior management. It is important to have at least one individual within the team to represent the customer (either internal or external).

Apart from providing computerised support for the diagramming techniques outlined above, technology has yet to make a big impact in this area. The models that we use to support the communication of ideas are largely supported by drawing tools.

Those businesses that wish to rely on external consultants to undertake large sections of the business analysis and re-design within a BPR initiative will almost certainly fail to achieve lasting, sustainable change. We believe that during the analysis and re-design phases external consultants should be used as either facilitators, trainers in modelling techniques, or brought in for specific expertise in the use of information technology, or to provide insight into varying approaches used by other companies (benchmarking).

The facilitator has an important role to play. They should lead the team in examining the criticality of each step and interaction within the targeted process. Only the specialists within the business really know what will work and what will not as external consultants can tell you more about your own business than you already know, and ideas must come from within if they are to be accepted and implemented. Certainly the facilitator can sow a few seeds and should be skilled in letting the team work it out for themselves.

For instance, in the RAD example, it might seem to make sense that the supervisor should not open mail, allowing the underwriters to handle the direct correspondence with the customers supported by a sophisticated system to establish a customer's credit rating (the only other real action in the example).

In reality there are likely to be very few underwriters within the business and the reason the process exists (as mapped) is to maximise the efficiency of their time, ie not answering phone calls from irate customers or dealing with the machinations of a complex credit scoring system. In general only the specialists from within the business have the prerequisite understanding to veto such a suggestion.

The study team should specifically look for the following:

- Roles within the process that do little more than pass or request information (a prime target for replacement with workflow systems).
- Hand offs – where responsibility for action moves from one individual to another without any value or meaningful action taking place (such as an expense claim which is routed to the first, second and third line managers before being authorised – ie the first and second line managers did not appear to add anything to the process).
- Disconnects – places where the responsibility for action appears to go into a grey area. All role transitions represent one of the areas of risk associated with a process.
- The physical location of a role, whether within a company office, outsourced or home based becomes an attribute of the role and should have no real bearing on the process definition.

Static Analysis

The second type of process analysis involves a static analysis of the process models, ie the direct calculation of the critical measures identified for the process. The measures built up within the process capture phases are manipulated to provide insights into the validity of alternative 'what if' scenarios or to show the implications of the existing process.

Spreadsheets, such as Lotus and Excel, are commonly used to build such static models. Some business modelling tools provide direct mechanisms for the calculation of these numbers. A static model might be used for a variety of purposes such as calculating the approximate number of resources needed, the cycle time for the process or the costs being incurred to support a particular product.

One of the constraints on this type of model is that all possible paths through a complex process will provide different implications for cycle time, cost or whatever other measure is being examined. It becomes increasingly more difficult to maintain an accurate image of the process being examined as the number of alternate paths increases.

Dynamic modelling

A dynamic model usually has a strong concept of time and tends to be based on statistical sampling techniques to maintain a more accurate image of the process and the various cases of work running through it. These types of model allow the analyst to take into account the influences of one case of work on another.

There are a variety of approaches that can be taken in building dynamic models of the process. The common techniques are based on Systems Thinking, Discreet Event Simulation and Time Slice Simulation. To discuss the implications and differences between these techniques is not possible in the context of this chapter (for further depth see Process Product Watch, volumes one and three).

Building a dynamic model with spreadsheet technology is possible but complex, time consuming and difficult to refine and maintain. Given the difficulty of building up dynamic models, their validity must be questioned within a BPR initiative. Generally, dynamic models have been used to prove the 'business case' or to reduce the risks associated with implementation.

Rules based modelling

An emerging area of process analysis is in the use of rules based modelling (sometimes known as Case Based Reasoning). This technique centres around the idea of 'exercising' the network of business rules within the model. These rules might be thought of as similar to the relationships of cells within a spreadsheet. Instead of restricting their activity to numbers (as in a spreadsheet), rules based modelling can just as easily operate on text strings, states, relationships and other elements.

Users may focus on the qualitative aspects of the model, removing the restriction for calculations to be purely quantitative (ie numerical). One does not always have to think of the model in a mathematical context – you build models in order to reflect the real world which is not always based on numbers.

Comparing analysis mechanisms

The best tool for the analysis of business processes is the human mind. No technology tools or products will replace the creative insights that people within the business produce when asked to examine the criticality of each action and interaction in the process, provided they have a suitably rich communication environment. The static analysis and dynamic modelling tools will provide ways of approximating the implications of change as a snapshot of the process and in some situations achieve greater understanding amongst the BPR team.

We believe that the use of simulation products should be limited to validating options described by the people working within the study team. Otherwise their practical use must be questioned, given the significant IT skills required to build and maintain models.

Dynamic modelling systems are good at calculating the implications of many cases running through the system, stacking statistical distributions on top of each other in various combinations to determine the best overall result. This is very difficult with static analysis tools, which might be used to calculate the cost or cycle time of one particular path through the process. Rules based modelling can more easily reflect the language and ideas which prevail in the business domain, although at present they are generally inaccessible to many business users as they require additional programming skills.

WORK MANAGEMENT AND PROCESS SUPPORT

The role for work management systems in re-engineering is to:

■ Provide options for the design of the re-engineered business process(es).
■ Support the re-engineered process in the live business environment.

There is a common, vendor driven, misconception amongst many organisations undertaking re-engineering. The belief is that by introducing a workflow system they will have re-engineered the business. We wish to emphasise the point that real and sustainable performance gains can only be achieved by affecting lasting changes in the mindset, attitudes and behaviours that created the current process design. Given this change in thought processes, it is then possible to achieve maximum value from IT-enabled work management systems as a component of the re-engineered solution.

The objective of work management systems is to provide generic software structures that can be built on and configured to provide automated support for repetitive and complex business processes. Ideally they should meet the changing needs of the organisation.

Particular care must be taken in managing the organisation's expectations of the value of work management and workflow technologies. Contrary to the claims of some vendors, technology is not a panacea that can be waived at a business process on the assumption that it will guarantee effective process performance.

As with any new software project, the key to successful implementation lies in having a clear understanding of the business opportunity for which the system will be used, and a properly thought-through and well-resourced implementation plan. This point can not be stressed too strongly. Alongside the success stories there are already a number of examples of firms that have suffered expensive and embarrassing failures with poorly thought-out workflow implementations. For most large businesses, transition from one method of working to another will involve many difficult issues at the systems level. For example, consider the problems faced by a large energy business with a history of regional autonomy trying to standardise their engineering systems.

Clearly, many vendors would have us believe that it is straightforward to implement process oriented working practices. However, the reality is that, in the majority of cases, users have not been encouraged or taught to think in process oriented terms. The hierarchical nature of the business and the decomposition of tasks has led them to think only of their own responsibilities. Typically few, if any, have a sufficiently broad perspective on the process to be able to describe its end-to-end structure with any accuracy.

Our true requirements only really emerge once we start to use the system and discover the steps in the process that it does not support. Hence, this places an ever greater importance on the need for work management systems that can be developed in an iterative manner as the needs of the business emerge and evolve.

Furthermore, when pushed, even higher level managers with a broader field of vision find it very difficult to define precisely all of the possible variations at any point in the process. This lack of process awareness and process thinking makes the task of implementing effective process support systems a difficult one.

It is especially true of work management products that they must be appropriate to the culture of the organisation. In particular we feel that the choice of products in this area will be influenced by the management philosophy of the business. For example a key decision criterion is whether the aim is to empower people within the business, or constrain their actions and activities and ensure adherence to strictly defined procedures.

The problem with the latter approach is that it is almost impossible to predict at the outset the full range of possibilities that might arise. The attempt to constrain workers to a tight definition of procedures results in a more mechanistic and inflexible approach to management of the business.

In the empowered organisation the situation is overcome by ensuring that all employees have a deep understanding of the logic and values that underpin the design of the business. It is this understanding that guides them to the right course of action in situations outside the norm. This in turn helps ensure that the business can respond more rapidly to the changing needs and expectations of modern society.

Of course management must realise that mistakes can and will happen in the empowered organisation (leading to learning inside the organisation). The challenge is to reduce the numbers of these mistakes through training and education programmes. (For a wider discussion of empowerment concepts please refer to Chapter 2 by Rohit Talwar.)

There is an inherent contradiction between empowerment on the one hand and the detailed and prescriptive specification and automation of business processes on the other.

Most businesses require a mix of the two concepts. For instance in the world of international banking, settlements are likely be highly procedural. One does not need creative office clerks when processing a million pound banker's draft. At the same time the service provided to the originator of the draft would tend to be oriented toward satisfying the customer's need as the account handler saw fit.

Hence, it would be almost impossible to build a highly structured process definition that would satisfy all the possible actions the account handler might take. However there is still a requirement to support this customer account representative in automating repetitive elements within their work. This highlights a key challenge for future generations of work management systems. They will need to balance enforcement and empowerment concepts within the one environment, sharing appropriate information between the various parts of the business.

At present, the vendors of work management systems have largely concentrated on prescriptive approaches that support only those work patterns which have been exhaustively defined at the time of implementation.

Approaches to work management

The implementation of work management systems is generally based on workflow products. Every vendor we have spoken to has a subtly different definition of the term workflow. Our definition of workflow is that it is a term invented by computer vendors to straitjacket the real world into matching the features that their products are delivering this month, ie the term means virtually anything you want it to mean.

Most realisations of workflow products are based on the automated routing of documents and tasks around the organisation. Given this definition there is still considerable work to do in developing commercially viable implementations that meet the full work management requirements of a modern business .

Along with process management, complex documents (sometimes called virtual or compound documents) have become an increasingly important factor within many spheres of business. Complex documents are constructed from fragments drawn from many other documents. These fragments are brought together dynamically to create new documents as required.

Typically, when we talk about work management we are including the overall system building and change control functionality that will be required. We believe that this activity should be placed as close as possible to the real users so that they can take ownership of the ongoing evolution of the system.

The problems encountered when building these complex systems often result more from attempts to ensure effective communication with other business applications such as word processing than from trying to ensure effective routing of cases to individuals within the business. For example, routing the responsibility for action to the correct user and linking in MS-Word to create a customer response at the appropriate point is relatively straightforward in most products reviewed. However it is far more difficult to provide that user with a selection of pertinent document templates and extract relevant information to be inserted into the selected template.

Workflow philosophy

Workflow systems work on the premise of routing the responsibility for action to the correct person within the organisation, and on providing them with the information they require to complete the task. More recently, products have provided the capability for users to initiate tasks on common third-party applications such as word processors and spreadsheets. Generally these systems constrain the user to undertake only that action that is defined at that point within the process definition.

Generally there are two ways of looking at workflow – from the point of view of what should be done, or who should do what. These approaches are often described as 'heads down' and 'heads up' workflow systems.

To explain the concepts we can draw on manufacturing analogies. Heads down workflow is akin to a production line where the conveyor belt brings the work to the operative who undertakes the same repetitive tasks on each item put in front of them. In contrast, heads up workflow systems are closer to the manufacturing management concepts popularised by Volvo and Nissan. Here, a small group of workers are empowered to build a number of cars from start to finish with total responsibility for the final output.

A workflow system can reduce the number of users involved in the process by providing an intelligent database system that helps individuals perform a wider range of tasks after appropriate training. If users are provided with relevant information such as instructions on which discrete tasks to carry out, and given access to all relevant data to carry out those tasks, not only is the individual more efficient, they can switch tasks more easily. Moreover, knowledge of the process is stored within the computer system, supporting users in undertaking a wider range of responsibilities and reducing risk for the business as a whole.

Workflow in the back office

The work of back-office staff is normally characterised by a low-trust relationship with management. Their response in any given situation tends to be controlled by tightly defined pre-specified procedures. The level of variation in back office tasks is relatively low, and such variations that do exist, have typically all been thought through carefully in advance.

The historical method of operation tends to be based around batches of work that are now being replaced with queues of tasks in the workflow environment. For example, in an insurance company batches were driven by the daily arrival of mail which was first sorted by the post room and then by supervisors for distribution to clerks for processing. These batches were then added to existing backlogs – creating the impression of a constant flow.

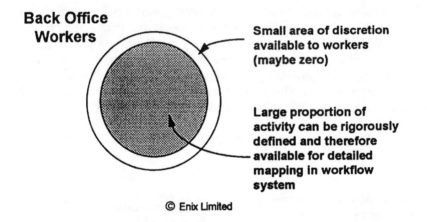

© Enix Limited

Fig. 8.6 *Small area of discretion for back office workers*

Back office workflow systems are typically heads down applications. They provide very little choice for the user apart from processing this task and accepting the next that automatically appears on the desk top.

Workflow in the front office

Front office workers tend to work in a more fluid environment. The levels of variation are relatively high, yet the alternative paths and consequences of action (or inaction) can usually be planned in advance. The focus of activities is outward from the organisation, dealing with customers and suppliers.

Systems for the front office are characterised by a higher degree of support for independent user action. These products are sometimes called 'case handling' systems because they aim to allow the user to process all the activities required to complete the case of work. The focus is oriented toward empowering the user to undertake what is thought necessary at the time in order to achieve case completion.

Workflow and knowledge workers

The focus of activity for knowledge workers is normally based around the completion of specialist and/or complex tasks and projects. The nature of their tasks implies high degrees of variation in the execution of individual activities. The knowledge worker will often be facing outward from the organisation dealing with customers and suppliers. This makes coordination with internal colleagues far more complex and less predictable than in the back office.

The needs of the knowledge worker and business professional have largely been ignored by existing workflow systems. At present this type of worker usually relies on personal productivity tools and paper to act as the focus of their collaboration with others.

Work management systems for knowledge workers are far more difficult to build and implement as complex process definitions must be capable of modification on a task-by-task or project-by-project basis. The additional infrastructure mechanisms required to support work management systems for knowledge workers should be accessible to the non-expert computer user. This class of user also requires *ad hoc* access to the system as it is impossible to predict all their support needs.

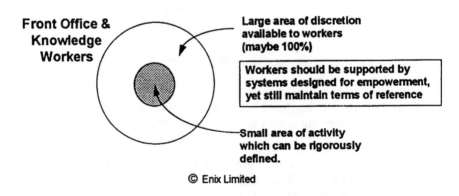

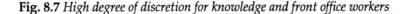

Fig. 8.7 *High degree of discretion for knowledge and front office workers*

Document management

In the absence of computerised workflow and document management systems, office procedures consist of paperwork physically routed from one desk to another. Documents perform two key roles – they act as the focus of knowledge and information about the process and they provide information about the specific case of work being processed.

The importance of document management is obvious in sectors such as pharmaceuticals, insurance, build-to-order manufacturing, bid management and telecommunications. In these industries a fragment of information is very seldom used in only one document. For example, a description of a new drug may appear in the company end-of-year report, an introduction in the submission to the Food and Drug Administration (one for each regulatory authority), packaging for the product and training materials for medical staff. The implication is that one only wants to enter the original data in one place and then re-use it many times, ensuring that if the data is changed this is reflected in all places where that data is used.

When authoring a new document, an average seventy per cent of the information already exists. For example, when addressing a letter to a customer the user needs to extract name and address information and combine it with an existing document template. All the information already exists, it has simply been recombined to create the standard letter response. When compiling an annual budget you might start with an existing document and edit the content – providing a relatively small amount of new information, with any analysis likely to be based on existing statistical information.

Workflow models

At the heart of workflow systems are a series of process models used to support the various cases of work flowing through the business. For example to support claims-processing in an insurance company, the workflow system will contain process models that define the routing rules and third-party applications to be called as cases of work flow through the business. While there are many different types of process model, two are of interest in the context of work management – descriptive models and executable models.

An understanding of the different models is essential if we are to build a true appreciation of the capabilities and limitations of the approach. Within this section we will also establish a more formal framework for considering the relationships between the different models, work management systems and the real world.

As outlined earlier, *descriptive models* are those that attempt to represent the business 'as is' or 'as desired'. Hence in the case of a business process they might represent the roles within a process and the flow of activity between them. They may also provide some of the underlying information about process performance. Such models are typically a combination of diagrams, text and performance measures. These models may have been built using some form of automated process modelling tool that may support the simulated running of the process as described.

Executable models are those models of desired business behaviour that are stored inside the computer systems to support business. Hence the process script and business rules stored inside a workflow system represent an executable model. It is these enactable models that govern the way tasks are actually accomplished within the system. Clearly the executable model should be an accurate representation of the descriptive model on which it is based, which in turn must reflect the real world. With many workflow products the translation from descriptive model to executable model is performed manually.

Executable models are used to support the actual *performances* of the process in the real world. These performances are the cases or jobs of work within the system (sometimes called 'episodes'). For example, in an insurance company the clerks and the claims they are processing are the individual performances.

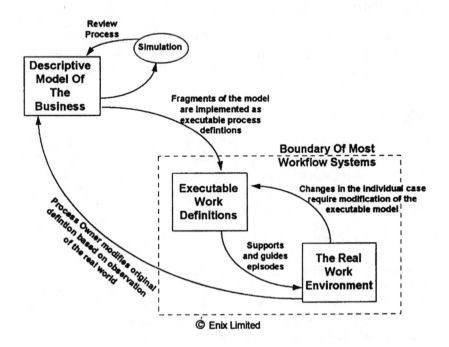

© Enix Limited

Fig. 8.8 *Life-cycle of a business model*

The important thing is the relationship between the executable model and the real world and how they are kept in step. This implies two challenges – the first is to ensure that the process as executed reflects accurately the process as defined. The second is to ensure that the executable model in the system provides adequate support at all the right stages for the process as it should be performed. In many cases we find that the users are having to work around inadequate descriptive and executable models. The relationship between these two types of model and the real world is shown in Figure 8.8.

The aim of work management systems should be to achieve a proactive support relationship within the modern office. The system should link user definable procedures both to the people who have to undertake them and to the information and documents required to achieve the goal.

However, at present, most products constrain the user to undertake only that activity that is defined within the model. At the other end of the spectrum some products attempt to empower the worker by providing a broader range of support mechanisms. Systems that support empowerment do not limit the scope of action, but should still monitor all actions (for audit purposes) and provide automated support for complex procedures where appropriate.

Feedback loops exist between individual performances and the descriptive and executable models. As process owners observe and measure a number of cases running through the system, modifications to the process may be identified. Initially the process owner might model and test the efficacy of these changes in one of the business modelling tools (reviewed in Process Product Watch, volumes one and three). Once a new design has been agreed, there will be a requirement to turn this new descriptive model into a new executable model to support the processing of new episodes as they are received.

With the emergence of object oriented techniques the distinction between the descriptive models and the executable models is becoming less clear. In true object oriented environments the descriptive and enactable models are one and the same – the model is the system.

CONCLUSION

Although the pundits would have us believe that BPR initiatives are based around the enhanced use of IT systems, we find that successful projects rarely focus on the technology issues alone. Achieving sustainable improvement in business performance is largely achieved as a result of changes in the attitudes, behaviours and mindset of the workforce. These cultural changes are often combined with technology implementations but it is the cultural change that must lead the initiative.

Through the ongoing research undertaken within Process Product Watch, we see new products appearing on the market every week. The business modelling and analysis tools are becoming more and more accessible to the average computer user although most techniques still concentrate on the flow diagram paradigm and the exhaustive mapping of processes. We have yet to see usable products that allow the business to model the degrees of empowerment placed on individuals within the business. Role Activity Diagrams probably offer the best vehicle for such a tool.

The vendors of work management and workflow products have tended to build products that constrain workers to follow precise processes, removing any flexibility or empowerment. There are a few exceptions to this rule but they are rare. Tomorrow's systems designed to support knowledge workers must do more than share data in a passive fashion. They will have to automate the procedural and repetitive elements yet provide support for the real expertise of the knowledge worker – ie the opportunity to exercise discretion, offering sufficient flexibility to allow individuals to vary the process as circumstances dictate.

There are many other potential uses of technology to enhance business performance that may be implemented within BPR initiatives. They include the use of telephony, executive information systems, application packages, hand-held data collection devices, mobile communications and many more. In this chapter it is impossible to address all potential product areas.

FURTHER INFORMATION

The Process Product Watch (PPW) service mentioned above is provided on a subscription basis to organisations interested in keeping in touch with the emerging use of technology in the field of BPR. PPW provides subscribers with practical advice and guidance on the selection and use of technology and tools to support the re-engineering, re-design and management of business processes. We investigate the technology and its applicability, rather than simply reporting the sales hype delivered by vendors.

PPW provides an extremely cost effective method of keeping the enterprise up to date with the implementation and selection issues, important developments and the products in this relatively immature sphere of technology.

Updated on a quarterly basis, PPW alternates its focus between reviewing:

■ Tools that support business or process modelling, analysis and re-design.
■ Process support and work management products.

Four volumes are published per year, two in each area. Each volume contains a detailed introduction and guide to the principles and technical approaches that underpin many of the tools reviewed (around a dozen product reports in each volume). We also outline the essential properties that products must exhibit in each area. Each individual product report is compiled following a five- to ten-day evaluation and usually comprise eight to ten pages detailing the approach taken, the underlying technology and usability issues.

Derek Miers can be contacted at:

Enix Limited
3 The Green
Richmond
Surrey TW9 1PL
Tel: 0181 332 0210
Fax: 0181 940 7424

or on the Internet with an address of miers @ enix.co.uk

NOTE

Details of 101 specific tools and techniques and an indication of their relevance at each stage of the COBRA approach to re-engineering can be found in: Colin Coulson-Thomas (Executive Editor) (1995), *The Responsive Organisation: Re-engineering new patterns of work*, London, Policy Publications, while the use of the approaches and technologies of electronic commerce in supply chain re-engineering is covered in: Peter Bartram, Colin Coulson-Thomas and Lee Tate (1996), *The Competitive Network*, London, Policy Publications. (Further information: Tel: +44 (0) 171 240 3488; Fax: +44 (0) 171 240 2768.)

9

The Practical Application of a Methodology for Business Process Re-engineering

Brian Fitzgerald and Ciaran Murphy

BACKGROUND

Microelectronic Devices Incorporated (MDI) is a multinational company that specialises in the design and manufacture of electronic components for the personal computer market. The company has four manufacturing sites: two in the Far-East, one in the US, and its European manufacturing headquarters is located in Cork, Ireland. This case study deals with the BPR exercise that is ongoing at the Cork plant.

Reasons for BPR

In 1992, demand for the company's products grew very significantly – in excess of 100 per cent. Sales projection figures in mid-1992 were found to have significantly underestimated product demand for late 1992 and early 1993. As a result, the company had to recruit a large number of temporary staff who had to be trained in a very short space of time. The company also had to reschedule its delivery dates with some of its customers. By mid-1993, problems had been addressed and the situation had stabilised. However, the general manager, mindful of the crisis that had been undergone, resolved 'never to go through an experience like that again'. He believed the failure to predict the upsurge in demand had been due to basic problems in the existing company processes for dealing with customers. Having recently become aware of the BPR concept, he felt that senior management at the company should investigate whether BPR could help analyse and address the problems that had arisen.

A researcher from the Executive Systems Research Centre (ESRC) who had some expertise in the BPR field, was invited to discuss the BPR concept with senior management at the Cork plant. A consensus emerged from this meeting that the BPR approach could be used. As a result, two researchers from ESRC undertook to facilitate the BPR project at the company. The name chosen for the project was *Smart Moves*.

A METHODOLOGY FOR BPR

The methodology followed was one that had been developed by the ESRC specifically for BPR projects. The methodology is expressed as a series of phases, each of which addresses a basic question, and is summarised below:

- Select process to be re-engineered: This addresses the basic question 'Where are we going to start?'
- Establish process team: Addresses the question 'Who is going to do it?'
- Understand the current process: Addresses the question 'Where do our stakeholders see us now?'
- Develop a vision of the improved process: Addresses the question 'Where do our stakeholders want us to be?'
- Identify the actions needed to move to the new process: Addresses the question 'What do we need to achieve?'
- Negotiate/execute a plan to accomplish these actions: Addresses the question 'How will we achieve it?'

It is worth noting that the methodology is expressed from a first-person point of view, reflecting the fact that it might be necessary to change the culture and mindset of those working in the company. This can only come from within the company itself rather than from any direct actions which external consultants can take. However, the phases of *understand the current process* and *develop a vision of the re-engineered process* take an external viewpoint, based on the necessity of adopting a detached stakeholder-oriented, outside-in viewpoint. Even though the above phases are presented as linear steps, a central tenet of the methodology is that it adopts an iterative approach (see Fig. 9.1). In the diagram, the links between the *understand current process* phase and the *develop a vision of re-engineered process* phase are shown as dotted lines to indicate that this is not an automatic progression. Each phase of the methodology is discussed in detail in the following sections.

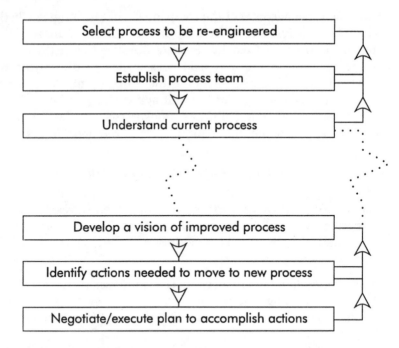

Fig. 9.1 *The ESRC methodology for business process re-engineering*

Select the process to be re-engineered

BPR requires a global view and an integrated approach to business rather than the traditional reliance on narrow departmental specialisations. There may be several candidate processes for BPR. However, it is necessary to focus in on a particular process to ensure that the project does not expand in many different directions. This phase ensures that such a focus takes place at the outset.

A number of processes emerged as candidates for re-engineering from interviews with key members of management at MDI. At this stage, a decision was taken that individual process re-engineering was more appropriate than overall business re-engineering. This more focused approach accepts the current business strategy and links the re-engineered process into it. The specific process chosen for re-engineering was Customer Handling/ Support. This process had been identified as a critical process by a number of managers in MDI. This was not altogether surprising given the extent to which customer service has become the dominant force in the supplier-customer relationship in all market sectors.

The specific output from this phase was a 200-word preliminary description of the process to be re-engineered. This helped to delimit the area, and even though it was modified later, it helped in the next phase when team members were being selected.

Establish the process team

Process re-engineering requires improved leverage of people and technology operating within the appropriate structure. The importance of people cannot be over-emphasised and the selection of the process team is critical. Process change is about challenging the most basic business assumptions, and may thus require significant cultural change. It was vital, therefore, that the process team be empowered, and this obviously had to come from the highest possible management level. Thus, an executive sponsor was appointed. This person's role was to initiate the project publicly, ensure that doors were opened, and necessary resources made available. The general manager at MDI fulfilled the role of executive sponsor. However, due to the intensive nature of the process re-engineering task, it was considered unlikely that the executive sponsor could be sufficiently involved on an ongoing basis, and so a process leader – the IS manager – was appointed. This person's role was to ensure that the project did not flounder and, for the duration of the project, the process leader reported directly to the executive sponsor. Additional team members were then chosen. One of the criteria used for selection was that good candidates would probably be those who felt they were too busy to involve themselves in such a team.

The size of the team posed a problem initially. Members were chosen from all the specialist areas relevant to the process, but the large team of experts resulted in meetings dragging on interminably as minor points of dispute were raised. Also, it was readily apparent that no one individual had a complete understanding of the overall business process. Compounding this, each team member represented their portion of the process with different graphical notations and narrative standards, thus making amalgamation difficult. These difficulties were resolved by reducing the size of the team to a small number of core people who were able to elicit any necessary information from other relevant personnel in the organisation. Also, a scribe was appointed to collate all information using a standard graphical notation with each process component underpinned by a complete narrative account.

Understand the current process

This phase involved the team acquiring a clear definition and knowledge of the current process that several writers have identified as an essential stage in BPR (Bevilacqua & Thornhill, 1992; Davenport & Short, 1990). This required detailed analysis of the current process. The nature of the analysis was both top-down and bottom-up. It involved the examination of relevant documentation, interviews with both internal and external personnel as customer concerns were vital in the current competitive business environment.

Benchmarking of the existing process took place at this stage and other metric data on the existing process were gathered to assist later evaluation of the re-engineered process. The explicit deliverable from this phase was a graphical model of the current business process. This model was greeted with considerable enthusiasm by all concerned. All the relevant personnel accepted the veracity of the model, and it helped to stimulate discussion. Also, several problem areas emerged that had not been previously articulated. For example, the timing of the computerised production scheduling and planning tasks followed a rigid timescale that was somewhat arbitrary and did not offer sufficient flexibility to the customer. This was very obvious from the model, and so the computer run was delayed to the latest possible time to allow fine-tuning of customer orders.

Develop a vision of the re-engineered process

The articulation of the current process in a graphical model helped to surface assumptions that needed to be challenged. To stimulate further desirable changes, the existing domain knowledge was supplemented by examination of similar processes in relevant industries and from world leaders in the process. The team identified a general need to flatten managerial and functional hierarchies and to align the process away from bureaucratic structure to a more customer-focused one. For example, corrective action reports, which gave customers feedback on the status of returned goods, were not being given adequate priority, with little inter-departmental co-operation. Consequently, one person was employed full-time to collate these reports from the relevant departments. However, this person was not having much success as individuals in the various departments did not give adequate priority to this task. Thus, there was a clear need to promote awareness of the importance of this task in the organisational culture. To facilitate the process, a Lotus Notes database was established that allowed individuals an easy and structured medium for formalising these reports.

Actions towards the new process

The actions needed to move to the new process must be detailed and prioritised. A number of basic flaws had been identified in core operations related to the process being studied, and these had to be rectified. For example, a number of problems emerged in relation to the working practices in the quality control section. First, the quality control department did not operate a shiftwork system. However, there was a continuous flow of materials coming from departments, which did operate shifts. Materials undergoing quality control inspections were consequently being buried under new material being received from evening shifts and early morning deliveries.

Second, the investigation of the quality control process revealed a basic flaw in how the company dealt with goods being returned under warranty. Typically, when a customer returned goods as faulty, it was assumed to be genuine and the customer's description of the fault was taken to be *bona fide*. However, it emerged that the lifespan for some products was shorter than the warranty period. Thus, customers were using their return of goods under warranty option to reduce stock levels by simply shipping back surplus stock on the pretext that it was faulty. In some cases, products still in their shrink-wrapping were returned as faulty!

A major problem was also identified in relation to stock levels. Too much stock was being held out of 'natural optimism' according to the general manager, and so an 'unbuying' policy was put in place to create some impedance in the procurement process. There was a need to change the prevailing culture in the company so that not having something in stock was seen as a lesser sin than having huge excesses. However, reducing stock in a coherent fashion was a major problem in that accurate stock levels were not available. However, a very simple solution to this problem presented itself. The company was already putting bar codes on all products to satisfy customer requirements, and these could be used to update stock levels automatically. This required a change to the stock control system in use in the company. The 'clean-up' of the stock area had a major impact. The general manager estimates that the stock value has been reduced by £3m, giving rise to annual savings of £300,000.

At this stage it was considered important to set audacious goals or 'stretch targets' to use Davenport and Short's term. This is necessary to avoid a half-hearted approach being taken, whereby BPR lapses back into an incremental improvement programme without any radical substance. Visible metrics were established wherever possible to verify that the re-engineered process is meeting expectations. If the efficacy and value of the re-engineered process cannot be reliably assessed, then it is difficult to tell if BPR has been successful.

Negotiate/execute an action plan

This plan must be negotiated, and again the executive sponsor plays a critical role here in ensuring that any cultural change will not be impeded. This is a vital but delicate stage and it is imperative that negative effects on employee morale be avoided. Relevant support mechanisms and management processes must be aligned. A formal presentation of the plan should be conducted to help win over those vital to ensuring its success. This step can be anticipated as being difficult. The organisation must present a 'business as usual' front, while at the same time accomplishing a smooth transition to new processes, which must then be institutionalised. Frequent monitoring is essential to ensure that the project does not fail at this stage, as this is where many BPR projects hit the rocks as radical change may not be fully undertaken.

In the case of MDI, this phase was iterated with the previous one. As actions were identified, meetings were held with the general manager, and he gave full and public support to the actions mandated.

LESSONS LEARNED

Although the BPR exercise at MDI is not yet complete, a number of lessons have been learned. First, BPR, while perhaps inevitable, is not an easy or automatic activity. If true re-engineering is to take place it is certainly not about half-measures taken by the half-hearted. The early phases of the methodology outlined here are perhaps not all that difficult to put in place: *select process to be re-engineered; establish process team; understand current process*. However, an appropriate process must be selected – one capable of adding value and which can be clearly and concisely defined. The team must be established and empowered, and to this end an executive champion/sponsor must be found. Second, getting a thorough understanding of the current process and representing this clearly and unambiguously in a graphical format can be tedious. However, as can be seen, major benefits can accrue from such an exercise.

The latter phases of the methodology from the *develop a vision* of the re-engineered process phase to the *negotiate/execute plan* phase are fraught with difficulty. A radical change may be identified by the team as necessary, but it is very difficult for management to commit themselves to a high-risk project, especially one that fundamentally alters the *status quo*. Also, in the case of multinational companies radical changes in business operations often cannot be mandated locally, but require head office approval. BPR recommendations may often involve a reduction in headcount – 'skimming management's midriff' to use Drucker's phrase (Drucker, 1986), but this may not be palatable in many organisations or cultures. Certainly, in Ireland, lateral transfer is more widely used than dismissal as a means of dealing with personnel problems, but such a policy is anathema to BPR.

The question arises whether, given these constraints, it is worth initiating BPR projects in the first place? However, the answer must be in the affirmative, if only due to the serendipitous benefits that BPR projects invariably provide. Certain fundamental problems may be identified by a thorough understanding of the current process, some of which can be rectified without radical change. Also, it may be possible to identify stages in the process where a richer approach could add value for the customer without too much extra effort. Therefore, even if the radical changes required by BPR are not feasible, business process *enrichment* may enable existing processes to add value whenever possible.

CONCLUSION

Even though BPR projects are extremely difficult to undertake, and the majority fail or are abandoned without achieving the desired objective, this should not deter organisations from initiating a BPR project. Ptolemy long ago declared that there was no royal road to geometry, and the same could be equally said of BPR. However, as can be seen from the evidence, the journey may provide benefits as significant as those of the destination.

BIBLIOGRAPHY

Andersen Consulting (1993), *Business process re-engineering*. Public lecture, UCC, April.

Bevilacqua, R. and Thornhill, D. (1992), Process modelling. *American Programmer*, 5, 5, pp. 2–9.

Davenport, T. and Short, J. (1990), The new industrial engineering: Information technology and business process redesign. *Sloan Management Review*, Summer, pp.11–27.

Deming, W. (1986), *Out of the crisis*. Cambridge, MA.

Drucker, P. (1986), *The frontiers of management*. London: Heinemann.

Hammer, M. (1990), Re-engineering work: Don't automate, obliterate. *Harvard Business Review*, July-August, pp.104–111.

Hammer, M. and Champy, J. (1993), *Re-engineering the corporation: A manifesto for business revolution*. New York: Harper Business.

Harrington, H. (1991), *Business process improvement*. New York: McGraw-Hill.

Scott Morton, M. (1991), *The corporation of the 1990s*. New York: Oxford University Press.

Waite, T. (1989), Business re-engineering. *Insights*, 1, 2, pp.9–12.

Zuboff, S. (1988), *In the age of the smart machine*. London: Heinemann.

10

Change Management in the French Steel Industry

Matthias Maier

INTRODUCTION

This chapter summarises a study that has been undertaken in order to describe and analyse change management practice in the French steel industry, where the use of a modified form of BPR has followed experience with Total Quality Management (TQM). Field research took place at Usinor Sacilor's Headquarters in Paris at the end of 1992. In addition to this, quality managers, personnel and production executives at several plants in France were interviewed and documents analysed.

Situated in a hypercompetitive international environment, French steel producers had no choice but to play on the two buttons that are today regarded as being the key to survival, not to say development in the market place: cost and value. TQM was adopted in France very early. Usinor Sacilor as well as Renault and Saint Gobain were among the first in Europe to adopt this Japanese approach to management. Already in 1986 TQM was declared as being a group-wide policy of Usinor Sacilor. One purpose of this approach was the integration of the different companies that were forged to become the national champion. At that time French steel production was highly inefficient – in comparison to the Japanese and German competition. Therefore improvements in cost and quality were the paramount targets of TQM. Only recently Usinor Sacilor's largest division Sollac has – additionally to TQM – adopted an approach to change management with a strong process focus.

The French steel industry

More or less unnoticed by the wider public the French steel industry has made huge efforts to keep up with international competition in the last decade. Once the European champion of subsidies, it can now be found at the cutting edge of competitiveness – at least compared with the majority of its European competitors.

Speaking of the French steel industry today means talking about Usinor Sacilor, the state-owned giant that accounts for about ninety-five per cent of French crude steel output. Usinor Sacilor is the second-biggest producer of crude steel worldwide (number one being Nippon Steel, Japan). The group is owned by the French state, with 80 per cent of its shares being directly held by the state and the remainder via the state-controlled bank Credit Lyonnais. Recently Usinor Sacilor has begun to pursue a strategy of internationalisation, realised by means of acquisitions mainly in the United States.

THE CONCEPT OF TQM AT USINOR SACILOR

The basic definition of TQM ('La Qualité Totale') at Usinor Sacilor, given by the former Directeur de la Qualité Totale Claude Barbier, is the following:

> Total Quality is a collection of principles and methods, set out as an overall strategy, which aims to mobilize the whole organisation in order to obtain the greatest customer satisfaction at the lowest cost.

Usinor Sacilor has formulated five core principles of TQM:

- *Conformity.* Each and every position and/or department shall be regarded as being a member of a chain of internal customers and suppliers, finally directed at the external customer. Conformity of the deliverables shall be realised between the elements of this chain.
- *Prevention.* The repair of defective products at the end of the process chain regularly causes massive costs. TQM aims at establishing organisational conditions to produce the right product from the beginning. In order to fulfil this, it is necessary to empower employees, to let them perform with minimised external constraints. Heavy investments in training have proven to lead to this.
- *Excellence.* This principle is synonymous with continuous improvement. Specific tools, that is to say problem solving techniques and techniques for the work in quality circles, are applied.
- *Measurement.* Every step in the improvement process is measured and translated into monetary terms. The effect is that the difference between the *status quo* and the aim as well as the realised improvement can be communicated. This is very important for motivating employees.

■ *Responsibility*. This principle refers to the general approach to the management of human resources. The French steel industry has switched from the traditional paternalistic or autocratic approach to a more consensus-oriented and more participative way of personnel management. As a result, motivation and identification with the enterprise seem to have improved. It can be regarded as a genuine novelty in French worker-management relations, that TQM is not obstructed by ideological arguments.

IMPLEMENTATION STRATEGY

Top management commitment is a basic condition for the success of TQM. The board of directors, especially the PDG (Président Directeur Général, CEO) has to devote continually a significant part of his time to the pursuit of TQM. This rule applies as well, but to a lesser extent, to middle management. In this sense, TQM is truly a top-down approach. Later on, when the programme has developed, the bottom-up aspect of the programme will come to the fore. Then the programme should run on the initiative of the employees. But till then, a lot of management input is necessary.

Usinor Sacilor distinguishes three steps in the implementation process:

■ Communication
■ Participation
■ Quality action plans (Plan d'Action Qualité, PAQ)

It has proven to be successful to follow this sequence when TQM is started at plant-level. Each step successfully passed, reinforces the effectiveness of the following step. In other words: no PAQ without participation and no participation without communication.

Communication

Traditionally French industry organisation has been quoted for being overly hierarchical and uncommunicative – for one main reason: the huge gap between executives ('cadres') on the one hand and workers on the other hand. These two social groups didn't have a common language, their backgrounds were too different.

Cadres are educated at highly elitist engineering or business schools (Grandes Écoles) and are trained to become leaders at a young age. They are separated from their less successful peers right after the high school degree (Baccalaureat) and have passed highly selective exams (Concours) for entry into Grandes Écoles. They are publicly regarded as having made it, whereas the other group finds itself on the far less prestigious side of professional life.

Workers were traditionally either not at all, or comparatively badly, trained. Consequently they lacked career chances. They acquired rather firm-specific skills, being trained on the job. Studies of French industrial relations always suggested that cold, distant relations were the norm in French organisations. Impersonal forms of communication instead of face-to-face contacts being preferred by management. Even departments at the same level of hierarchy were traditionally not in close contact. In brief: internal communication problems – horizontally as well as vertically – were common in French enterprises.

To overcome these difficulties, Usinor Sacilor established specialist departments for corporate communication at holding, division and plant level. Their main mission is internal communication, with a priority upon the propagation of TQM. It is believed that effective communication is a necessary condition for improving efficiency.

Participation

Participation of employees in quality circles ('Cercles de Qualité') is voluntary at Usinor Sacilor. In group work, a general problem-solving method and both all-purpose and specialist tools are applied by the quality circles – if necessary assisted by specialists or line managers.

Participation of personnel differs significantly between the different plants of the French steel industry. Usinor Sacilor's flat products division Sollac, is well known in French industry for its high participation rates – especially at the biggest works like Fos sur Mer (75 per cent personnel participation in 1992), Dunkerque and Florange (each 48 per cent). But many other sites experience great problems in motivating their employees. It is worth mentioning that workforce participation is only seen as a *necessary condition* for the success of TQM, whereas middle management commitment is seen to be all-important. A high ranking quality manager coined the phrase: 'Middle management is the drive belt. All actions come from engineers, foremen and technicians.' (Dapère, 1990). This statement is in line with a conclusion of this study, that the qualificational background of employees has a major impact on the degree of participation that can be accomplished. This is one reason why the enterprise's investment in workforce training is significantly above the average of French industry.

Quality action plan

The 'Plan d'Action Qualité' (PAQ) is a cyclical improvement plan. In 1992 85 per cent of the French plants of Usinor Sacilor were running under PAQ. 'Normally' the PAQ is started when a 30 per cent participation is reached in the preceding stage. The PAQ combines the more participative elements of stage 2 with more directive features, more management control via annual improvement plans. It works top-down, whereas the participation phase is more bottom-up and concerns the initiative for concrete improvement ideas. Whereas stage 2 builds on voluntarism and individual initiative, this stage is designed to let management coordinate the improvement efforts. The PAQ is much more effective than the pure quality circle stage and it receives a lot of attention from top management. The PAQ works best in production units, whereas in administration only a few attempts to apply it have been successful.

This administrated approach to continuous improvement typically has four steps:

- Establishment of an inventory of non-quality
- Evaluation of the weak points
- Selection of targets in Pareto-order and
- Problem-solving one after another

IMPLEMENTATION TOOLS

There are two sets of tools for quality circle work at Usinor Sacilor: so-called *all-purpose tools*, applied to make group work effective, and *special tools*, which are in effect complex programmes for the improvement of specific problem areas.

The first set (all-purpose tools) consists of internationally well-known techniques like Brainstorming, Euler Diagram, Fish Bone Diagram, Weighted Votes, Pareto Chart, Weighting Table and Blocking Evaluation. These are not unique to Usinor Sacilor, so it is not necessary to explain their design and function.

The special tools are in fact TQM programmes of their own, designed to meet the requirements of specific problem areas. One of them is Total Productive Maintenance (TPM), transformed into French by Usinor Sacilor into 'Topomaintenance'. TPM has been introduced recently and soon became a success in terms of realised participation and quality and cost improvements.

TPM is focused on the improvement of the reliability of machines in order to improve maintenance efficiency. The success of 'Topomaintenance' is easily understandable, as the steel industry has on average maintenance costs in the range of 8 to 15 per cent of turnover (International Iron and Steel Institute, 1989). So a huge potential for improvement exists and the commitment of plant managements was assured.

The approach is to reorganise maintenance work. Machine operators are trained to do standard repairs. In addition they acquire basic technical knowledge concerning the functioning of the machine. By establishing cleaning and examination routines – jointly by the responsible engineer and the operators – the acquired maintenance standard is preserved. This causes lower machine down times, more stable product quality and generally results in significant cost savings, also because specialised maintenance technicians have to be called far less often for repairs.

Statistical Process Control (SPC), one of the other special tools, has long been used and this technique can be regarded as the backbone of any TQM programme. Other special tools in use at Usinor Sacilor are Single Minute Exchange Die (SMED) and One Touch Exchange Die (OTED), Failure Modes and Effect Analysis, Kanban, Design review and Experimental design. The latter have in common, that their application is not as widespread as that of TPM and SPC.

IMPLEMENTATION PROBLEMS

In the longer term, one problem is the necessity constantly to 'push' the employees in order to get results. At Usinor Sacilor, TQM didn't become a programme that runs by itself. But too much 'push' can also be destructive. Finding the balance requires lots of experience, as some plants had to learn painfully.

Perhaps a specific of the French approach is heavy internal marketing for 'la Qualité Totale'. Employees in certain units became fed up by being too often told why, that, and how TQM would be 'the thing' to pursue. Also linking personnel participation in quality circles closely with material benefits proved to be counterproductive. As a result TQM could have had a short corporate life, after initial euphoria had ended.

Diminishing returns of PAQ are another problem, closely correlated with the problem just mentioned. TQM practice tends to concentrate on problems that are easily solvable whereas basic structural problems are not attacked. Although internal customer-supplier relations are at the centre of TQM, radical questioning of the inherited basic structure is not an element of TQM. Unlike BPR *continuous* improvement leads to incremental rather than dramatic improvements.

Finally, TQM has not yet been shown to work successfully in administrative areas. The official answer by Usinor Sacilor to this question is, that lay-offs are more likely to be the effect than would be the case in production areas, so that resistance to change is greater. What could be meant by this is, that administrative areas have traditionally – not only in France – been protected against close supervision of performance.

According to TQM-executives a huge potential of performance improvement is buried in offices. A structural specific of French organisations is the high degree of control that is performed by the administrative and supporting technical functions. Compared with Germany, shop floor employees enjoy a much smaller degree of autonomy concerning the organisation of work. As lateral communication (as mentioned earlier) is another crucial aspect, the French system of work organisation tends to carry daily operational decisions remarkably high in the hierarchy. Higher ranks in French organisation are indeed much more concerned with coordinating routine processes than is the case, for example, in Germany. Introducing hard performance improvement programmes like Quality Action Plans into an administration area is difficult for this reason. Or, in other words: French corporate administrators have always been the ones who did the job of control, while not themselves being the object of control.

USINOR SACILOR'S FLAT PRODUCTS DIVISION

Constrained by TQM's incremental design – to change organisational structures and practices step by step, the management of Sollac – internationally renowned as being one of the French benchmark companies in TQM-practice – decided to start a new approach to organisational change. It could best be described by the terms 'business process redesign' or 'simplification'. 'Rationalisation des Opérations Administratives' (ROA) is an element of the strategic vision *Sollac 2005*. Its focuses are the administrative sectors of the company, but also certain technical areas that are not directly attached to production.

A fundamental rethink of organisational structures was initiated. Project teams were assigned to identify the core functions (grandes fonctions) of Sollac. The core functions are: human resource management, procurement, information systems, finance, management, maintenance, incoming logistic, new buildings, communication, and quality. An eleventh category was preserved for remaining functions that were regarded as not central. ROA is described as a horizontal, 'transversal' approach, applied across all functions of the flat products division. Complete functions are the object of reorganisation, and 9000 employees were involved at the end of 1992.

Edmond Pachura (PDG of Sollac) describes ROA:

> This time it is a question of looking at the organisation both in its entirety and horizontally, function by function. The rules of behaviour are different, because they imply work on the interfaces between sites, divisions and functions, and call for the organisation to go beyond a sector-based vision and to work out how to strive for overall progress.

The analysis of the value chain is at the centre of the ROA approach. Its aim is to simplify processes by removing non-value-adding activities. Take for example the core function of procurement: 80 per cent of the staff employed there was occupied by the administrative work that didn't produce value for the internal customer. The project group identified a potential for cost reduction in the order of 10 per cent of the total value of the purchasing volume, which is around seven billion French Francs (Pachura, 1992, p.854). At divisional level potential savings of 30 per cent have been identified, to be realised within three years.

In effect:

- The organisational structure will be simplified and the hierarchical pyramid flattened. In some advanced sectors of Sollac the number of organisational levels has already been reduced by three layers.
- Processes will be simplified and correspondingly the competencies of the employees concerned will be broadened and enriched.
- The redesign shall be focused on the creation of value for both the internal and the external customer.
- Modern information systems will be applied.

As this process initiative had just been started at the time of the study, it would be premature to judge its success. However, salient features of its design indicate that ROA is not as radical as BPR, as it is currently being discussed all over Europe. Rigby (1993, p.25) defined re-engineering as an approach that is characterised by:

- A fundamental rethinking of process organisation with the aim of drastically improving productivity and cycle times.
- A reorganisation of organisational structure aimed at breaking functional hierarchies into cross-functional (horizontal) teams.
- Implementation of a new state-of-the-art information system, providing information to the places where it is really needed.
- A strong focus on the company's customers.

What Sollac has chosen, is an approach that can be characterised as process improvement or simplification. On a continuum from incremental to fundamental change, process re-design takes a middle position between TQM (incremental) and BPR (fundamental). Whereas re-engineering radically questions the ways work is done at company level, 'a process redesign focuses on a lower level, such as a single process, a single product, or a single work group, department, or division' (Skinner, 1994, p.6). Another aspect of re-engineering – the integration of new ways of work, for example, telework, has not yet received much attention at Usinor Sacilor.

INSTEAD OF A CONCLUSION

Ask a top-executive of a European steel producer what is the greatest threat to the long-term survival of his company: is it quality? Volatile prices? Or rising competition from East Europe? The answer would most probably be: it's the competitive threat of the *mini mills*.

American and Japanese mini mills are a significant step away from the traditional way to produce crude steel. Traditional integrated steel works consume iron ore and coke that are processed into iron in blast furnaces (the production of coke is itself a complex production process). After that the iron becomes converted into crude steel, the basis for finishing work in rolling mills.

As mini mills produce steel out of scrap their layout in terms of size, labour force, and capital requirement can be a quarter of that of integrated steel mills. Because of quality requirements in other product sectors their core market has until recently been commodity steel products for construction. Now, 'new casting technology. . . has given them access to the much larger market for flat-rolled steel used in cars, domestic appliances and tubing,' (*The Economist*, 1993).

All the ingredients of a truly radical and 'greenfield' BPR now exist. The difference is that the new mini mill business has been started from scratch, and without having to take into consideration existing structures.

Continuous adaptation of an organisational entity is a *conditio sine qua non* in today's volatile environment. But TQM still relies on existing structures, techniques and methods. When everybody talks about re-engineering today, here is an example of a very successful 'white sheet' approach. While it would be premature to discuss the reasons for European myopia (with rare exceptions) to grasp the growing importance of this new way to produce steel out of scrap, this example might serve as a reference (or benchmark) against which TQM and other approaches should be judged. Incremental change even when successful can be overtaken by fundamental innovation and radical breakthroughs.

REFERENCES

Barbier, C. (1992), La qualité totale. *Techniques de l'ingénieur*, 5, pp.1–20.

Dapère, R. (1990), The Usinor Sacilor way to total quality control. In: International Iron and Steel Institute (Ed.), *Total quality control*. Bruxelles. pp.1–7.

The Economist (1993), *The European steel monster*. 6 March.

International Iron and Steel Institute (1989), *Maintenance for the 1990s*. Bruxelles.

Pachura, E. (1992), Productivité et management des hommes. In: Institut Renault de la qualité (Ed.), *Qualité totale. La voie vers l'enterprise au plus juste*. Paris. pp.843–873.

Rigby, D. (1993), The secret history of process reengineering. *Planning Review*, 3, 4, pp.24–27.

Skinner, C. (1994), Does reengineering equal success? *Focus on Change Management*, 1, pp.3–6.

11

The Community as an Electronic Proving Ground

Eric Benhamou

It is not only business that is undergoing a transformation in the 1990s. The pattern and scope of people's entire lives are changing too.

PEOPLE AND INFORMATION

Usually when we talk about BPR, we mean a top-down overhaul of the way an organisation works. We identify what is essential to corporate survival and prosperity, sweep aside all habitual practices, clear the mind of received wisdom, and decide from first principles how we're going to carry out those essential activities in future.

Customer focus, teamwork, employee empowerment, performance-related pay, cross-divisional task forces – these are some of re-engineering's key ideas. Computer networks are essential to support these key changes by connecting the workforce to information they need. The re-engineered business needs information delivered quickly to the places where it most valuable – that is, where it can be put to work immediately.

In business, the two most valuable assets are people and information. This connection is fundamental. The dynamic relationship between employees and information technology lies at the heart of BPR. Managing that relationship is crucial to the success of re-engineering projects – and the profitability of any business.

Communications links with the office, for example, can enable employees to 'telecommute' – accessing the same information in their own home as at their office workstation. This fits perfectly with the idea of bringing information to people rather than requiring people to come to the information. From the organisation's point of view, it shows in microcosm the problems and opportunities of BPR.

Telecommuting employees often get more done, with productivity increasing by fourteen to twenty per cent. Headquarters and field real estate can be reduced saving space and money. A successful contribution to re-engineering on both counts. On the other hand, newly empowered employees, working away from headquarters supervision for the first time, may get distracted, underperform and create problems for their managers. So, human relations issues are central to BPR: its success depends on effective personnel management.

Let us look at this another way. How do people experience business process engineering? Only if it is a two-way process, where individuals enjoy benefits as well as the organisations they work for, does it have a long-term future? There is already evidence to show that it does.

People who have learned transformational skills in business play a key part in ushering in the next wave beyond BPR. They can transform communications among people in their communities, states and even society at large. By re-engineering corporate IT systems to reach out beyond their local boundaries, they can create wide-access social networks. They have the opportunity to lay the communications foundation of the information highway that will transcend geographic borders linking nation with nation.

This process has started already in most of the advanced countries of the West. But essential to its favourable outcome is partnership between individuals and their communities, businesses, and government. In Europe especially, some hard decisions must be taken first.

Although discussions of process re-engineering usually concentrate on changes within commercial organisations, here we intend to step across the boundary between what is work and what is 'everything else' in people's lives. We shall give a view from both sides of that frontier on what process re-engineering has to offer us, as individuals, as employees of organisations, and as members of society.

THE ELECTRONIC COMMUNITY: POLICIES

The will to bring the power of networked computers into all sectors of life has been there from the beginning. Now the enabling technologies have become pervasive enough, and of a low enough cost and simple enough to use to make the dream happen. A personal computer, useful software and on-line services are now within the reach of most households.

Nearly 35 years after the early experiments at MIT – that is, more than three-quarters of the way forward up the evolutionary ladder of digital computing – the federal government has swung in behind the concept of the electronic community.

As the Clinton administration took office, it created a technology policy that put the National Information Infrastructure (NII) at its centre. The NII is both a symbol for economic growth, and a practical investment in overcoming the most pressing problems the US faces, in education and healthcare reform. In effect, federal government's vision of the NII is a blueprint for re-engineering society through information technology.

It remains true that perception is not necessarily aligned with policy. The government has done a great job publicising the information super-highway but most Americans have a rather different idea of what it is for. They have no doubt that the information superhighway connects with their life but many perceive it as an entertainment proposition. We shall lose a great opportunity if we let this happen.

The most urgent need is to reclaim the agenda from sectional interests and put the electronic community back on track as a general-access resource and not as a medium for the distribution of entertainment. Government can only do so much by articulating policy – the rest must come from effort at the grass roots. Smart Valley in California's Silicon Valley – described later – is one model of how this can be done.

Countries other than the US are tackling the issue of public policy. This is vital in providing the environment in which particular electronic communities can thrive and deliver benefits to their citizens, and in ways that reflect their own political and social beliefs.

China's vision of its information infrastructure is especially interesting. As a country it has enormous – seemingly limitless – people resources. Its economic growth is running at about thirteen to fourteen per cent a year. China has a very small information technology base. Its Ministries of PTT and of Information and Technology have formulated a pragmatic vision to solve specific business and government problems.

China's Golden Bridge Projects plan to use information technology to interconnect about thirty or forty of the provincial capitals, about five hundred cities in total. The aim is to provide an infrastructure for finan-cial trading, interbank electronic funds transfer, the national value-added tax system, and foreign trade. It is moving very quickly and on a grand scale to solve particular problems – in effect re-engineering the nation's commercial business. Here, unlike in the countries of the West, the government has also the power to implement as well as to legislate.

Just about everywhere in the world is prepared for an information society. Canada has the Canarie project, Singapore IT2000, Japan its 2015 ISDN milestone. But the countries of the European Union appear to have no similar co-ordination. The exceptions that demonstrate this are the

SuperJANET network that interconnects research institutions and universities across Europe on a high-speed network, and France has its Minitel network as a result of a large-scale government funding.

Europe may have a vision at the senior level – the European Commission recently published a White Paper that urged the creation of a European information infrastructure. However, to my mind there is no unifying vision of what the information society can offer individuals on the European continent. Only if individuals are convinced that it is in their own interests will they join in and contribute. Building an infrastructure requires builders as well as planners and engineers. The builders must be drawn from the grass roots.

Even when government takes the initiative and succeeds in gaining grassroots support, success is not assured. In the countries of the West, where governments cannot simply mandate infrastructural change, translating vision into action is a delicate balancing of public and private interests.

SMART VALLEY

Businesses own most of the communications infrastructure and need to see a proper case to cede any control over assets in which they have invested for commercial advantage. Individuals may be reluctant to invest their highly-paid skills for no direct reward, particularly when the beneficiary of their voluntary work is vaguely identified as 'the community'. Nevertheless, it is up to communities where there is a concentration of expertise, and where businesses and individuals have a high level of understanding of the issues, to show the way.

One such community, Smart Valley, already exists in California's Silicon Valley, located 35 miles south of San Francisco and the birthplace of today's electronics. Its declared vision is 'to create an electronic community by developing an advanced information infrastructure and the collective ability to use it . . . to benefit all sectors of the community – education, healthcare, local government, business and the home' – remarkably similar to the ideals of the pioneers of computer networking.

The Smart Valley concept grew out of Joint Venture: Silicon Valley, a grass-roots effort to generate ideas to create balanced economic growth and improve the quality of life in Silicon Valley. Smart Valley draws its volunteers from universities, local government, businesses and private citizens. Their common belief is that the convivial electronic resource is central to re-engineering the life of their community – to the benefit of all its citizens.

Of course, the Silicon Valley is fertile ground for this project. Its modern history is intimately bound up with that of the digital computer.

Much of the early work on computer networking was done here; it can trace an unbroken line back to the pioneers. World-class laboratories and research institutions thrive synergistically with high-technology businesses. Computer skills are widely spread throughout its two million population. Local government takes seriously its role to safeguard and promote the quality of its citizens' lives. The technologies and skills to build a networked community are available now.

Smart Valley's mission is to deploy these tools to build an information infrastructure for the 21st century that will benefit the entire community. This will involve applications such as telecommuting, geographic information systems, distance learning, networked classrooms and community information services.

COMPUTER NETWORKING

For 'entire community' read an area rather beyond the boundaries of Silicon Valley. Although specific applications with direct benefits such as collaborations between suppliers and vendors, government and citizens, healthcare providers and patients, are primarily for residents, Smart Valley's regional connectivity is part of a much larger picture. In effect, this is the practical, grass-roots realisation of the NII vision of a computer network that will span not just the United States, but the entire globe.

This bottom-up, grass-roots approach to delivering benefits from computer networking offers, I believe, the best model for the future. It is clearly focused on certain key initiatives:

■ to revitalise education by connecting schools to libraries and research resources;
■ to improve the responsiveness and drive down the costs of healthcare;
■ to deliver local government services to people's homes and reduce the time spent on administration;
■ to connect distributed businesses for closer teamwork;
■ to enable employees to telecommute, so reducing the volume of traffic on the roads, with obvious environmental payback;
■ to create new jobs installing, programming; and
■ offering new services on the network.

These benefits are equivalent, at the grass-roots or community level, of the competitive advantage sought by businesses who re-engineer. And at the heart of it, in just the same way, is the rapid movement of information to where it can be used to best effect.

An infrastructure already exists to support this model: the many thousands of local networks already in use in business. It takes only a small leap of the imagination to see these networks spreading out as telecommuting takes hold, and connecting to form a global resource: the super-highway.

That is why the contribution of businesses, with their vast under-utilised computer network resources, are the key to the creation of an information society. It is much easier, more economical and more rational, to build a global network from many smaller, overlapping and inter-communicating networks.

The 'entertainment proposition' of wiring up America and the world for 500 channels of video-on-demand, interactive game shows, and teleshopping is an irrelevance in the mean time. This top-down model is offered by cable operators, telephone circuit providers, and Hollywood bosses, who see an opportunity to distribute consumer-only choices into homes. The connections on the information highway, I believe, need to be made at local user level. If the highway is to achieve its potential, I believe its power must be distributed at the perimeter. It must be simple to use and offer productivity enhancements for business, the home and education.

EXTENDING BUSINESS NETWORKS

Local area networking is already a vast industry, said to be worth $10 billion a year. The number of connections to local area networks – ports – is estimated at 35 million, with a further 28 million ports to be delivered this year. And connectivity among individuals is already happening. CompuServe has 1.7 million members, America Online 600,000; the Internet, largely non-commercial but spinning out of the same technology, already has more than 20 million users. Some of the traffic on these networks is commercial; much of it is cyber-chatter.

Businesses don't generally have much time for this. They tend to view their connectivity strictly as a means to an end: to link the people in their own organisations with electronic mail – recognised by senior managers as a useful way of speeding up decision-making; to keep in touch with their people in the field; to exchange documents and plans with suppliers and trading partners; to collaborate in design and planning work.

So while Smart Valley's aims are excellent, why should businesses, which already pay a social levy in the form of corporate taxes, readily give up any of their own resources to the community? One of Smart Valley's most crucial tasks was to answer that question, and show why it was in businesses' own interests to reach out beyond the boundaries of their own organisations, and help provide the pervasive connectivity that the information society needs.

Smart Valley teamed up with Enterprise Integration Technologies (EIT), a Palo Alto-based R&D company, to raise funds for a project to show businesses that public computer networks such as Internet have commercial benefits – specifically, that they could be made robust enough for business applications.

Late 1993, Smart Valley and EIT were able to announce Commercenet, backed with funds from the US government's Technology Reinvestment Programme, the State of California, and local businesses. Participants include Apple Computer, Hewlett-Packard, Lockheed, National Semiconductor, Pacific Bell, and Sun Microsystems, and Stanford University.

Among the first points CommerceNet had to prove is that business networking no longer has very high barriers to entry. New technologies such as Integrated Services Digital Network (ISDN) offer high bandwidth at much lower cost than the slow, protocol-bound computer-to-computer networks of the past.

The latest remote routing equipment allows speedy but secure multi-protocol access to local area networks, and provides the ideal linkage for LAN-to-LAN connections without the excruciating technical mumbo-jumbo and ever-present fear of unauthorised access by hackers. Laying to rest the twin problems of cost and security are among the key objectives in making public networks 'industrial-strength', and bringing on board the many smaller and medium-businesses which have previously considered networking strictly for corporates.

CommerceNet, tapping into the resources of Silicon Valley's innovative networking technology firms, gives business a real motive to grow into and contribute to the growing resources of the information highway.

SOCIAL AND BUSINESS BENEFITS

Two phenomena, one universal in the Western world, one particularly associated with California, kicked the Smart Valley project into life by highlighting the social and business benefits of the information network.

The first was the recession: California and Silicon Valley business led the way as technology firms retreated from the State's hostile regulatory environment. It made business leaders wonder what they could do to mitigate the effects of savage competition from the newly industrialised countries of the Far East, where labour rates are typically one-tenth of those in California. The prescription was: work smarter to overcome competitive disadvantage, and invest in technology to extend the business's reach into global markets. These lessons are the new orthodoxy in Europe equally as in the US.

Since the recession and the earthquake, the will to get networked, present from the beginning of the computer era, has converged with the innovative, low-cost technology solutions produced and used by local businesses. The only remaining component for a networked community was organisation. And that is what Smart Valley, Inc. did by bringing together over 100 people from 70 companies, schools and governments to:

- Build awareness of the potential of new information technologies and services in the community.
- Work with providers to develop a communications technology and information services road map and strategy.
- Facilitate grassroots efforts to identify and implement a diverse set of applications.
- Drive a few, selected focused projects to demonstrate the value of the network.
- Work with state and local agencies to resolve public policy issues that affect the implementation and management of the information infrastructure.
- Develop a governance structure that reflects strong ties to Joint Venture: Silicon Valley Network and to the community.

California deploys some special advantages in this pilot of the information superhighway and the kind of convivial community it will support. Its intense concentration of high-technology firms, for instance, is very helpful, though by no means unique: similar clusters of enterprise are springing up in Europe, in the Thames Valley, or Bavaria for example.

But the technology Smart Valley deploys is by no means unique to California. The solutions it proposes answer questions that are being asked throughout the world. Questions such as: In this new community, do I do something different when I get up in the morning? Will it be more enjoyable? Will it help me get more satisfaction from my life?

That is why, of all the many possibilities opened up by the information society, few have evoked such widespread interest as telecommuting. Telecommuting – the use of a remote office or office services, often in the home, networked to the employee's main business centre – is an outward and visible sign of 'applied re-engineering'. Employees have access over the network to all the tools they would use in the office, and waste no time moving themselves to their place of work to have their use.

Several Silicon Valley organisations affiliated to Smart Valley are trying teleworking, including 3Com, Hewlett Packard, Pacific Bell, Silicon Graphics, Cisco Systems. Other participating organisations include Stanford University, Santa Clara University, Regis McKenna, Inc., and the law firm Gray Cary Ware & Freidenrich.

Around 50 of 3COM's employees telework, carrying out tasks ranging from programming and technical writing to purchasing and compensation. The trial, which began early 1994, also helps assess the performance of the company's own communications products in a 'live' situation. Hewlett Packard is devolving much of its technical support department to teleworkers, and already has around 300 people telecommuting from its Response Centre. Deloitte, Touche is starting around 50 people on teleworking, saving valuable real estate in their downtown San Francisco offices and enable hiring of new personnel for their booming information technology practice. Silicon Graphics even goes so far as to encourage product development work from home.

The benefits include easier recruiting of quality staff, retaining existing staff, reduced requirement for floor space in prime head-office districts, improved individual productivity of the order of ten to thirty per cent, reduced absenteeism, and less air pollution as fewer employees drive to the office. Employees can fit their work better to the patterns of their individual days, use their time more creatively and effectively, and reduce stress in their lives.

INFORMATION TO THE PEOPLE

At the level of individual experience, telecommuting can be a profound change for the good. And here we move back over the boundary between work and 'not-work'. For what is good for the individual is good for business too. Telecommuting demonstrates in microcosm exactly what the information superhighway is about: moving information to people, rather than moving people to information.

If we manage this dynamic relationship between people and information intelligently to build a strong infrastructure, then there will be immeasurable benefits for individuals, businesses, and nations. It will transform the quality of life and make business more competitive. But like all transformational projects, it is at the microcosmic level that it will be proven. If the information society is to work, then they must work to enhance individuals' lives. When it does that, it works for business, and for society at large.

BIBLIOGRAPHY

JALA International Inc. (1993), *City of Los Angeles Telecommuting Project*. Los Angeles, California.
Smart Valley Inc. (1993), *Smart Valley Telecommuting Guide*. Palo Alto, California.

12

Organisational Structures, People and Technology

Hamid Aghassi

THE CHANGE IMPERATIVE

The traditional command and control structures based on information being available to the select few are becoming increasingly irrelevant to today's organisation competing in a shrinking world:

- The decade of the empowered knowledge worker and the high emphasis placed on customer focused business processes necessitates a fundamental change in hierarchical organisational structures and their inherent functional oriented way of working.
- Intense competition on a global scale demands value to be added by every member of the organisation at all levels. This includes functional and middle management who have to date survived mainly through their privileged access to, and manipulation of, information.
- Strategic deployment of information technology and the resulting availability and sharing of information across the organisation is transforming the roles and activities performed in today's organisation.

A demand-driven organisational structure places the emphasis on customers and their closest contacts within the organisation: the senior management and the knowledge worker (see Fig. 12.1). Such an organisational structure provides a continuous and effective feedback mechanism to the decision-makers who can develop the appropriate strategies aimed at satisfying future customer needs. The reactive management style resulting from inherent delays within the supply chain becomes the exception rather than the rule.

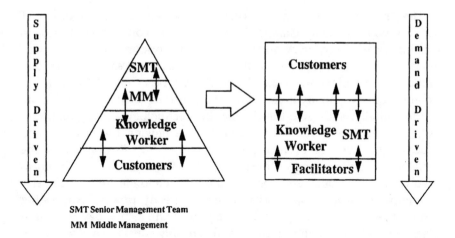

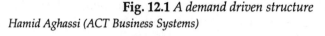

SMT Senior Management Team
MM Middle Management

Fig. 12.1 *A demand driven structure*
Hamid Aghassi (ACT Business Systems)

TECHNOLOGY AND PEOPLE ISSUES

For many large organisations changes in business processes often involve changes in information flows, and the consequent changes in the supporting business systems. Harmonisation of base technologies and consolidation of international and European standards have now resulted in the availability of stable yet flexible technical infrastructures. This level of infrastructure flexibility and the ability to develop appropriate business systems rapidly are critical to achieving sustained competitive advantage in a continually changing business environment. The transition process, however, is often severely constrained by people's resistance to change and by the organisation's existing and inflexible infrastructure on which the business systems are built.

It is ironic that the so-called enabling technology has, and continues to present, such a significant barrier against achieving the transformational goals. The reasons for this is twofold. Firstly, strategic and business-objective driven use of technology is disappointingly rare, and secondly, customer involvement in development of the end systems is alarmingly limited. Both factors illustrate the existing supply driven nature of the development and delivery mechanisms for information technology.

The responsive organisation's ability to match its business systems effectively to business objectives and to underlying processes is clearly of fundamental importance. A highly responsive systems development and delivery capability based on end-user active participation and a flexible but well-controlled technology infrastructure become critical to successful transformation.

The use and application of a flexible infrastructure and responsive IT services will inevitably change the way people work. Purely based on existing technology, teleworking and homeworking are now serious alternatives to long journeys to the office. Substantial savings in accommodation and increase in quality of life can be achieved through the organisation's capability in facilitating the required technology and, more fundamentally, managing the change. But technology although a necessary enabler, has never been sufficient in achieving the business and process effectiveness promised by re-engineering. Realisation of the benefits demands taking an holistic view of the organisation's business involving people, business processes and information technology issues.

Identification of people issues is not a speedy process. Addressing those issues can be so lengthy that the underlying technology is often in place before the human impacts have been fully considered. Availability and distribution of information is threatening to functional and middle management who see their perceived value diminishing. Distribution of knowledge and know-how development is also threatening to specialists who fear erosion of their influence. Empowerment of the knowledge worker is potentially threatening to the organisation's traditional sales teams. They see the knowledge worker as being in an ideal position to understand and respond effectively to the customer's needs. Today's technology presents teleworking as a viable business proposition, but the majority of people are either unwilling or simply not capable of undertaking such a fundamental change in their way of working.

The organisation's sensitivity to people issues, despite the prospect of dramatic change, is the key to success of a re-engineering programme. A process oriented organisation with minimal functional departments is not contradictory to being a people sensitive enterprise. Indeed process oriented organisations must, and often do, integrate human resource management with their business processes rather than treating it as an add-on entity. Such an approach often identifies critical issues such as trust, motivation, empowerment, communication, teamworking, skills development, and cultural shifts in the context of the re-engineered organisation.

Motivation and empowerment

The cliché 'our people are our most valuable asset' is not readily identifiable with today's socioeconomic environment of intense tactical competition and high unemployment. People are becoming notoriously unreliable for strengthening balance sheets in cost driven organisations. Large scale redundancy programmes can be disguised as re-engineering initiatives resulting in lack of trust at all levels of the organisation. The inevitable restructuring that follows the departure from a functional perspective hurts staff morale.

A recent survey[1] of the 285 organisations found that some 62 per cent had recently experienced changes that would impact employee morale to a great extent. According to the majority of HRM directors that responded to the survey, workplace counselling was used primarily for reducing employee stress (67%), handling redundancy/outplacement (59%) or as part of the process or organisational change (57%). The survey indicates that 78 per cent of UK major employers had provided some sort of counselling in order to cope with such rapid and widespraed change. Sadly, these statistics can indicate a reactive and damage limitation stance taken by the employers as shown by distinctly low levels of professional presence. Only 11 per cent of personnel staff had attended a 1–2 year counselling course, but 43 per cent had attended an external 1–2 day course.

Another country that has been subjected to relentless change is the new united Germany. The results of a two-year research programme[2] supported by the Anglo-German Foundation have confirmed the damage limitation approach adopted by personnel functions during a period of rapid change. Ariane Hegewisch, a key member of the research project team confirms that 'the current crises in the labour market have temporarily prevented personnel from addressing the more fundamental issues of motivation and development', and that 'the introduction of short-term fire-fighting structures may impede long-term development of organisations in the east'.

In a re-engineering environment dominated by change and uncertainty, motivation becomes a critical issue. Lifelong investment in current skill sets may have to be written off, either due to the enabling power of technology or as a result of new ways of working. Moreover, the natural human response to uncertainty is often led by fear and denial of change rather than flexibility and embracing the inevitable. Clearly the adoption of a reactive management style will act as a major obstacle to the organisation's long-term ability to change.

Furthermore, in a changing environment where the full scale of benefits is often not known at the outset, motivating factors such as growth, recognition and achievement play a significant role in increasing the driving forces that direct behaviour away from the *status quo*. Technology-enabled and accountability-based empowerment becomes the key to improving motivation during the period of major change.

Re-engineering requires a controlled transition towards new products, services and delivery mechanisms. To be successful, it must take place before the restraining forces intent on hindering movement from the existing equilibrium gather momentum. These forces tend to propagate fear, and act as the main cause of decline in staff morale during a period of change.

COMMUNICATION AND SHARING OF KNOWLEDGE

Notwithstanding sustained top level commitment, poor communication of the need for, and consequence of, change, is the single most destructive element in a re-engineering environment. BPR concepts both challenge and reinforce the most basic of human instincts: the desperate urge for belonging to well-defined cultural groupings and the need for stability. Moreover, the different interpretations of re-engineering principles can be contradictory or at best unclear to the majority of people within the organisation. This is especially true in the case of people at the junior levels who, in general, are distant from the wider objectives, strategies and, more importantly, organisational politics.

Communication of the reasons behind re-engineering and articulating the benefits to the individuals at all levels of the organisation is a major issue facing the committed chief executive.

A clear two-way communication strategy must be developed at early stages of the re-engineering programme. The strategy should convey clear messages on the organisation's goals and determination to increase the driving forces that direct behaviour away from the *status quo*, and decrease the restraining forces that hinder movement from the existing equilibrium, or both[3].

Ironically, those who display active resistance do not, in general, present a significant threat to the re-engineering programme. It can indeed be argued that they are merely travelling through the 'denial of change' phase on the transition curve. Experience has proved that the major threat to re-engineering is presented by those who appear to have accepted re-engineering, but choose politics and passive resistance techniques to delay or invalidate the change programme.

The key lies in clear and agreed goals, accountabilities and ways of monitoring progress in the achievement of individual objectives.

The communication plan must provide people with information on skills development programmes, reward structures and the use of enabling technology. Moreover, a formal process for capturing and sharing of organisation-wide knowledge must be defined. Such a process is the key to process oriented teams' ability to operate effectively within an empowered environment.

Teamworking

The human being's desperate urge to belong to groups that share the same knowledge base, skills and attitudes is the most significant factor in the formation of functional departments within organisations. This situation is exacerbated by the inherent hierarchical nature of functional groups resulting from reward structures based on levels of superiority in specialist skills. Such functional groups are often composed of extremely effective team players, but the critical issue is that organisational objectives are often sacrificed in favour of achieving functional aims.

Team working provides the foundation on which a customer focused and process oriented organisation responds to its rapidly changing business environment. The organisation's ability to form effective cross-functional teams who share the overall business objectives, provides a reliable measure of organisational responsiveness. However, this capability is often hindered by the existence of procedures that reflect functional organisational structures rather than take a process oriented view aimed at achieving the team's objectives.

In practice, re-engineering does not remove functional departments, but aims to focus their operations towards the delivery of value to both internal and external customers. This is achieved through dynamic utilisation of functional specialisation in the form of process oriented teams that respond to changing customer needs. The key to success lies in the definition of customer focused processes and, more importantly, the establishment of appropriate appraisal schemes and reward structures based primarily on achieving the process team's objectives. The level of contribution to organisational learning and development of new and marketable skills present other elements of an appraisal scheme relevant to a re-engineering environment.

The findings of a recent survey[4] involving 65 organisations who have undertaken re-engineering, indicated the critical importance of introducing teamwork to re-engineering success and, especially, the relative ease with which it can be achieved. However, customer focused, process oriented and output driven teamwork is a cultural issue requiring a very specific mindset. It demands much more than the definition and introduction of teams. The organisation's ability to inspire and propagate this way of thinking at an early stage will determine its success when embarking on a re-engineering programme.

CULTURAL VALUES AND BELIEFS

Radical changes resulting from a re-engineering programme often affect the entire organisation and hence the chief executive's commitment is critical to success. Once the need and the risks associated with a re-engineering programme have been identified, top-level commitment is normally gained from a vision-led chief executive with relative ease.

However, changing the roles of functions and achieving organisation-wide buy-in requires careful planning and implementation.

Not surprisingly, cultural change and acceptance of new ways of working are seen as central to successful implementation of a re-engineering programme. These often involve individuals contributing to multiple teams and fulfilling multiple roles concurrently, which can be location independent. Such flexibility in working practices demands definition of appropriately planned management processes aimed at setting the goals and measuring the re-engineering success.

Organisational structures and cultural values are inextricably linked, often reflecting the senior management's attitudes and way of thinking. Human nature in general lends itself to bureaucratic organisational structures primarily due to their inherent perceived stability. This stability is fundamentally dependent on people in key positions tasked with the communication of cultural norms to the next level of hierarchy. Although open to misinterpretation by middle management in the hierarchy, the communication activity can be propagated throughout the organisation with relative ease. In contrast, sharing the appropriate cultural values in a flat organisational structure requires a well-planned and methodically executed communication strategy, primarily due to the high degree of cross-functional relationships within the organisation.

The main problem arises when, due to the pursuit of cultural change, re-engineering is not fully achieved because of the extensive time required for cultural shifts to take effect. The key to successful implementation therefore lies in achieving cultural change as a by-product of the more tangible changes in goal setting, know-how development and dynamic reward structures.

Consideration of the impact of change and goal setting activities should be propagated throughout the organisation and applied to every individual and team. Once the goals have been agreed, a dynamic reward structure capable of responding to over- and under-performance can be put in place. The appropriate structure should be designed to reward value added activities rather than those based on bureaucracy and lack of trust. Contribution to the organisation's strategic and tactical goals, ability to fulfil multiple demanding roles, team working and self-development represent other measures appropriate to a re-engineering environment.

Clearly cultural change can only be achieved if those influencing the change both understand and are fully committed to the re-engineering success. Creation of a customer focused, supportive, coaching and accountability based culture must therefore be the ultimate goal and measure of successful transformation.

CONCLUSIONS

The specialist has, to date, been treated with respect, albeit at a superficial level. Ironically, the ineffectiveness of technology itself has contributed towards further business reliance on the specialist who has been tasked with delivery of the promised benefits. This has given rise to the continued prosperity and stability of functional departments who more often than not pursue departmental goals at the expense of business objectives and, more importantly, the end customer.

Research indicates that in a relatively stable bureaucratic environment motivational factors, irrespective of the assumed motivation theory, are simpler to address. Functional teams are often motivated by sharing of interests in their specialist area of knowledge and skill. However, in the re-engineering environment, which is based on flat organisational structures, the distribution of power and where change is considered to be the norm, motivation becomes a far more critical issue.

The European experience confirms that a reactive approach to people issues during a period of significant change will damage staff morale and impede the long-term development of organisations. If re-engineering is to succeed, the reward structures must aim to motivate every member of the organisation. In the long term, however, neither the temptation of the carrot, nor the threat of the stick will work if people do not understand, or share, the organisational aims.

Empowerment is a much overused term in the BPR literature, but it generally aims to release the inherent creative capabilities that have been locked within the organisations. In practice however, people working in organisations have been functioning within well-defined structures and responsibilities that have become a foundation for their working and social lives. Unplanned liberation of this suppressed energy can lead to chaos, anarchy and the inevitable failure of a re-engineering programme.

The answer lies in controlled liberation that allows people to operate creatively within well-defined accountabilities and standards. Control and liberation may appear to be contradictory, but the transition to full liberation can be achieved as people learn to understand and share the organisational aims. As with any other learning process, education plays a significant role, which in the context of re-engineering, is nothing but facilitating the cultural shift that is so fundamental to the success.

The reality therefore is that the cultural change towards full empowerment needs to be both planned and controlled. Clearly defined terms and standards must be communicated in a manner that is understood by the majority of people within the organisation. These standards must provide clear guidelines on each individual's attitude towards customers, suppliers and colleagues alike.

Re-engineering and its principles of fundamental change introduce major shock waves into the stagnant waters of traditional organisations. The released energy could, and often does, destroy the organisation that has attempted to move from controlled to empowered, functional to process oriented, and stability to change.

However, stability and change are not mutually exclusive. Stability can be achieved within a continuously changing environment if an appropriate level of control is exerted. Those organisations that understand the nature of the BPR shock wave and the need to control both the shock and its effects, while moving towards a totally liberated environment will have a better chance of succeeding. The high failure rates of BPR initiatives are witness to the reality that in the frenzy of empowerment, the control and accountability elements are often ignored.

The ultimate question involves the social effects of successfully re-engineered organisations. As liberated workers break out of their suppressed working environments and taste the joys of empowerment, what will be the effect on their social lives? How will the class oriented hierarchical European society respond to the liberated mass, and when will the need for stepwise improvement end?

REFERENCES

1. TDA Consulting Ltd (1993), *The Counselling at Work Survey*, by the Marketing Shop and Woodside Communications Ltd.
2. Hegewisch, A. (1994), *Challenges to human resource management in the new German lander*.
3. Robbins, S. P. (1989), *Organisational behavior, concepts, controversies, and applications*. Prentice-Hall International Editions.
4. Braganza, A. (1993), *Business process redesign; beyond planning . . . towards implementation*. Cranfield, UK: Information Systems Research Centre, Cranfield University.

13

Cultural Values, Workplace Democracy and Organisational Change: Emerging Issues in European Businesses

Edna Murphy

. . . We must distinguish between innovators who stand alone and those who depend on others, that is, between those who, to achieve their purposes, can force the issue and those who must use persuasion. In the second case, they always come to grief, having achieved nothing; when however, they depend on their own resources and can force the issue, then they are seldom endangered.

That is why all armed prophets have conquered, and unarmed prophets have come to grief.

. . . the populace is by nature fickle; it is easy to persuade them of something, but difficult to confirm them in that persuasion. Therefore one must urgently arrange matters so that when they no longer believe they can be made to believe by force.

Niccolò Machiavelli (1469–1527), *Il Principe*. Chapter 6, De principatibus novis qui armis propriis et virtute acquiruntur.

INTRODUCTION

Everywhere we read that today's enterprises are undergoing rapid and often profound change. Businesses are being challenged by aspects of both the external and internal environments. The external considerations include markets, competitors, macroeconomic factors, industry sector factors and country-specific factors. The internal pressures are demands for more flexible, family-friendly employment practices, demands for consultation and information, and concern for training and quality standards. The introduction of information technology, along with intensified competitive pressures and the impact of recession in Europe have all combined to create a business environment in which job security is perceived to have been reduced, and where change is often synonymous with job losses and increased work stress. Consequently industrial relations in Europe in the last year or so has concentrated on disputes concerning job losses.

To what extent, in this context, is the Machiavellian prescription correct (ie that a ruthless, authoritarian, coercive approach is the only way to effect change)? Is there a role for a democratic approach within the difficult process of bringing about organisational change? And how can the devolving notion of 'empowerment' sit alongside the strongly directive approach required in a vision-led process such as a BPR programme?

This chapter sets out to explore some of the relationships between democracy in the workplace, organisational change and the rhetoric of change management in Europe's businesses today. It also contains some of the conclusions of the COBRA project. These aim to match the factors enabling successful organisational change with those organisational preconditions for introducing effective teleworking/telecommuting programmes.

PEOPLE POWER IN ORGANISATIONAL CHANGE

Resistance to change as well as fear of job losses provide a stressful and difficult environment in which many organisational change exercises take place. Thus, according to the many leading exponents of BPR and change management, the level of managers' communication skills and the ability to empower the workforce are viewed as being critical to the success of the organisational change exercise.

Much of the success of change management in general and BPR in particular hinge on effective harnessing of people's talents and co-operation. Thus core aspects of labour-management relations are critical to the success of BPR programmes. For example behind notions of 'empowerment', 'people power', and 'valuing the people in an organisation' lie concepts of workplace democracy, the quality of industrial relations and the nature of the decision-making processes in the workplace. Also related is the much more diffuse area of employee involvement, which cuts across different areas of traditional industrial relations concern, and covers a wider range of matters including job performance and career development. Employee involvement is usually referred to in the context of a certain type of workplace 'culture', one in which there are individualised contracts, a non-unionised workplace, and probably a service sector employer.

The language of change management and industrial relations converges particularly in the concept of empowerment. In the growing BPR literature and in many case studies, it is clear that empowerment is meant to be limited to the project team – those selected to bring about the changes necessary in the programme. Here, on closer inspection, empowerment means simply that this select group should have the authority to carry out the tasks that are required of them – not that the workforce should be empowered in the sense of consultation and negotiation, co-determination or other industrial relations concepts. Thus the apparent initial promise of many change management programmes to liberate or empower the bulk of the people in an industrial relations sense can remain unfulfilled.

However, in other cases it is clear that broad consultation or employee involvement has occurred and indeed has played an important part in the success of the BPR programme. In particular managers and the project team recognise that the people directly involved in existing processes are best placed to identify the shape of the problems, as well as to think creatively about new ways to deliver value to customers. In consulting these workers about process re-engineering the project team is doing two things: it is getting the best possible input to its programme as well as valuing and harnessing the talents of a wider group of employees – employee involvement in action.

Indeed, early experience of BPR in Germany suggests that *Mitbestimmung*, their highly consultative framework of labour-management co-operation (ie where workers' representatives are on the company's board), is a significant factor in the effectiveness of corporate BPR programmes. Co-determination means that the fear that the board has a hidden agenda, such as having plans to make large numbers of people redundant, is very much diminished – such secrets cannot be kept easily in an environment which is open. Furthermore, values such as co-operation and consensus-seeking enable the vital ingredient of trust to develop. Thus it is not surprising that the early evidence from Germany as captured in the COBRA project, suggests that BPR programmes in German companies seem to take a little longer than the norm to get started due to the consensus-building required, but then run very smoothly.

Nevertheless, it is important to remember that it seems that it is neither a necessary nor sufficient condition of effective consultation that there is a statutory framework in existence that mandates consultation and union recognition. The UK has a relatively low level of statutory labour market regulation and no framework of rights around negotiation and consultation. Despite this, there are many examples where companies that do not even recognise unions – such as Mercury Communications Ltd – have undergone programmes of radical organisational change but have done so with real attention to employee involvement. This has taken the form of re-training, awareness-raising, consultation and empowerment.

Studies published this year (Fernie *et al.*, 1994; Guest, 1994) look to the way in which the 'new industrial relations' fares in terms of creating good industrial relations climates, employee rights and corporate performance. These results tend to support the notion that in non-unionised organisations there may very well be a very progressive, consultative environment without mandatory statutory requirements for consultation.

PARTICIPATION AND CORPORATE PERFORMANCE IN CHANGE PROGRAMMES

There is some significant research evidence suggesting that the levels of industrial democracy have an impact on corporate performance, particularly in the context of introducing new technology.

One recent study carried out on behalf of the European Foundation for the Improvement of Living and Working Conditions, focuses on the relationship between levels of employee participation and the success experienced in introducing technological change in European organisations. It reveals workplace culture factors that contribute to making the introduction of IT successful. This study (European Foundation, 1990a; 1990b) is significant because of its size and methodology. For example, it asked managers and employee representatives of the same organisations identical questions and compared the responses to get a balanced view.

Nearly 7300 managers and employee representatives were interviewed in 12 member states in five sectors (mechanical engineering and electronics in the manufacturing sector, and banking, finance and retailing in the service sector). The study focuses on the role of participation in technological change. In particular, it explores participation in training, health and safety aspects of new technology, work organisation, investment, product quality, and the benefits of participation to both managers and employee representatives.

This study clearly links the factors of management style, industrial relations and communications and finds that they are directly related to the levels of acceptance of change in the workplace. This research identifies the acceptance as far as it relates to change involving IT. Although BPR is not specifically the subject, it is suggested that the findings are highly relevant and applicable to BPR programmes involving change and the introduction of IT.

Participation in the context of the European Foundation study is viewed as a continuum ranging from information dissemination by managers to employees (the weakest form) through consultation to nego-tiation/joint decision-making. The findings that are relevant to BPR are as follows:

■ There were substantial benefits – including straightforward business benefits – resulting from participation. Importantly, participation:
  – does not slow down managerial decision-making;
  – does not delay the implementation of new technology;
  – enhances the mutual understanding between managers and employees in companies;
  – improves the knowledge and utilisation of skills on the part of employees;
  – leads to a better industrial relations climate;
  – does not adversely affect the quality of managerial decision-making;
  – over half of all managers throughout Europe reported that partici-pation had positive effects on the acceptance of new technology by employees and enhanced their utilisation of skills;
  – four out of ten managers reported that participation improved the quality of managerial decision-making;
  – provides an effective means of resolving the problems that employ-ees in various occupational groups may have about the impact of new information technology on their jobs.
■ Participation is essential in the management of any organisational change.
■ Different levels of participation were exhibited at different phases of the programme of introducing technological change.

The four phases identified were planning, selecting (both strategic), and implementation and post-evaluation (both operational). Least participa-tion was present in the former, whereas much greater levels of employee involvement were recorded in the latter.

The form and quality of participation in technological change depends greatly on the way in which each member state's industrial relations system has been shaped by political, economic and historical forces. Five factors in particular helped/hindered opportunities for participation:

1. management's dependence on the skills/co-operation of its workforce to achieve its objectives for introducing new technology;
2. management's style and attitudes towards participation;
3. the bargaining power of organised labour to force management to negotiate or consult with its representatives in the absence of any voluntary disposition to do so;
4. regulations that lay down participation rights for employees or their representatives on a range of matters at enterprise level;

5. the degree of centralisation of the industrial relations system that exists in the country concerned.

The 'top-ranking' countries, with the most favourable factors were Denmark and Germany. Middle-ranking countries were Ireland, the Netherlands and Belgium. The low-ranking countries were (in descending order): the UK, France, Spain, Greece, Italy, Luxembourg and Portugal.

Only in France and the UK was there found to be a dependence by management on the labour force's skills and co-operation/problem-solving abilities. Management style in low-ranking countries was generally unfavourable with the UK's participation levels shifting away from negotiation towards a more paternalistic consulting style (although this does enable workers to be more involved at the planning phase). In France the Auroux reforms were thought to be working very slowly. The dictatorial past of Spain, Greece and Portugal was thought to manifest itself in current management style and a traditional reaction against participation rights. Of the low-ranking countries only in the UK and Greece were unions not divided on political or religious lines.

In the works councils (some form being present even in most low-ranking countries) it was found that unions were reluctant to be involved in the decision-making concerned with technological change. Their preference was for it to form part of collective bargaining.

One of the major concerns of employee representatives about introducing new technology was the danger that it would be accompanied by forms of job design and a division of labour based on 'Taylorist' principles of 'scientific management'. There is a diversity in approach to work organisation across Europe. For example in Denmark, Germany and to a lesser extent in the Netherlands, unions have taken a strong interest in job design, unlike unions in other European countries.

WAYS IN WHICH CULTURE CONTRIBUTES TO WORKPLACE DEMOCRACY

Several studies exist that explore the cultural context in which people work in Europe. The importance of culture was highlighted for example in one study (Ronen, 1986) that suggested that unconscious cultural identification was the root cause of the majority of problems arising in international business transactions. The culture of an organisation is also related to the quality and form of its industrial relations, and across Europe there are differentiating cultural factors affecting the workplace.

For example, one group of authors (Leeds, Kirkbride and Durcan, 1994) reviews studies that identify and describe differentiating cultural dimensions in Europe. One study identified, (Hofstede, 1980), describes differentiating cultural values that have most bearing on the issues of change management and workplace democracy. These differentiating factors are:

Power distance index
This measures the extent to which the members of a society accept that power in institutions and organisations is distributed unequally, thus a low score indicates that people expect that power in institutions should be used legitimately. All northern European countries have low scores, with the implication being that generally the following organisational factors are generally relatively highly valued:

- flatter hierarchies preferred;
- drives to reduce bureaucracy;
- tasks delegated;
- consultative management style;
- belief that power should be used legitimately;
- delegates autonomy.

Southern European countries (including France, Greece, Italy, Portugal, Spain) by contrast had higher scores, thus expected organisational characteristics would include:

- hierarchical structures;
- management style paternalistic/autocratic/directive;
- senior staff have status symbols or privileges, and employees regard them with ambivalence;
- employees are dependent on superiors and tend to conform/afraid to disagree.

Uncertainty avoidance
The extent to which the culture programmes its members to feel either comfortable or uncomfortable in unstructured and ambiguous situations. Uncertainty avoidance is low in the UK, Denmark, Holland and Ireland and these societies are characterised by:

- tolerance of different views;
- not many rules, informality;
- low reliance on experts;
- self-control in dealings/actions.

UK and Danish organisations value managers who are action-oriented, good decision-makers and practical, placing less emphasis on intellectual or academic skills and qualifications. German organisations by contrast exhibit high uncertainty avoidance and place great store on expert advice, detailed rules, and value managers with high levels of qualifications who are thorough in their dealings. All Southern European societies (including France, Spain, Greece, Italy, Portugal) are high in uncertainty avoidance, and this shows in the desire for long career structures, rules for every situation, formalism in procedures. Sometimes the need for formalism results in the existence of many rules that are overreaching and therefore ignored in practice.

Individualism
The extent to which in society ties are loose, everyone looks after themselves or their families, and where emphasis is placed on individual achievement and identity. In highly collectivist societies the culture is characterised by:

- strong in-group/one-group dichotomy, extended family and other networks;
- individuals' dependence on group in exchange for strong loyalty;
- strongest values at work include achieving consensus, co-operation, group decision-making, achieving group aims.

In highly individualistic societies, people in organisations tend to value personal achievement, look to individuals' contributions to achieving collective goals, more motivated by self-advancement and where collectivist characteristics are less prominent. In another study by Hofstede (Hofstede, 1991) all Europe is defined as being individualistic, with the exceptions of Portugal and Greece, with UK being the second most individualistic society in the world after the USA.

Masculinity/femininity
This dimension measures the influence of gender roles in societies, with 'masculine' societies (such as Germany, Greece, Italy, Spain and the UK) emphasising values of competitiveness, personal achievement, materialism, action-orientated work, and profit. 'Feminine' societies (such as Denmark, Finland, Norway, Portugal, Sweden) put emphasis on values such as co-operation, caring, quality of life, and egalitarianism.

Much cross-cultural research can be criticised for over-simplifying national cultures. However, it does provide insight into the cultural diversity within European workplaces, and how the multi-faceted issues of consultation and worker empowerment in BPR or other change management programmes might be approached.

COBRA'S FINDINGS ON INTRODUCING NEW WAYS OF WORKING

COBRA set out to make links between factors enabling successful change management using IT, and the possibilities for introducing new ways of working in such an environment.

Teleworking (performing work for a distant employer by means of telecommunications and information technology) and telecommuting (working part-time from the main office and part-time at a distance, often from home, and facilitated by telecommunications) are not yet very common forms of working in Europe. Recent research (Huws, 1993) indicates that only six per cent of UK employers use teleworkers as compared to five per cent employing non-telework home-based workers. However, many employers feel that they may take up teleworking in the future.

There is a great deal of interest in teleworking, not only for business reasons (reducing the fixed costs of labour, improving productivity and quality) and to meet employees' demands for better working conditions, but also for environmental reasons as teleworking could result in a reduction of car-based transport.

Introducing teleworking requires that certain criteria are met, including:

- the work is suitable;
- technology infrastructure is appropriate;
- the employee is psychologically suited to the way of working (self-motivated, organised, gains satisfaction from eg increased productivity made possible from teleworking, problem-solver, good social and out-of-work networks);
- the organisational culture will support this innovation in workstyle.

The last point is the most crucial and is where most teleworking projects fail. Broadening this out, 'organisational culture' means:

- management style;
- internal communications systems;
- social attitudes to work;
- flatter organisations, minimal hierarchies;
- human resources policies (including training, pay policies, career development);
- management attitude to change;
- management/labour co-operation and the general industrial relations climate.

These match many of the organisational factors that support the successful implementation of BPR programmes.

CONCLUSIONS

Culture and attitudes towards employee involvement, though complex and multi-faceted, can be seen to play a crucial role in the development of a workplace culture that supports innovation and change. Importantly the link between consultation and business performance has particular lessons for those involved in change management. This is especially true for those who are tempted to follow Machiavelli and push through changes without full support and co-operation, not only of the Board, but also the workforce in general.

Changes may result from process innovation, the need for better customer service, or teleworking to improve productivity and meet employees' aspirations, but the demands on managers are often very similar. Thus we may expect to see teleworking as an outcome of successful, progressive BPR programmes in the future.

REFERENCES

European Foundation for the Improvement of Living and Working Conditions (1990a), *Roads to participation in technological change: Attitudes and experiences*. Luxembourg: Office for the Official Publications of the European Communities.

European Foundation for the Improvement of Living and Working Conditions – C Gill (1990b), *Issues of participation in technological innovation: Attitudes and experiences in the European Community*. Luxembourg: Office for the Official Publications of the European Communities.

Fernie, S., Metcalf, D. and Woodland, S. (1994), *Does HRM boost employee-management relations?* London: Centre for Economic Performance and Industrial Relations Department, London School of Economics.

Guest, D. and Hoque, K. (forthcoming), Employee relations in non-union greenfield sites: The good, the bad and the ugly. *Human Resource Management Journal*.

Hofstede, G. (1980), *Culture's consequences: International differences in work-related values*. USA: Sage.

Hofstede, G. (1991), *Cultures and organisations*. UK: McGraw-Hill.

Huws, U. (1993), *Teleworking in Britain*. A report to the Employment Department, Research Management Branch, Employment Department. Analytica.

Leadbeater, C., Mulgan, C. et al., (1994), *The end of unemployment: bringing work to life*. UK: DEMOS.

Leeds, C., Kirkbride, P. and Durcan, J. (1994), The cultural context of Europe: A tentative mapping. In: *Human resource management*, P. Kirkbride, (Ed.), UK: Routledge.

Ronen, S. (1986), *Comparative and multinational management*. USA: John Wiley.

14

Reflections on Business Process Re-Engineering

Wanda D'hanis

BPR, A UNIQUE OPPORTUNITY

During his visit to Antwerp in September, 1993, Gary Hamel stated that it is not so much the currency or wage costs that determine the success of a business but rather the outlook of the management: 'The way managers think is a greater danger than the financial strength of the competitors . . . The real challenge for most companies is not "better tools and better techniques" but "better principles, better paradigms"'[1].

Does BPR offer this new paradigm? It presents itself as such: 'fundamental', 'radical', even 'dramatic'[2].

As is the case with all promising concepts, the idea of BPR is also open to incorrect interpretation. The word itself, 're-engineering', does refer to the rich symbolism of *homo faber*, tinkering, producing, 'ingenious' man. But at the same time there is the danger that this ingenious genius will limit his actions to the world of machines. Re-engineering is then narrowed down to the redesigning and reorganisation of production processes.

In itself such a revolution is, without doubt, the only possible answer to the 'crisis that will not go away'[3]. And many a technocrat will soon become acquainted with its dramatic character. As long as the revolution does not penetrate to the very foundations of economic reality the wound beneath the plaster will never heal. Is not the BPR concept also based on the rather naive belief that every low will necessarily be followed by a high?

If BPR is not to remain limited to the sensible but merely operational answer to the end of Taylorism then other answers are required. And not least the answer to the fundamental alienation, which today more than ever before characterises economic and therefore also human life. If Karl Marx[4] regarded the total impoverishment of the nineteenth-century worker as the historic moment that could reveal the degeneration of economic life then perhaps the moment has come in 'the crisis that will not go away' when revolution will not only cause substantial commotion on the surface but can finally set in motion the turnaround and positive evolution of economic life.

Alienation, the ontological condition of human beings

The demand for change in business life requires radical restructuring of the way business is done. 'Radical change' means changes to the 'radies' or roots of business life itself. This need has arisen now because, as a result of its historical evolution, Western society has increasingly developed an alienating as well as an alienated way of dealing with the world of wealth and goods.

Georg Wilhelm Friedrich Hegel[5] described the origins of this alienating development. He referred to the exterior world with its constant otherness and multiple changes and the pleasing medium of human development, as the starting point of his reflective thinking that leads him to true freedom, and the origin of stagnation and human slavery.

The conflict between nature and the ambiguity of the material world has been revealed repeatedly since ancient times. In antiquity, Epicurian and Stoic thinkers warn constantly of the seductive vanities caused by civilisation and its successful way of dominating natural calamities. And right at the beginning of the young industrial revolution Jean Jacques Rousseau[6] was one of the first authors to pay attention to the ambivalent consequences of man's struggle with nature.

The more industrialisation increases, the more the inherence of its alienating nature is emphasised in the work of important thinkers. Marx's contribution to the analysis of the origins of human alienation still remains an undeniable masterpiece of critical approach to the industrialised free market itself. As industrialisation creates a distance between the worker and the product of his labour, Marx shows its connection with the alienation of man from his own essence as a working being. According to him, the ultimate result of this fundamental negation of the essence of human work consists of the mutual struggle for work and the perversion of man's social character.

Private dream versus business life

Marx's sharp analysis has not solved the problem of alienation. On the contrary, his proposals seem to entail as high a level of alienation as the system he complained of. Moreover, the interventions – both those in capitalism itself and the alternative of communism and socialism – have led to the development of Herbert Marcuse's 'one-dimensional man'[7] and his 'cynical' behaviour[8] in the 'culture of contentment'[9].

And finally, as stated above, we come face to face with the profound realisation that the 'crisis' phenomenon is apparently inherent in the economic system itself. In other words, economic life itself is currently revealing its alienating character. It is up to us to recognise it.

What are the typical features of today's alienation? They are no different from those to which Marx drew attention in his authoritative analysis in 1844: the origin of the alienation still lies in the fact that 'working' man is separated from his product and therefore from his work itself. But the consequences have a very modern countenance: we live – and now even against better judgement – incorrigibly believing in an ever-accelerating growth economy, which increasingly places its calculating laws in direct opposition to and even in place of the laws of life itself.

In short, economic alienation is today expressed by the contradiction between the ethos of personal life and that of the practices of industrial organisations. In particular, in the opposition between the calculating rationality that determines economic action and the wide range of ways of thinking, moral considerations and emotions that ensure the completeness of human life.

Therefore, before business re-engineering can call itself 'fundamental' and 'radical', space must first be created for thorough business re-animation. And the fundamental question then is: what is the original purpose of the *homo economicus* and his activities? What is the true nature of his means and instruments, management tools and organisations? How can economic life regain its human face?

Business re-animation and its presuppositions

The first prerequisite for a fundamental healing process is both simple and improbable: slow down, both in time and space. Everyday experience shows that the dream of unchecked growth and speed is irretrievably over.

Time and space have acquired an almost exclusively negative meaning in life. Speed and size are the means with which not only the economic competitor but also the fellow citizen is threatened, overwhelmed and finally eliminated. Speed claims its victims every day on the roads but also at work. There its symptom is called 'stress' and its victims are cast aside as weaklings: the winners are the fast career makers, the fast decision makers, the fast growers, the fast salesmen and the fast consumers.

But now fundamental changes seem to be occurring in Western culture and probably in world culture, too. The Superpowers are loosing their grip on their satellite states and must simply stand and watch, almost powerlessly, as small national units adopt independent status. The idea of federalism is gaining ground and states held together artificially can no longer hide their divisions from the outside world. It would appear that the end of totalitarian thinking is in sight. And it is becoming more and more difficult to unite larger entities under one central administration.

The political world is not playing a game of its own. Its evolution reflects what is happening elsewhere: the changeover from large to small, the increase in mutual interdependence and the move from an economy of mass production and ditto consumption to computer-controlled tailor-made production. Mass media, which held the world in its spell of uniformity, is being supplanted by a diversity of specialised forms of communication resulting in fast-changing image formation. The rather well-established 'general opinion' of the past is disappearing and individuals are being forced to create their own world from the many small pieces of puzzles offered to them.

In this world of high technological demands, small scale is no longer synonymous with weakness, nor is large scale synonymous with strength. Fortunately, the time that the Little Ones were only there to be eaten by the Big Ones is past. Following reckless gluttony the Big Ones have been known to suffer from indigestion and the wild stories about superfast growth, amalgamations and takeovers do not always have a happy ending. The instant recipes for the winner's success sometimes show signs of going mouldy.

Economy and harmony

Economy – at least according to the original meaning of the word – does not require such toughness and display of power. In the origins of the word lies the concern for the welfare of the members of a community, the estate, the family in a broad sense, and the internal measures that have to be taken in order to be able to withstand periods of shortage. Little reference is made to power and lack of power, nor to equality, in fact.

Economy is about welfare and this entails much more than just surviving during times of shortage. Only in this limited sense does it provide an opportunity for greed, grasping behaviour and exclusivity. Apart from that, it extends, by definition, further than the material preconditions for individual existence. It relates to the quality of life, which must include the harmony of the community. A welfare society cannot be one of internal displays of power.

Concepts such as power, rule, mutual competition and elimination only appear in the economy following the occurrence of the fundamental misunderstanding concerning human needs. This latter cannot of course be proved historically, but is a feature that is as indestructible and omnipresent as the human desire for well-being itself. Every civilisation produces its 'idle' desires and is, in its progress, itself the source of social conflict. To deny this would be naive but to simply accept it would be to fail.

The interaction between large and small therefore becomes an essential precondition for the life of both parties.

'The good life': Stability a central issue once again

But if space for that which is small scale and, perhaps in consequence, a different experience of time, have to become features of the organisations of the future, then the irrevocable demand for stability arises. In the prevailing economic climate smallness is mercilessly devoured and slowness harshly punished. In the case of such a mentality the processes that occur lead inevitably to repression, destruction, uprooting and, not least, to generally feared chaos.

Hence the necessity of a second step, that of business re-validation, the reunification of business ethics – in so far as it is used as something other than a trendy marketing tool – and moral awareness itself, which is also not in the best of health. This means that a number of features and attitudes that make human life 'good', ie which do one good and make life good to live, features that heal the disunity of modern society, have to be revalidated. And economic activity immediately regains its original and inalienable objective, namely the 'good life' itself, success, successfulness and happiness, as specified by Aristotle[10] in ancient times.

Economy, which comes from *oikos*, Greek for house, and *nomos*, Greek for the law of the house, has always been the path to happiness. It is the means by which, and way in which, people within a certain culture develop their life as they deal with the natural preconditions of existence and thus give shape to the purpose of human life itself. It is therefore obvious that the 'laws of the house' and the 'laws of the economy' cannot be in opposition to each other.

Business ethics versus private ethics?

This means that it has been a typical Western mistake to attribute to economic activity a separate, so-called value-free order as if it is separate from the rest of life. Or that – as can sometimes be read in literature about business ethics – the economic order has its own laws, its own morals, which do not necessarily have to concur with the standards of what is called private life. And that it is not in the least peculiar – let alone alienating – that in economic reality it is open season on the competitor while in private life individuals long for mutual respect and support. Nor that in business life profit is the only aim while in the non-profit sector the sympathy and generosity of the citizen is constantly appealed to on behalf of those who are weaker.

The Golden Mean

First and foremost the 'good life' strives for stability, which should not be confused with rigidity. This means that it provides reasons for long-term confidence, separate from and beyond the multitude of its many possibilities and moments.

Therefore, above all, stability requires courage and insight to foresee, point out and integrate unavoidable changes, the readiness to bear the less favourable aspects and to hold open a safety net for the weakest. It also requires perseverance and resolve to fight alienating and dividing powers. On the other hand it asks for reserve and even a certain forbearance in order to resist its unmistakable temptations. At an intellectual level this forbearance leads to the quality which in ancient Greece was among the most praised of virtues, ie level-headedness, intellectual moderation which draws its power from its fundamental love of truth and aversion to manipulation.

Thus, a feeling for stability does not threaten economic growth at all. On the contrary, didn't Mintzberg[11] recently show that highly praised and, above all, unscrupulous, extremely fast flexibility is not so much inherent in the so-called 'turbulent times' but rather in the actions of 'inflated egos' which attempt to remain on their feet? 'Flexibility' is sometimes simply a very nice word for 'aggression'.

Justice again in full

If the aforementioned conditions are satisfied, then the sense of justice in its full meaning can be restored.

In the history of Western Europe the meaning of justice has become considerably narrower. At the end of the eighteenth-century the fight of the citizens for political and legal equality leads to the realisation of a new model of society. The class of hardworking, resourceful citizens who have become financially powerful want to be treated on an equal footing with nobility. For them 'equality' (égalité) means: the right to political involvement and certainty regarding fair treatment in legal conflicts, ie the fight for equality meant eradicating the differences that existed between nobility and the other classes in a feudal society and in the realm of absolute monarchs. This fight was led by craftsmen and tradesmen, ie by the forerunners of modern industrialised society.

It is therefore not surprising that these people borrowed the concept of equality from their familiar world of exchange and trade. When more and more goods are exchanged and traded, authentic exchange is only guaranteed via the external criterion of mathematical equality, on the basis of mutual agreements and arrangements, called 'prices'. The devised equal treatment, the price, makes it possible to make extremely diverse goods and services perfectly exchangeable. The sterile mathematical figure brings about that the taste of apples can be compared with that of lemons! With the price as criterion exchange occurs 'correctly'.

Money, the ultimate equaliser

And since this neutral link has a form of its own, namely money, it is therefore not surprising that it quickly started to lead a life of its own and in turn displayed a specific alienation. Money degenerates from an authentic means of exchange to a product and goal in itself, with all the alienating consequences of this, both individually and socially. The ultimate result of this development is the present uncontrollability of the mood of the stock market: money even gets away from its owner.

With the rise of the growth economy the concept of exchange justice (*iustitia commutativa*), as if inevitable, gained more and more ground. It is an attitude of calculating reasonableness which, with not undeserved success, drives the entire technological evolution. Under the influence of the latter grew the almost spontaneous conviction that everything should be exchangeable with everything.

The value of the differences in quality

Nothing is less true. Even the very hard fight for equality is fought in an unequal way. And now that the growth economy no longer appears to be perpetual and unthreatened those aspects that were previously neglected are becoming more important. The value of the differences between people and the diversity of things start to be discovered again. And the realisation that the balanced well-being of the whole can only be achieved by the multicoloured but stable interaction of the unequal parts. In former times this was the ideal on which the limited community of the Greek city-state was built.

The difference between people is part of their being. Their physical appearance varies and they do not even wish to discuss their taste. Even the most neutral approach of biological sciences cannot deny the unique character of every organic construction.

In social life, distributive justice (*iustitia distributiva*) recognises that the differences between people are as essential as equality itself. They guarantee, above and beyond all differences, the humanity of mutual relationships. Only in such a climate can the categoric imperative, as Kant formulated it, thrive: 'Act in such a way that you always uses humanity, both in your own person and in the person of any one else, as an end in itself and never as a means'[12]. In this formulation the essence of man undoubtedly reaches one of its most sublime heights.

In addition to this universal right to a human approach, people also have the right to be different. In an organisation this means that different work and effort, different aptitude and ability, are evaluated in a different way. The idea that equal work deserves equal pay is salutary. But the question is whether equal work exists? Employees inevitably display differences in aptitude and possibilities, they do not all have the same energy and not everyone is prepared to make the same effort. How, therefore, can their work be identical? Only an abstract approach, alien from reality, is able to assume such equality and even make it measurable.

Culture, the safety net of the differences

The habit that has developed in Western companies of defining 'equal work', identical positions and jobs in the same way and also to reward them thus is the direct reason for the concept of 'culture' disappearing from business life. When jobs, people and their wages can be made identical via mathematical links then they can also be exchanged. And, in the flow of changes, they also become immediately mutually threatening.

The promising concept of 'culture' offers the lifeline that will bind the employees to companies and vice versa. The culture of a company is said to show its irreplaceable face to the outside world. Initially it is not yet very clear what this actually means and in many cases the concern about so-called business culture is limited mostly to outward appearances, a beautiful logo, representative writing paper and ditto secretary, a nice entrance hall. But all this can easily be found at the competitors, too.

However, 'culture' is more than that which outward appearances suggest. These are definitely part of it but are the consequences not the cause of what the inherent culture is. 'Culture' is, as Jürgen Habermas aptly describes it, the underlying bedding, the 'store of knowledge' of which individuals make use when they interact with each other. In a business the culture is therefore the stable foundation on which not only everyday action but also radical projects and changes can be built without upsetting the whole. Culture is therefore associated with 'ethos', standards and customs, with dialogue and interaction.

Within an unadulterated culture, human characteristics such as friendship and playful sociability have a place in business life and stress and destructive competition disappear.

ELEMENTS OF A NEW BUSINESS CULTURE: FROM STRUCTURAL POWER TO INTERSUBJECTIVE PROCESS

Considerable interaction, both internal and external, will be required of both the large and the small businesses in the future. This assumes, in the first place, the explicit readiness for mutual exchange of knowledge and ability. However, without tangible points of comparison this will not be possible and will degenerate into an unparalleled competitive struggle.

All the parties involved will have to look for common objectives and these cannot be found in the isolation of exclusive self-interest. A more universal point of view should be sought, products, services, methods and strategies that seek and find alliance with the social trends themselves and for which it is worthwhile for all parties to make an effort. In this way the ideal limit of economic life even becomes visible: a world in which everyone's needs are satisfied.

Interdependency: a new form of ignorance

Technological evolution occurs as 'a totally anonymous, irresistible revolution planned by no one'[13]. The result of this is that reasonableness itself is seriously threatened. The time is past when sufficient solace was provided by naive confidence in one's own knowledge and ability and a belief in the future. In today's human and world view concepts such as 'autonomy', 'perfection' and 'verticality' have made way for ideas such as 'solidarity', 'relativity' and 'horizontality'. We are aware that, without always knowing the results of our actions, we are nevertheless constantly engaged in developing our power in an 'exorbitant'[14] way as 'collective, cumulative technological action', as Jonas aptly describes it. This action is entirely unfathomable.

Once aware of this, the concept of 'responsibility' not only becomes the central theme of morality but also takes on a wider meaning. Let us apply this to the world of managers for a moment.

The manager works on the authority of the owners, the financial shareholders and is therefore accountable to them in the strictest sense. As a result he often finds himself in an unenviable position in between the owners and the business's employees or workers. His policy will therefore tend to put his self-preservation first instead of the interests of the business or those of the employees. Although with regard to the latter he hardly differs from the owner/employer who is often suspected of putting his personal interests before those of the employees.

As indicated above it appears from recent developments in social and natural sciences and from the present day economic confusion itself that the necessary solidarity of the knowledge and ability of the various individuals is irrevocably under discussion, not only within the whole of society and science but also within the life of businesses.

Communicative action

No single individual nor group holds the absolute truth or absolute skill. And this is only normal. Yet for some this appears to just be the result of scientific progress. Nothing could be less true. The authentic way to develop science and skill is not that of the isolated scholar but that of dialogue, the exchange of words between partners in a conversation. The truth must be passed on. It is not the monopoly of an individual or institute, it is also not an inviolable, everlasting unchangeable institution, it is the constant, shared work of the community. In short, truth is communication.

The fact that this view has not yet penetrated to any depth is shown by the fact that communication can still be easily reduced to the transfer of information. This minimal, purely psychological technical level already requires considerable attention in order to avoid difficulties and interference between the famous 'transmitter' and 'receiver'.

Authentic communication is based on three corner-stones: in addition to the aforementioned psychological conditions, there are also the logical and ethical presuppositions.

The logical presuppositions concern sensible and valid reasoning. Numerous discussions degenerate into hopeless misunderstandings or remain without any tangible conclusion because the participants are not able to assess the nature and effect of the arguments used. Although Western culture is one of the few that has fully developed the instrument of logic. Conventional logical insight provides a sharp instrument not for telling the truth from the untruth but for recognising valid or invalid ways of reasoning. It is, therefore, the best instrument for effectively eliminating manipulation.

Finally, there are the ethical conditions that are presupposed to lie at the basis of communication. Following on from the aforementioned formulation of Kant[15], Habermas pleads for what he calls 'herrschaftsfreier Dialog', with which mutual recognition and acceptance enter the economic world and the in-built reserve provides the ultimate counteraction to every form of extension of power.

New forms of organisation: Networking, virtual organisations

Just as the truth and social power are not monolithic, neither can organisations continue to exist in the future as the large pyramidal entities of olden days. It is not sufficient to speak of the antithesis of vertical and horizontal or level organisations. The only antithesis – if it can be called an antithesis – is that the number of levels of power are limited in the latter form. But essentially 'power' remains the key to the whole in both cases.

Two thousand years of Western civilisation should have made it clear that power is a contraindication of everything that is assumed in a present-day organisation. In the aforementioned uncontrollability of the mood of the stock market, in particular, the economy of today shows that 'power' in the sense of quantitative 'superior power' has become extremely vulnerable. Which is the reason for the increasing necessity of forming worldwide networks, safety nets instead of monolithic power blocks. And the ideal of 'virtual' organisation is gaining more and more ground for the same reason. 'Teleworking' is not only a dream to enable parents of young children to work at home but quite possibly the realistic new 'way of life' of the generations of the future.

Networks, virtual organisations and teleworking require, first and foremost, trust and mutual recognition. It is necessary that the boundaries of competition are crossed, both at individual level among the employees of one particular organisation and in the relationships between the organisations themselves. Competition is a peripheral phenomenon, unavoidable where two or more parties pursue, for purely material reasons, the same objectives, the same place in the market, the same buyer for products of different origin. But in essence intelligent beings should be able to avoid these unpleasant situations or at least not invite them.

The breaking point of a network is the loyalty of its members. It is not necessarily the largest or the strongest partner that is the source of the long-term security which organisations strive so hard for. Perhaps the 'best' is not either, if the awarding of the qualities of 'good', 'better' and 'best' is mathematically based. Quantitative criteria are there to be exceeded. And the beaten enemy always tries to get up again and hit back. Competition is only encouraged in this way, not reduced.

Long-term security is to be found in the 'loyal' co-operation of the employees in the organisation and in the interaction with the 'loyal' partners, co-makers, suppliers or customers outside the organisation. Loyalty goes beyond competition and places the role of profit and self-interest within a realistic framework, namely as a means of achieving and setting the pace of common objectives and not of the mutual extension of power.

Managerial responsibility versus power

One of the features that is immediately to be seen in the Western economic model – both capitalism and communism – is the constant confusion of the ideas of 'responsibility' and 'power'. In spite of all the overblown theories on horizontal and other structures, economic life is still based on an archaic, hierarchic, pyramidal model. Like in the ancient realm of the Pharaohs, it is still considered normal in the companies of today that a few decide on the (economic) life or death of many. And, in addition, that they can autonomously control the standard by which their decisions are judged. In political and social life we violently dismissed this for good at the end of the eighteenth-century, in the French Revolution. Or at least we tried to safeguard the future from this.

However, we are forced to ascertain that today, still, the highly praised 'democracy' has hardly developed past the embryonic stage in business life. Economic capacity is immediately identified with (financial) power. 'Being' is still identical to 'having', as was sharply condemned by Marx. And the accompanying extension of power over people and things requires no legitimacy and is not questioned. On the contrary, it is even held in social esteem, if we are to believe the reports in the media on the 'winners' and 'fast growers'.

The fact that responsibility is the correlate of power does not seem to have penetrated through to the practice of the economic rulers themselves. In the games of musical chairs, which are not only to be seen on the political scene, liability still has to be invented and accountability has long since ceased to exist.

Responsibility and accountability in Rome

The concept of responsibility was originally part of the legal and political language of the Roman Empire. In the Roman constitutional state 'being responsible' (*respondere*) means that the free citizen is accountable for the things and events which he himself – either consciously or unconsciously – has caused. The law adheres to material factuality and therefore also includes those cases in which negligence and carelessness are the cause for others suffering loss or damage. The Roman citizen is materially liable because he is able to account for his actions and must do so in the place of those who come under his control.

In addition, in the periods in which its organisation was at its most flourishing the Roman state also introduced the personal liability of the political mandatary. As we are still in the habit of doing today, it was the custom of Roman citizens to place control expressly and voluntarily and the execution of matters of general but also of individual importance in the hands (*mandare*) of an elected few. This task was regarded as being the highest honour, in particular where it concerned interests of the state, and did not include any obligation of remuneration and incurred for the person in question as many duties as rights. During the execution of the political mandate the mandatary enjoyed a general immunity of his person and his deeds. But at the end of his period of office he could be called to account by the democratic authorities and public sentencing occurred when fraud, mismanagement and, in particular, the pursuit of personal gain were proven. Accountability was not just an empty word.

This demonstrates the close relationship between being able to exercise power and the idea of responsibility. The German scientist and philosopher Hans Jonas[16] describes the phenomenon of 'power' in the human sense as the place where the cause of superior power combines with 'knowledge and freedom'. There is a difference between human power and the strength and superior power of animals and natural elements. In nature the cohesion of the whole sets the necessary boundaries within which the different force fields are balanced. The power of animals and natural elements is 'blind and not free', according to Jonas, and as a result subject to the inherent purposiveness of nature itself. Man, on the other hand, enjoys the ambiguous privilege, in consequence of his 'knowledge and ability', of being able to disrupt this natural coherence and as a result is able not only to fundamentally threaten the object of his power but also himself. The toll of the increased value of man is responsibility itself.

Growing power and growing responsibility

Hans Jonas also describes the reasons why the concept of responsibility only received minimal attention as a part of morality in the past and could mainly only continue to function as a political-legal concept. He considers the vertical orientation of conventional Western morality to be the main reason. As already stated, the concept of 'responsibility' has been irrevocably linked with the ideas of 'will' and 'knowledge' since time immemorial. As long as human knowledge and ability were fairly limited, responsibility for the future, and even liability for the wide horizontal reality in which man operates, lay to a large extent beyond the ruler himself. Jonas does not see any place for the development of any sense of responsibility in such a context.

However, this has since undergone a radical change. The superfast high development of modern Western sciences and the possibilities of high technology insistently push the problem of responsibility to the fore and this is evident in all areas. In the present circumstances it is no longer only about what happens here and now. And the careful preservation of the ruling order and balance of power is pure Utopia.

Western man knows and experiences his own possibilities as powerful instruments with which he can constantly move the world and reality for himself and for others. And the most important driving force of this evolution is to be found in the economy. He who acquires superior power in economic life acquires superior power in life itself. And is therefore accountable in the developed democracy in which we are assumed to live.

CONCLUSION

Reconciliation through Reflective Management

Responsibility lies, of course, in the answer to others, the employees, the stakeholders, society. But also, and possibly mainly, in self-criticism and the inherent dialogue that those in charge in business life conduct with themselves, ie in their critical reflective ability itself. If they wish to be honest and efficient, then such reflection must extend to the basis of business life itself and not be limited to the rethinking and restructuring of technical processes. Consequently, BPR is only effective if it is supported by the wide background of Reflective Management.

Traditional 'management by objectives' conceals a double danger. In the first place it encourages the fragmentation of the activities and the departments of an organisation. It is quite possible that the various objectives of different departments within one company are in opposition to each other and can even hinder each other. Everyone has heard the story of the financial director who announces general savings on personnel costs while at the same time the sales manager has to increase the output of his slimmed-down department. Result: a shortage of marketing means, dissatisfied and overworked employees and probably even, in the end, the fall of the final results with the ultimate consequence: the dismissal of those who are the victim of the contradiction of the objectives set from above, namely the sales staff.

Another hidden risk in management by objectives is the consequence of the unstoppability of the series of objectives. Confrontation with fear and uncertainties are easily masked by the inexhaustible number of possible objectives. Business people sometimes present themselves as do-people, active, practical, always able to show more and more initiative. Do-people always have to be do-more people. The result is that more is done but less person is left.

However, Reflective Management recuperates the possible fragmentation by drawing attention to the integration possibilities of part solutions. A technical innovation of the information policy for the sales organisation of one of the major European hotel chains appeared to include the possibility of doing something about one of the key problems of this sector, namely the problem of the large turnover in personnel. However, the precondition was that the role of the solution provided was situated and worked out within the whole.

But, above all, Reflective Management breaks through the narrowing of the calculating reasonableness that tends to control economic activities. The first result is an authentic strategic vision, a far-sighted outlook that extends further than the compulsiveness of the immediate moment and its problems. Stability and calm flowering are mainly features of thought and not of reality. Awareness of the past is extremely important in the above reasoning. As Kierkegaard says: life is lived forwards but understood backwards – and it is the same for business life. A second consequence is authentic leadership. This is not just the consequence of a fortunate coincidence in a lightning career. And it is certainly not without obligation. On the contrary, it is based on the ability to develop and continue to support a shared system of values. Its intention is focused on the essence of leadership itself, 'the responsibility of people for people'[17].

REFERENCES

1. Hamel, G. (1993), In: *De Financieel-Ekonomische Tijd*, Saturday 11th September.
2. Hammer, M. and Champy, J. (1993), *Re-engineering the corporation*.
3. idem, p.7
4. Marx, K. (1884), *Nationökonomie und Philosophie*.
5. Hegel, G. W. F. (1806), *Die Phänomenologie des Geistes*.
6. Rousseau, J. J. (1762), *Du Contrat Social*.
7. Marcuse, H. (1964), *One-dimensional man*.
8. Sloterdijk, P. (1983), *Die Kritik der Zynischen Vernunft*.
9. Galbraith, J. K. (1992), *The culture of contentment*.
10. Aristotle, Nicomachean Ethics I & V.
11. Mintzberg, H. (1993), *The rise and fall of strategic planning*.
12. Kant, I. (1775), *Grundlegung der Metaphysik der Sitten*.
13. Jonas, H. (1980), *Das Prinzip Verantwortung*. pp. 229–230.
14. idem, p. 231.
15. See 12.
16. idem, p. 232.
17. Jonas, H. op. cit.

BIBLIOGRAPHY

Boehme, G. and Stehr, N. (1986), *The knowledge society: The growing impact of scientific knowledge on social relations*. Dordrecht: D. Reidel Publishing Company.

Hammer, M. and Champy, J. (1993) *Re-engineering the Corporation: A Manifesto for Business Revolution*. London: Nicholas Brealey Publishing.

Kratky, K. W. and Wallner, F. (1990), *Grundprinzipien der Selbstorganisation*. Darmstadt: Wissenschaftliche Buchgesellschaft.

MacIntyre, A. (1984), *After virtue: A study in moral theory*. Notre Dame: University Press.

Mintzberg, H. (1993), The rise and fall of strategic planning. *Californian Management Review*.

Sora, S. A., Natale, S. M. and Sora, J. W. (1994), Quality as a permeatic ethic. *International Journal of Value-Based Management*, 7, 1, pp.25–37.

Wilson, J. Q. (1993), *The moral sense*. New York: The Free Press.

15

BPR Sources and Resources

Nigel Courtney

The expression 'Business Process Re-engineering' (BPR) first entered the management lexicon in the late 1980s. Several leading management thinkers claim to have coined the phrase and, although the consultancy firm CSC Index holds the copyright to the phrase 'Business Re-engineering', these are now widely used generic terms attributed to radical organisational change. The concept encompasses a range of variations on this theme, including 'Business Process Re-Design', 'Business Transformation' or simply 'Re-engineering'.

In the summer of 1990, papers were published almost simultaneously by two prestigious journals which are widely seen to bridge the academic and business domains. One article, by Davenport and Short, appeared in the *Sloan Management Review*; the other, in *Harvard Business Review*, was by Michael Hammer. These authors, who are both academics and practicising business advisers, brilliantly unveiled BPR as a new phenomenon which they had observed to be occuring in a small number of US companies. Although their arguments were short on evidence, their hyperbole caught the imagination of recession-weary American managers and was eagerly siezed upon by consultants. The rest, as a journalist might say, is history.

The purpose of this chapter is to provide the reader with a relevant and accessible store of sources and resources that not only documents this history but attempts to deliver a handbook for future reference.

Few could have failed to notice that the burgeoning public interest in BPR has resulted in a plethora of publications for a seemingly insatiable audience in an ever-increasing variety of fields. Application of the keywords 'Business Process Re-engineering' to one proprietary database of leading US and UK journals from January 1990 to June 1993 delivers no fewer than 555 references. There are many such databases.

This chapter sets out to make some sense of this plurality and present the results in a usable form. In so doing, two issues must be addressed. First, the author makes no pretence to have read every available or listed item. Second, the process of compiling a selected list means that an element of subjectivity is unavoidable.

The adopted process has produced 316 references together with a number of sources of further information and the way in which this selection was acquired and assembled is explained below. Even this reduced listing presents an unwieldy mass of data. Accordingly the items have been arranged under a variety of headings which, it is hoped, will assist the reader to locate information of relevance to a particular need or interest.

Of necessity the choice of headings is somewhat eclectic. Some categories have been chosen to meet a perceived need while others emerged simply because – as can be seen – more has been written to date about BPR in certain domains. Once defined, this segmentation led to the issue of allocation. The placing of a paper about the role of IT within an insurance company case study is a case in point. As a result, readers who browse beyond topics of immediate interest may find things to intrigue. A guide to these headings precedes the full listing of BPR Sources and Resources.

The literature search has encompassed the following activities:

■ The City University Working Party on BPR:
During the first half of 1994 members of a Working Party have conducted a shared study of books, specialist reports, articles and papers on BPR. Members have submitted copies, summaries or abstracts to a central compendium and index, and also exchanged information via a group email-box. This process has enabled individuals to investigate aspects of BPR from the standpoint of their own discipline and also to gain a wider appreciation by accessing the collected contributions of members from other disciplines.

■ Conferences, seminars and special interest groups on BPR:
These have been attended by Working Party team members, both as speakers and as delegates. Examples include the IoD's special conference in London on 16 February, the UK's first annual BPR conference and regular attendance at meetings of the special interest groups of the British Computer Society and the Strategic Planning Society concerned with BPR.

■ Electronic discussion groups:
Electronic discussion groups and lists on the Internet have been monitored for the last six months; in particular, 'bpr@mailbase' based at Lancaster University, UK and 'bpr-l@is' which is moderated at Delft University of Technology, Holland.

- City University library resources:
  The collection and the Inter-Library loan system have been accessed.
  CD-ROM databases also used include:
  - ABI-INFORM (from UMI of Ann Arbour, Mich.) for US and UK journals
  - IMID directory of books and periodicals
  - Whittacker/Bowler Global's directory of publications
  - ProQuest UMI's Dissertation Abstracts (listing 1,200,000 UK and US theses)
  - The British National Bibliography.
  It should be noted that, in general, these proprietary sources rely on publishers to submit information. Updates tend to be several months behind the market.
- The author's doctoral studies related to BPR:
  These include, *inter alia*, a number of in-depth case studies of companies engaged in BPR experiences, in consultation with senior executives in those organisations. Longitudinal studies of on-going developments are being conducted so that post-event rationalisation will not colour published results.

These sources have produced nearly 1000 references. Had additional keywords been used on the databases this number would undoubtedly be larger, if less focused. As far as has been feasible, the references have been read or the abstracts inspected. Material which contained book reviews, was repetitive or appeared to be frivolous was discarded. Arguably, there is a definition of 're-engineering' that characterises certain systems development work by the IS/IT community. At the risk of controversy, items in this category have been omitted from the list – although care has been taken to reflect the importance of IT as an enabler for successful BPR.

The final list also reflects the growth of the literature of BPR. Of the 316 listed items, 5 appeared in 1990, 11 in 1991, 29 in 1992 and 199 in 1993. A further 70 appeared during the early months of 1994. The total is made up by two earlier items included as background reading. Items that include case studies, surveys, or methodologies are flagged by a note in square brackets.

These figures clearly indicate that interest in BPR continues unabated and, indeed, is increasing. Perhaps more importantly, they also reveal the growing range of communities considering BPR. We know from case studies that manufacturing and financial services industries were early users and can now see evidence of heavy industry, process industry, the health sector, and local government joining the throng. Examples exist of organisations in, *inter alia*, real estate, advertising, chain stores, security, printing, and even nuclear power. Additionally, there is evidence that management consultants have started to take their own remedy – surely a case of 'Physician, heal thyself'!

If this pervasive tendency is a sign of BPR's growing maturity then it is matched by the increasing desire of authors to place BPR in a historical and social context (examples would include Grint, 1993; Earl & Khan, 1994). At the same time more writers are now challenging BPR – mainly either as 'not new' or as a destructive influence characterised by 'Big People Reductions'.

The progenitors of BPR define it to be radical, fundamental, dramatic and contemporary (Hammer and Champy, 1993 p.32). Any one of these qualities tends to threaten the *status quo*; it is hardly surprising that, now in concert, they provoke hostility. Those sceptical of Dr Hammer's teachings may draw comfort from a few lines written 175 years ago by Percy Bysshe Shelley, entitled 'Ozymandias':

> I met a traveller from an antique land who said:
> 'Two vast and trunkless legs of stone stand in the desert.
> Near them on the sand, half sunk, a shattered visage lies
> whose frown and wrinkled lip and sneer of cold command
> tell that its scupltor well those passions read
> which yet survive, stamped on these lifeless things.
> The hand that mocked them and the heart that fed.
> And on the pedestal these words appear:
> *My name is Ozymandias, King of Kings.*
> *Look on my works, ye Mighty, and despair.*
> Nothing beside remains. Round the decay
> of that collossal wreck, boundless and bare,
> the lone and level sands stretch far away.'

But these words also remind us that time marches on. People and organisations are not immortal and must constantly adapt to change and find better ways to cope with their turbulent environment. There is little doubt that BPR has enabled organisations to achieve remarkable performance improvements. However, the disturbingly high failure rate and the long-term consequences are yet to be fully understood.

This chapter is offered to help readers to develop such an understanding. No doubt some will spot glaring omissions – for which, apologies. It is hoped that experienced practitioners and newcomers to BPR alike will find it a useful and balanced source.

GUIDE

SUGGESTED CORE LIST

Books and Discussion Papers:

CCTA (1994) *BPR in the public sector: An overview of business process re-engineering.* (London: HMSO). 44 pages.

DAVENPORT, T. (1993) *Process innovation: Re-engineering work through information technology.* (Boston: Harvard Business School Press).

GRINT, K. (1993) *Reengineering history: An analysis of business process reengineering.* (Oxford: Templeton College) Working Paper: ref # MRP 93/20.

HAMMER, M. and CHAMPY, J. (1993) *Reengineering the corporation: A manifesto for business revolution.* (London: Nicholas Brealey).

HARVEY, D. (1994) *Re-engineering: The critical success factors.* (London: Business Intelligence in association with Management Today).

MORRIS, D.C. and BRANDON, J. (1993) *Reengineering your business.* (New York: McGraw-Hill).

VENKATRAMAN, N. (1991) IT-induced business reconfiguration. In: *The corporation of the 1990s: Information technology and organizational transformation,* M.S. Scott Morton (ed) (New York: Oxford University Press).

Academic, Professional and Trade Journals:

CHARETTE, R. (1994) Management by design: Business process re-engineering. *Software Management.* Feb:10–15.

DAVENPORT, T.H. and SHORT, J.E. (1990) The new industrial engineering: Information technology and business process redesign. *Sloan Management Review.* Summer:11–27.

EARL, M. and KHAN, B. (1994) How new is Business Process Redesign? *European Management Journal.* 12 (1) Mar:20–30.

LAWRENCE, A. (1994) Tools of controversy. *Computer Business Review.* March:11–14.

HAMMER, M. (1990) Reengineering work: Don't automate, obliterate. *Harvard Business Review.* Jul/Aug, 68 (4):104–112.

SHORT, J.E. and VENKATRAMAN, N. (1992) Beyond business process redesign: Redefining Baxter's business network. *Sloan Management Review.* Fall:7–21. [case study features Baxter International, incorporating American Hospital Supply].

TALWAR, R. (1993) Business re-engineering: A strategy-driven approach. *Long Range Planning.* 26 (6) Dec:22–40.

I/S Analyzer (unsigned) , Rockville, MD (1993) The role of IT in business reengineering. 31 (8):1–16. [cites case studies of AT&T Co, L L Bean Inc., US Dept of Defense].

GENERAL SELECTION

1. Books

1.1 General reading

BARTRAM, P. (1992) *Business re-engineering: The use of process redesign and IT to transform corporate performance.* (London: Business Intelligence).

CROSS, K.F. (1994) *Corporate renaissance: The fine art of re-engineering.* (US, Blackwell).

HAMMER, M. (1992) *Re-engineering work: A manifesto for business revolution.* (Warner Books).

HARRINGTON, H.J. (1991) *Business process improvement.* (New York: McGraw-Hill).

HUBER, G.P. (1993) *Organisational change and redesign: Ideas and insights for improving managerial performance.* (New York: Oxford University Press).

JAYACHANDRA, Y. (1994) *Re-engineering the networked enterprise.* (McGraw-Hill).

JOHANSSON, H.J. and others (1993) *Business process reengineering: Breakpoint strategies for market dominance.* (Chichester: John Wiley).

KING, R.A. (1992) *Breakpoint: Business process redesign.* (US: Coopers Total Quality).

MITROFF, I.J. (1994) *Framebreak: The radical redesign of American business.* (Jossey-Bass).

RUMMLER, G.A. and BRACHE, A.P. (1990) *Improving performance: How to manage the white space on the organizational chart.* (Jossey-Bass).

TOWERS, S. (1994) *Business process re-engineering: A practical handbook for executives.* (Technical Communications).

1.2 Sector-specific monographs

ADAIR, C.B. (1994) *Breakthrough process redesign: New pathways to building customer value.* (US: AMACOM).

COATE, L.E. (1993) *Re-engineering administrative processes.* (NACUBO).

CURRID, C. (1994) *Twelve re-engineering tools.* (Rocklin, CA: Prima Publishing).

DONOVAN, J.L. (1994) *Business re-engineering with technology.* (Prentice-Hall).

EMBLEY, D.W., KURTZ B.D. and WOODFIELD S.N. (1992) *Object-oriented systems analysis: A model-driven approach.* (Prentice-Hall).

HANSEN, G.A. (1994) *Automating business process re-engineering: Computerised quality & productivity improvement.* (Prentice-Hall).

KAVANAUGH, P. (1993) *Downsizing: Re-engineering business for open client-server systems.* (Bantam).

KILOV, H. and ROSS, J. (1994) *Information modeling: An object-oriented approach.* (Prentice-Hall).

PEARSON, J.R.W. and SKINNER, C. (1993) *Business process re-engineering (BPR) in the UK financial services industry: The first research into BPR programmes.* (University of Bristol: Dept of Continuing Education) 106 pages. [survey and analysis].

SPURR, K. and others. (1993) *Software assistance for business re-engineering.* (Chichester: John Wiley).

SWATMAN, P.M.C. and SWATMAN, P.A. (1993) *Business process redesign using EDI: An Australian success story.* Proceedings of the 6th International EDI Conference. Bled, Slovenia. June 7th-9th. [case study of BHP Steel of Australia].

2. Academic, Professional & Trade Journals

2.1 General Reading
In-depth analyses & discussions

BARRETT, J.L. (1994) Process visualization. *Information Systems Management.* 11 (2) Spring:14–23.

BASHEIN, B.J., MARKUS, M.L. and RILEY, P. (1994) Preconditions for BPR success. *Information Systems Management.* 11 (2) Spring:7–13.

BELMONTE, R.W. and MURRAY, R.J. (1993) Getting ready for strategic change: Surviving business process redesign. *Information Systems Management.* 10 (3) Summer:23–29.

BROWNING, J. (1993) The power of process redesign. *McKinsey Quarterly.* 1 pp.47–58.

CYPRESS, H.L. (1994) Re-engineering. *OR/MS Today.* Feb:18–29.

DAVENPORT, T.H. (1993) Need radical innovation and continuous improvement? Integrate process reengineering and TQM. *Planning Review.* 21 (3) May/Jun:6–12.

DAVIS, T.R.V. (1993) Reengineering in action. *Planning Review.* 21 (4) Jul/Aug:49–54. [cites four US case studies].

DUCK, J.D. (1993) Managing change: The art of balancing. *Harvard Business Review.* Nov/Dec:109–118.

GLECKMAN, H. (1993) The technology payoff. *Business Week.* Iss: 3323 Jun 14th, pp.56–68. [cites five US case studies].

HAGEL, J. (1993) Keeping CPR on track. *McKinsey Quarterly.* 1:59–72. [CPR means 'core process redesign'].

HALL, G., ROSENTHAL, J. and WADE, J. (1993) How to make reengineering really work. *Harvard Business Review.* Nov/Dec 71 (6):119–131.

KAPLAN, R.B. and MURDOCK, L. (1991) Core process redesign. *McKinsey Quarterly.* (2):27–43.

KEENAN, W.Jr. (1993) If I had a hammer. *Sales & Marketing Management.* 145 (15) Dec:56–61.

KENNEDY, C. and ROCK S. (1993) We knew that if we didn't get it right it would be the end of the road for the whole company. *Director.* Aug, 47 (1):20–27. [case study featuring Barr & Stroud, defence engineers].

LAU, R.S.M. (1993) Business reengineering: The ultimate productivity gain. *South Dakota Business Review. 52* (1) Sep:1–4.

LUFTMAN, J.N., LEWIS, P.R. and OLDACH, S.H. (1993) Transforming the enterprise: The alignment of business and information technology strategies. *IBM Systems Journal. 32* (1):198–221.

MOAD, J. (1993) Does reengineering really work? *Datamation. 39* (15) Aug 1st, pp.22–28. [cites three US case studies].

OLIVER, J. (1993) Shocking to the core. *Management Today.* Aug:18–22.

OMRANI, D. (1992) Business process reengineering: A business revolution. *Management Services.* Oct, 36 (10):12–14, 16.

OSTROFF, F. and SMITH, D. (1992) The horizontal organization: Redesigning the corporation. *McKinsey Quarterly.* (1):148–167.

SCHERR, A.L. (1993) A new approach to business processes. *IBM Systems Journal. 32* (1):80–98.

STALK, G., EVANS, P. and SHULMAN, L.E. (1992) Competing on capabilities: The new rules of corporate strategy. *Harvard Business Review.* Mar/Apr:57–69.

STANTON, S., HAMMER, M. and POWER, B. (1993) Reengineering: Getting everyone on board. *I.T. Magazine. 25* (4) Apr:22–27.

STEWART, T.A. (1993) Welcome to the revolution. *Fortune.* Dec 13th pp.66–76.

STEWART, T.A. (1993) Reengineering: The hot new management tool. *Fortune International. 127* (17) Aug 23rd pp.32–37. [cites eight US case studies].

van ACKERE, A., LARSEN, E.R. and MORECROFT, J.D.W. (1993) Systems thinking and business process redesign: An application to the beer game. *European Management Journal. 11* (4) Dec:412–423.

VANTRAPPEN, H., (1992) Creating customer value by streamlining business processes. *Long Range Planning. 25* (1):53–62.

VENKATRAMAN, N. (1994) IT-enabled business transformation: From automation to business scope redefinition. *Sloan Management Review. 35* (2) Winter:73–87.

VOGL, A.J. (1993) The age of reengineering. *Across the Board. 30* (5) Jun:26–33.

WHEATLEY, M. (1994) De-engineering the corporation. *Industry Week. 243* (8) April 18th pp.18–26.

Chief Executive (unsigned), US (1994) *Approach to transformation.* Mar:2–5.

Concise, pithy articles and cameos

ASBRAND, D. (1993) Re-engineering demands expert management. *InfoWorld.* 15 (27) Jul 5th, p.51.

BALDWIN, S.R. (1994) Winning the performance-improvement stakes: Radical change isn't always the answer. *Industry Week.* 243 (3) Feb 7th, p.48.

BOOTH, C. (1993) Rules of re-engineering. *Computing Canada.* 19 (14) Jul 5th, p.9.

BURGETZ, B. (1991) Gold flakes not gold nuggets. *CMA Magazine.* Oct, 65 (8):38.

BYRNE, J.A. (1993) Reengineering: Beyond the buzzword. *Business Week.* Iss: 3320 May 24th, pp.12–14.

CAFASSO, R. (1993) Re-engineering: Just first step. *Computerworld.* 27 (16) Apr 19th, p.94.

CHAMPY, J. (1990) Organizational revisionism. *Chief Information Officer Journal.* Dec 20th.

CLASSE, A. (1993) Don't tinker with it: BPR it! *Accountancy.* 112 (1199):64–66.

DAVIDSON, W.H. (1993) Beyond reengineering: The three phases of business transformation. *IBM Systems Journal.* Jan.

ELIOT, L. (1992) Five approaches to re-engineering. *CASE Trends.* Sep:50–54.

FUREY, T.R. (1993) A six-step to process reengineering. *Planning Review.* Mar/Apr:20–23.

GANTZ, J. (1993) Surviving the re-engineering revolution. *Networking Management.* Jan:16–24.

HAMMER, M. and CHAMPY, J. (1993) Reengineering the corporation. *Small Business Reports.* 18 (11) Nov:65–68.

HERBKERSMAN, J. (1994) Taking the confusion out of re-engineering. *National Underwriter.* 98 (4) Jan 24th, p.5.

HOBBY, J. (1994) The truth behind the hype. *Computer Weekly.* Feb 3rd, pp.32–33.

HUFF, S.L. (1992) Reengineering the business. *Business Quarterly.* 56 (5):55–58.

ISHAM, P. (1993) Beware the erosion of the human touch. *Computer Weekly.* Dec 9th.

KAWALEK, P. (1993) BPR – a revolutionary manifesto? *Computer Bulletin.* Dec:18–20.

KEENAN, W.Jr. (1993) Reengineering salespeople out of a job. *Sales & Marketing Management.* 145 (15) Dec:61.

KING, J. (1993) Re-engineering repercussions: Kodak. *Computerworld.* 27 (26) Jun 28th, p.151 [case study features Eastman Kodak Co].

KING, W.R. (1994) Process reengineering. *Information Systems Management.* 11 (2) Spring:71–73.

KINNI, T.B. (1994) The reengineering rage. *Industry Week. 243* (3) Feb 7th, pp.11–14.

KINNI, T.B. (1994) Reengineering: Righting wrong organizations. *Industry Week. 243* (3) Feb 7th, pp.14–16.

KRPAN, J. (1993) Re-engineering the right way: 10 tips. *CMA Magazine. 67* (5) Jun:14–15.

LOWENTHAL, J.N. (1994) Reengineering the organization: A step-by-step approach to corporate revitalization: Part 2. *Quality Progress. 27* (2) Feb:61–63.

MARCUM, J.W. (1993) Process innovation: Reengineering work through information technology. *National Productivity Review. 12* (4) Autumn p.582.

MARCUM, J.W. (1993) Re-engineering your business. *National Productivity Review. 12* (4) Autumn:584–585.

NEWMAN, G. (1994) Neo-Luddites on the loose. *Across the Board. 31* (1) Jan:8–9.

MAGLITTA, J. (1994) Michael Hammer: One on one. *Computerworld. 28* (4) Jan 24th, pp.84–86.

MANGANELLI, R.L. (1993) Define 're-engineer'. *Computerworld. 27* (29) Jul 19th, pp.86–87.

MANGANELLI, R.L. (1993) It's not a silver bullet. *Journal of Business Strategy. 14* (6) Nov/Dec:45.

MEYER, N.D. (1993) Theory X lives on. *Computerworld. 27* (25) Jun 21, p.96.

MILL, J. (1994) No pain, no gain. *Computing.* Feb 3rd, p.26–27.

NORMAN, D. (1994) BPR – how to spot the pitfalls. *Strategic Planning Society News.* Feb:6–7.

PARKER, J. (1993) An ABC guide to business process reengineering. *Industrial Engineering. 25* (5) May:52–53.

RANDALL, R.M. (1993) The reengineer. *Planning Review. 22* (3) May/Jun:18–21.

RYAN, H.W. (1994) Reinventing the business. *Information Systems Management. 11* (2) Spring:77–79.

SALAMA, E. (1993) Henley Centre: When the measure of success fails. *Marketing.* Jul 29th, p.6.

SHERIDAN, J.H. (1994) Reengineering isn't enough. *Industry Week. 243* (2) Jan 17th:61–62.

SHOREY, E. (1993) Process redesign. *Executive Excellence. 10* (10) Oct:16–17.

STRASSMANN, P.A. (1993) Re-engineering: An emetic in a perfume bottle? *Computerworld. 27* (33) Aug 16th p.33.

TANSWELL, A. (1993) Business restructuring: The key to radical change. *Professional Engineering. 6* (1) Jan:24–25.

THACKRAY, J. (1993) Fads, fixes & fictions. *Management Today.* Jun:40–42.

TICHY, N.M. (1993) Revolutionize your company. *Fortune.* Dec 13th pp.114–118.

TOWERS, S. (1993) Business process reengineering lessons for success. *Management Services.* 37 (8) Aug:10–12.

VITIELLO, J. (1993) Reengineering: It's totally radical. *Journal of Business Strategy.* 14 (6) Nov/Dec:44–47.

VOWLER, J. (1993) The reluctant revolution. *Computer Weekly.* Sep 2nd p.20.

VOWLER, J. (1993) The medicine men of BPR. *Computer Weekly.* Sep 16th p.20.

WARD, J.A. (1994) Continuous process improvement. *Information Systems Management.* 11 (2) Spring:74–76. [a Total Quality viewpoint].

WHITMAN, A.R. (1994) Virtual reengineering. *Industrial Engineering.* 26 (3) Mar:17–18.

Economist (unsigned), London (1994) *Re-engineering Europe.* 330 (7852) Feb 26th, pp.63–64.

Industrial Engineering (unsigned), US (1994) *Dramatic results possible when reengineering entire company.* 26 (2) Feb:8–9.

Industrial Engineering (unsigned), US (1993) *Companies applying reengineering worried about managing change.* 25 (6) Jun:9–10.

Japan 21st (unsigned), (1993) *Forrester Research Inc. finds corporate re-engineering requires workflow computing.* 38 (4) Apr:33–34.

Management Review (unsigned), US (1994) *Measuring the success of reengineering.* 83 (1) Jan:59.

National Underwriter (unsigned), US (1993) *30 reengineering pointers for CEOs.* 97 (39) Sep 27th, pp.18–19.

2.2 *Texts for interest-groups*

Accounting/Purchasing/Sales/Marketing viewpoints

ARNOLD, G.W. and FLOYD, M.C. (1992) Reengineering the new product introduction process. *AT&T Technical Journal 71* (6):12–19.

EVANS, E. (1993) Business process redesign: A purchasing opportunity. *Purchasing and Supply Management.* Nov:30–33.

LAYNE, C.R. (1993) Re-engineering the payment process using EDI, ERS and imaging technology. *Journal of Cash Management. 13* (5) Sep/Oct:10–19. [case study features R J Reynolds Tobacco Co.].

MONCZKA, R. and MORGAN, J. (1994) Reinventing purchasing. *Purchasing. 116* (1) Jan 13th, pp.74–79.

RICHMAN, T. and KOONTZ, C. (1993) How benchmarking can improve business reengineering. *Planning Review. 21* (6) Nov/Dec:26–27.

SCHMIDT, D. (1994) The credit manager's reengineering primer. *Business Credit. 96* (1) Jan:29–31.

WEBER, R. and Kelly, J. (1993) Business reengineering: With the customer in mind. *Business Communications Review. 23* (11) Nov:44–48.

An HRM viewpoint

ASH, P.R. (1993) Reengineering compensation and benefits management. *Journal of Compensation & Benefits. 9* (3) Nov-Dec:26–31.

CAUDRON, S. (1993) Are self-directed teams right for your company? *Personnel Journal. 72* (12) Dec:76–84.

CIAMPA, D. (1993) Reengineering with caution. *Management Review. 82* (10) Oct:50.

FILIPOWSKI, D. (1993) Is reengineering more than a fad? *Personnel Journal. 72* (12) Dec:48L.

GREENGARD, S. (1993) Reengineering: Out of the rubble. *Personnel Journal. 72* (12) Dec:48B-48K.

GREENGARD, S. (1993) HR's role in the reengineering process. *Personnel Journal. 72* (12) Dec:48H.

GREENGARD, S. (1993) How to create the corporate reengineering committee. *Personnel Journal. 72* (12) Dec:48J.

HERZOG, J.P. (1991) People: The critical factor in managing change. *Journal of Systems Management,* Mar:6–11.

KATZENBACH, J.R. and SMITH, D.K. (1993) The rules for managing cross functional reengineering teams. *Planning Review.* Mar/Apr:12–13.

KAVIN-LOVERS, J. and KEILTY, J. (1993) Designing incentives to support business reengineering. *Journal of Compensation and Benefits. 8* (5):55–58.

MIRON, D., LEICHTMAN, S. and ATKINS, A. (1993) Reengineering human resource processes. *Human Resources Professional. 6* (1) Summer:19–23.

RAYNOR, M.E. (1993) Reengineering: A powerful addition to the arsenal of continuous improvement. *CMA Magazine. 67* (9) Nov:26.

RICHARDS-CARPENTER, C. (1993) How a CPIS helps re-engineering. *Personnel Management. 25* (11) Nov:23.

SMITH, B. (1994) Business process reengineering: More than a buzzword. *HR Focus. 71* (1) Jan:17–18.

THOMAS, M. (1994) What you need to know about: Business process re-engineering. *Personnel Management.* Jan:28–30.

WHITE, W.L. (1993) Compensation support for the reengineering process. *Compensation & Benefits Review. 25* (5) Sep/Oct:41–46.

HR Focus (unsigned), US (1994) *10 rules of thumb for reengineering. 71* (1) Jan:18.

An IS/IT viewpoint

ABUAF, A. and MEDINA, A. (1993) Technology's role in business process reengineering. *Wall Street & Technology*. 11 (3) Sep:72.

ALTER, A.E. (1994) Re-engineering tops list again. *Computerworld*. 28 (5) Jan 31st, p.8.

ARYANPUR, S. (1993) On the mend. *Computer Weekly*. Mar 25th.

BEATTY, R.W. and MURRAY, R.J. (1991) Getting ready for strategic change: Surviving business process redesign. *Information Systems Management*. Summer pp.16–30.

BOZMAN, J.S. (1993) Framing re-engineering plans. *Computerworld*. 27 (47) Nov 22nd, p.10. [open IS architectures for BPR: eg US Dept of Defense].

BROCHU, E. (1994) System project re-engineering could catch on. *Computing Canada*. 20 (2) Jan 19th, p.17.

BROUSELL, D. (1993) A word with Michael Hammer. *Datamation*. 39 (15) Aug 1st, p.24.

CAFASSO, R. (1993) Re-engineering plan preserves mainframe role. *Computerworld*. 27 (15) Apr 12:63, 68. [case study features US loans business, Key Corp].

CANTON, A.N. (1994) BPR: The arguments every CIO hears. *Information Systems Management*. 11 (2) Spring:87–89.

CAREY, D. (1993) Nine I.T. executives tell you how to get reengineering success. *I.T. Magazine (Canada)*. 25 (11) Nov:12–20.

CHAMBERLAIN, W.W. (1993) CIO, reengineer thyself. *Chief Information Officer Journal*. 5 (7) Sep/Oct:20–25.

CHARAN, R. (1991) How networks reshape organizations – for results. *Harvard Business Review*. Sept/Oct:104–115.

COLLINS, B.S. and MATHEWS, S. (1993) Securing your business process. *Computers & Security*. 12 (7) Nov:629–633.

CURRID, C. (1993) Everyone's re-engineering except the computer companies. *InfoWorld*. 15 (35) Aug 30th, p.62.

ERRICO, S.G. AND SULLIVAN, A.D. (1993) Radical I.S. change: Can we get there from here? *CASE Trends*. 5 (2):16–19.

FRIEDLANDER, P. and TOOTHMAN, W.E. (1994) Reengineering done right: Intermediate solutions that are cost-effective. *Information Systems Management*. 11 (1) Winter:7–15.

FUREY, T.R., GARLITZ, J.L. and KELLEHER, M.L. (1993) Applying information technology to reengineering. *Planning Review*. 21 (6) Nov/Dec:22–25.

GARRETT, J.G. (1994) Reengineering, outsourcing and all that. *Business Quarterly*. 58 (3), Spring:116–120. [outsourcing case studies, eg Blue Cross of Atlantic, Canada].

HALLBERG, C. and DEFIORE, R. (1993) Reengineering the information services function. *SIM Network*. 8 (3):1–4.

HOSSEINI, J. (1993) Revisiting and expanding Taylorism, business process redesign and information technology. *Computers & Industrial Engineering. 25* (1–4) Sep:533–535.

MONTELEONE, F. (1994) Re-engineering: Don't miss this train. *Computerworld. 28* (5) Jan 31st p.35.

SEYBOLD, P.B. (1994) Closing the gap to save your business. *Computerworld.* Feb 21st, p.35.

SCHNITT, D.L. (1993) Reengineering the organization using information technology. *Journal of Systems Management. 44* (1) Iss.379:14–42.

SCHRERR, A.L. (1993) A new approach to business processes. *IBM Systems Journal. 32* (1):80–89.

SULLIVAN, P. (1993) Re-engineering: Worth another visit. *Computing Canada. 19* (21) Oct 12th p.43.

WALLACE, S. (1993) How many successful managers of reengineering and imaging initiatives can dance on the head of a pin? *Inform. 7* (6) Jun:32–34. [on the role of imaging technology in BPR].

WANG, S. (1994) 'OO modeling of business processes: Object-oriented systems analysis. *Information Systems Management. 11* (2):36–43.

National Underwriter (unsigned), US (1994) *Reengineering top challenge for IS execs in '94.* 98 (10) Mar 7th, p.36 [CSC's annual survey of CIO priorities].

Planning Review (unsigned), (1993) *IT in reengineering.* 21 (3) May/Jun:11.

2.3 Sector-specific articles

Banking/Financial Services/Insurance sectors

BOLLENBACHER, G.M. (1992) Reengineering financial processes. *Bankers Magazine. 154* (4) Jul/Aug:42–46.

DAY, J. (1992) Going beyond the buzzwords. *Bank Systems & Technology. 29* (12) Dec:52.

DOLAN, N. (1993) Insurance industry leads pack in reengineering. *National Underwriter. 97* (31) Aug 2nd, p.12.

GREENGARD, S. (1993) IDS Financial Services reengineers to reduce turnover, improve customer service. *Personnel Journal. 72* (12) Dec:48D. [case study features IDS Financial Services].

HAZELL, M.(1992) Activity mapping for business process redesign. *Management Accounting.* Feb:36–38.

HELLDORFER, S. and DALY, M. (1993) Reengineering brings together units. *Best's Review. 94* (6) Oct:82–85. [case study features CIGNA Corp].

HOFFMAN, T. (1993) Re-engineering pays off at Cigna. *Computerworld. 27* (32) Aug 9th, p.70. [case study features CIGNA Corp].

INMAN, P. (1993) High Roller. *Computer Weekly.* Sep 16th, p.26. [case study features National Vulcan Engineering Insurance, UK].

JANSON, R. (1993) Thanks to its employees, this re-engineering effort worked. *Journal for Quality & Participation.* 16 (7) Dec:78–80. [case study features American Modern Home Insurance Group, of Cincinnatti, Ohio].

JONES, D.C. (1993) 'Reengineered' cos. must keep eye on customers. *National Underwriter.* 97 (24) Jun 14th, p.2.

LaPLANTE, A. (1993) MasterCard SWAT team tackles re-engineering. *InfoWorld.* 15 (16) Apr 19th, p.74. [case study features MasterCard International Inc].

LAWRENCE, P.J. (1991) Reengineering the insurance industry. *Best's Review.* May:68–72.

MORRALL, K. (1994) Re-engineering: Buzzword or strategy? *Bank Marketing.* 26 (1) Jan:21–25. [case study features First Commerce Corp].

MORRALL, K. (1994) Re-engineering the bank (part 2). *Bank Marketing.* 26 (2) Feb:67–71.

MOTLEY, L.B. (1994) Re-engineering should help marketers. *Bank Marketing.* 26 (2) Feb:60.

PELTZ, M. (1993) Reengineering the finance department. *Institutional Investor.* 27 (10) Oct, pp.151–155 [case study features EDS Corp].

RIFKIN, G. (1993) Reengineering Aetna. *Forbes.* Jun 7th, pp.78–86. [case study features Aetna Life & Casualty Co].

SEAVOR, P.G. (1993) How to: Reengineer statement rendering. *ABA Banking Journal.* 85 (12) Dec:50.

STAINTON, J. (1993) How information technology contributed to business process re-design in the UK's third largest health insurer. *Document Image Automation.* 13 (3) Fall:4–6. [case study features health insurer Western Provident Association, UK].

VINCENT, D.R. (1993) How eight firms transformed – with technology. *Financial Executive.* Mar/Apr:52.

WOOLLACOTT, E. (1993) People power. *Computer Weekly.* Sep 16th, p.30. [case study features National & Provincial Building Society, UK].

Bank Management (unsigned), (1993) *Study cites re-engineering as top I/S issue for 1993.* 69 (4) Apr:21.

Health sector

BECKHAM, J.D. (1993) The longest wave. *Healthcare Forum.* 36 (6) Nov/Dec, pp.78–82.

BERGMAN, R. (1994) Reengineering health care. *Hospitals & Health Networks.* 68 (3) Feb 5th, pp.28–36.

BERND, D.L. and REED, M.M. (1994) Re-engineering women's services. *Healthcare Forum.* 37 (1) Jan/Feb:63–67. [case study features Women's Health Pavilion at Sentara Norfolk General Hospital].

DEEVY, E. and MacINNIS, P. (1994) Re-engineering service in an acute care hospital. *Journal for Quality & Participation.* 17 (1) Jan/Feb:84–87. [case study features Hale Municipal Hospital, Haverhill Mass.].

DIX, J. (1994) Changing the way business works. *Network World.* 11 (2) Jan 10th, p.34–36.

HAIGH, P.J. (1993) Healthcare reengineering via network technologies: A critical combination. *Computers in Healthcare.* 14 (12) Nov:36–40.

MASONSON, L.N. (1993) Reengineering is here to stay. *Healthcare Financial Management.* 47 (11) Nov:84–85.

McMANIS, G.L. (1993) Re-engineering: Are you ready, willing and able? *Hospitals & Health Networks.* 67 (19) Oct 5th, p.44.

MORRIS, D. and BRANDON, J. (1992) Reengineering: More than meets the eye. *Computers in Healthcare.* 13 (11) Nov:52–54.

NICH, D.L. (1994) Finding internal auditing's role in work reengineering. *Internal Auditing.* 9 (3), Winter:76–79. [case study features a 300-bed hospital].

Heavy Industry, Mining & Plant

EVANS, J. (1993) Juggling powers. *Computer Weekly.* Dec 16th. [case study features Trafalgar House Engineering, UK].

GODDARD, W.E. (1993) Rethink – in 6 steps – then reengineer. *Modern Materials Handling.* 48 (13) Nov:37.

HOLZHAUER, R. (1993) Reengineering to success. *Plant Engineering.* Dec:20. [review of Re-engineering: leveraging the power of integrated product development, by V. Daniel Hunt].

McMANUS, G.J. (1994) Re-engineering the steel industry. *Iron Age New Steel.* 10 (1) Jan:17–19.

MORLEY, D. (1993) Reengineering: Art or science? *Manufacturing Systems.* 11 (9) Sep:8.

TORREY, E.E. (1993) Why should IEs be involved in reengineering? *Industrial Engineering.* 25 (5) May:4 [on the BPR role for Industrial Engineers].

TORREY, E.E. (1993) BPR offers opportunity for IEs to shine. *Industrial Engineering.* 25 (10) Oct:4.

Manufacturing Industries

CHESTER, A.N. (1994) Aligning technology with business strategy. *Research-Technology Management.* 37 (1) Jan/Feb:25–32. [case study features Minnesota Mining & Manufacturing Co].

COLE, C.C., CLARK, M.L. and NEMEC, C. (1993) Reengineering information systems at Cincinnati Milacron. *Planning Review.* 21 (3) May/Jun:22–26.

deJONG, J. (1993) Redesigning design. *Computerworld.* 27 (47) Nov 22th, pp.87–90. [case study features Black & Decker Corp].

DUTTON, B. (1993) Reexamining reengineering. *Manufacturing Systems. 11* (11) Nov:4.

GOLL, E.O. and CORDOVANO, M.F. (1993) Construction time again. *CIO. 7* (2) Oct 15th, pp.32–36.

INGLESBY, T. (1993) Reengineered out of a job. *Manufacturing Systems. 11* (7) Jul:4.

KLEIN, M.M. (1993) IEs fill facilitator role in benchmarking operations to improve performance. *Industrial Engineering. 25* (9) Sep:40–42.

KRUGER, P.D. (1993) Reengineering: A competitive advantage. *Appliance Manufacturer. 41* (9) Sep:31–32.

LAYDEN, J.E. (1993) Reengineering the human/machine partnership. *Industrial Engineering. 25* (4) Apr:14.

RASMUS, D. (1992) 'Reengineering', or evolution through violent overthrow. *Manufacturing Systems. 10* (9) Sep:52–58. [cites BPR in Aerospace industry].

SANTOSUS, M. (1993) No pane, no gain. *CIO. 7* (3) Nov 1st, pp.46–52. [case study features window manufacturer Andersen Corp. of Bayport, Minn.].

SCHAADT, P. (1993) Successful pilots: Using pilots for successful reengineering. *Inform. 7* (5) May:28–30. [on BPR of production systems].

VASILASH, G.S. (1993) Reengineering: Your job may depend on it. *Production. 105* (6) Jun:9–16.

WILKINSON, R. (1991) Reengineering: Industrial engineering in action. *Industrial Engineering. 23* (8):47–49.

Industrial Engineering (unsigned), US (1994) *Survey shows tendency to reengineer new product development processes. 26* (1) Jan:6.

Industrial Engineering (unsigned), US (1993) *Manufacturing lags behind other industries in reengineering. 25* (7) Jul:12.

Oil/Chemical/Pharmaceutical Industries

CALLAHAN, C.V., QUARLS, H.F, and TREAT, J.E. (1993) Restructuring opportunities: New rules and new tools for today's oil-company managers. *Oil & Gas Investor.* Summer:4–6.

HYMAN, H. (1993) The French have no word for it – but Rhone-Poulenc does it. *Chemical Week. 153* (20) Nov 24th, p.46. [case study features Rhone-Poulenc].

MULLIN, R. (1993) Top management's prescription for successful reengineering. *Chemical Week. 153* (20) Nov 24th, pp.46–48.

MULLIN, R. (1993) Reengineering: Confronting the challenge of clean-sheet redesign. *Chemical Week. 153* (20) Nov 24th, pp.28–30.

MULLIN, R. (1993) Instrumentation expo takes a reengineering spin. *Chemical Week. 153* (11) Sep 29th, p.16.

MULLIN, R. (1993) Reengineering's uneasy guru contemplates the changes. *Chemical Week. 153* (5) Aug 11th, p.40.

STOW, R.P. (1993) Reengineering by objectives. *Planning Review*. 21 (3) May/Jun:14–16. [case study features CAT Pharmaceuticals Corp].

Public/Not-for-Profit Sectors
McCRINDELL, J.Q. (1994) Value-added invoice processing: A re-engineering case study. *CMA Magazine*. 68 (1) Feb:30. [case study features US federal government's 'administrative re-engineering'].

SAVAGE, M. (1993) Rethinking city management empowers workers. *American City & County*. 108 (10) Sep:90.

TOREGAS, C. and WALSH, T. (1993) Out with the old, in with re-engineering. *American City & County*. 108 (6) May:49–56. [cites case studies of five US local authorities].

Environment Today (unsigned), US (1993) *'Reinventing government' plan full of advice for EPA, OSHA*. 4 (10) Oct:8.

Telecommunications Industry
BRITTAIN, C. (1994) Reengineering complements BellSouth's major business strategies. *Industrial Engineering*. 26 (2) Feb:34–36. [case study features BellSouth Telecommunications Inc].

HOUSEL, T.J., MORRIS, C.J. and WESTLAND, C. (1993) Business process reengineering at Pacific Bell. *Planning Review*. 22 (3) May/Jun:28–33. [case study featuring Pacific Bell].

HOUSEL, T.J., BELL, A.H. and KANEVSKY, V. (1994) Calculating the value of reengineering at Pacific Bell. *Planning Review*. 22 (1) Jan/Feb:40–43. [reports Pacific Bell's Process Value Estimation methodology].

Utility Industries
HILL, G.M. (1993) Re-engineering electric utilities: What works, and what doesn't. *Electrical World*. 207 (12) Dec:8–9.

HOWARD, C. and JUHL, G.M. (1994) AM/FM: Tuned in to utility reengineering. *Fortnightly*. 132 (2) Jan 15th, pp.36–38. [case study features North Queensland Electricity Board in Australia].

KUEHN, S.E. (1993) The process of reducing nuclear O&M costs. *Power Engineering*. 97 (5) May:18.

Other Types of Activity & Enterprise
BARTON, R.S. (1993) Business process reengineering. *Business Quarterly*. 57 (3) Spring:101–103. [case study features Xerox Canada Inc].

BLACKWELL, G. (1993) Re-engineering financial systems. *I.T. Magazine*. 25 (8) Aug:14–18. [case study features Royal LePage Real Estate Ltd].

BUDAY, R.S. (1993) Reengineering one firm's product development and another's service delivery. *Planning Review*. 21 (2) Mar/Apr:14–19. [case study featuring Hallmark, greetings card manufacturer].

BUTTON, K. (1993) Internal affairs. *Computer Weekly*. Sep 2nd. [case study features Andersen Consulting].

COSCO, J. (1993) Reengineering: The razor's edge. *Journal of Business Strategy*. 14 (6) Nov/Dec:58–61. [case study features GTE (directories)].

COUGER, J.D., FLYNN, P. and HELLYER, D. (1994) Enhancing the creativity of reengineering. *Information Systems Management*. 11 (2) Spring:24–29. [case study features Federal Express Corp of Colorado Springs].

DAVIDSON, C. (1993) Driving ambition. *Computer Weekly*. Sep 16th. [case study features Eurodollar].

deROULET, D.G. (1993) Reengineering the order-to-delivery cycle. *Transportation & Distribution*. 34 (6) Jun:57.

FAHEY, A. (1993) Here come clusters, CBUs, super groups... *Adweek [US Eastern Ed.]*. 34 (33) Aug 16th, p.6. [cites five agency case studies].

FOX, B. (1993) The pitfalls of reengineering. *Chain Store Age Executive*. 69 (11) Nov:76.

HAROWITZ, S.L. (1993) Reengineering security's role. *Security Management*. 37 (11) Nov:36–45.

JAFFE, A. (1993) One cure for agency ills: 'Reengineering'. *Adweek [US Eastern Ed.]*. 34 (39) Sep 27th, p.68.

JOHNSON, S.J. (1993) Reengineering: What works, what doesn't. *Retail Business Review*. 61 (5) Jun:28–30.

ROWAN, R. (1993) Business process engineering case study: TI Semiconductor Group order fulfillment reengineering. *SIM Network*. 8 (4):1–4. [case study features Texas Instruments].

THERRIEN, L. (1993) Consultant, reengineer thyself. *Business Week*. Iss: 3314 Apr 12th, pp.86–88. [case study features Andersen Consulting].

Frozen Food Age (unsigned), US (1994) *Frozens hold key to 're-engineering' restaurants*. 42 (7) Feb:25–26.

Global Trade & Transportation (unsigned), (1993) *Re-engineering business processes for EDI*. 113 (12) Dec:49.

3. Newspaper Articles

CANE, A. (1994) Re-engineering's all the rage. *Financial Times*. Jun 24th, p.14.

CANE, A. (1993) Back to square one – or two. *Financial Times*. Apr 20th, p.16.

De JONQUIERES, G. (1993) A clean break with tradition. *Financial Times*. Jul 12th, p.12. [case study cites Elida Gibbs].

DEVINE, M. (1994) Riding the re-engineering tiger. *Sunday Times*. Jun 26th, section 6 p.2.

LORENZ, C. (1994) Re-engineering in small doses. *Financial Times*. Jul 1st, p.14 [cites survey of BPR experiences by CSC Index].

LORENZ, C. (1993) Square pegs in round holes. *Financial Times*. Dec 10th, p.13.

LORENZ, C. (1993) Sculptors in jelly. *Financial Times*. Jul 28th, p.8.

LORENZ, C. (1993) Time to get serious. *Financial Times*. Jun 25th, p.13.

LORENZ, C. (1993) The very nuts and bolts of change. *Financial Times*. Jun 22nd, p.11.

LORENZ, C. (1993) The uphill battle against change. *Financial Times*. Jun 18th, p.11. [cites case study at Rank Xerox].

LORENZ, C. (1993) A new concept placed in context. *Financial Times*. Jun 11th, p.10.

LORENZ, C. (1993) Stepping out in a new direction. *Financial Times*. May 24th, p.11. [cites case studies at AT&T; IBM Credit].

LORENZ, C. (1993) The side-effects of a cure-all approach. *Financial Times*. Apr 2nd, p.11.

LORENZ, C. (1993) Restoring the order from chaos. *Financial Times*. Jan 2nd, p.11 [case study features Reuters].

MAY, M, (1993) Chip, Chop – jobs on the line. *The Times*. Jul 9th, p.27.

MICHAELS, A. (1993) Culture vultures. *Financial Times*. Jul 23rd, p.15. [case study cites CIGNA Corp (UK)].

MICHAELS, A. (1993) Taking it from the top. *Financial Times*. Jul 5th, p.9. [case study cites National and Provincial Building Society, UK].

RAWSTHORN, A. (1992) Re-engineering the Paris stock market. *Financial Times*. Mar 24th, p.23.

TRAPP, R. (1994) Company culture: Key to successful change. *Independent on Sunday*. May 5th.

TRAPP, R. (1993) Gearing up for change brings the revolution. *The Independent On Sunday Business*. Jul 18th, p.21.

Financial Times (unsigned), London (1993) *The tough nuts to crack*. Apr 7th, p.18. [cites case study at Leeds Permanent, UK building society].

The Independent (unsigned), London (1993) *Breaking the Mould*. Jun 30th, p.27.

4. Theses

DUR, R.C.J. (1992) *Business reengineering in information intensive organizations*. PhD thesis. Delft University of Technology (The Netherlands).

HEERDEN, S. van (1992) *Preparing the work environment and workers for the implementation of information technology with special reference to office automation* (Afrikaans text). MCom dissertation. University of Pretoria (South Africa).

MEEL, J.W. van. (1994, forthcoming) *The dynamics of business engineering: Reflections on two case studies within the Amsterdam Municipal Police Force.* Doctoral dissertation. Delft University of Technology.

UPDIKE, L.R. (1992) *The identification of key business processes.* MS dissertation. San Jose State University (Ca., USA).

5. BPR Tools

BALLOU, M-C. (1994) Market for re-engineering tools burgeons. *Computerworld.* 28 (6) Feb 7th, p.95. [appraisal of tools].

BORTHICK, A.F. and ROTH, H.P. (1993) EDI for reengineering business processes. *Management Accounting.* 75 (4) Oct:32–37 [case study features Northern Telecom].

GATES, W(Bill). (1994) Role of client/server in re-engineering. *Computer Reseller News.* Feb 7th, p.186.

HANNA, M. (1993) Reengineering aims for legacy salvation. *Software Magazine.* 13 (13) Sep:41–50. [examples of platforms and tools].

KIRKPATRICK, D. (1993) Groupware goes boom. *Fortune.* 128 (16) Dec 27th, pp.99–106.

KLEIN, M.M (1994) Reengineering methodologies and tools. *Information Systems Management.* 11 (2) Spring:30–35.

LOPES, P.F. (1993) Fine-tuning reengineering with workflow automation: Blueprint and tool. *Industrial Engineering.* 25 (8) Aug:51–53. [on 'automated workflow technology'].

WANG, S. (1994) OO modeling of business processes. *Information Systems Management.* 11 (2) Spring:36–43.

Details of 101 specific tools and techniques and an indication of their relevance at each stage of the COBRA approach to re-engineering can be found in: Colin Coulson-Thomas (Executive Editor) (1995), *The Responsive Organisation: Re-engineering new patterns of work*, London, Policy Publications, while the use of the approaches and technologies of electronic commerce in supply chain re-engineering is covered in: Peter Bartram, Colin Coulson-Thomas and Lee Tate (1996), *The Competitive Network*, London, Policy Publications. (Further information: Tel: +44 (0) 171 240 3488; Fax: +44 (0) 171 240 2768.)

On-going appraisals and reports on this constantly changing field may be obtained from, for example:

Process Product Watch. Quarterly review of re-engineering and process management products; produced by Enix Ltd, Tel: (44) 181 332 0210.

Lists of firms and individuals offering BPR consultancy services are available from professional institutions and trade associations or from market research firms and publishers of specialist reports such as those referred to above.

6. Re Techniques and Methodologies

CARR, D.K. and others (1992) *Breakpoint: Business process redesign.* (Arlington VA: Coopers and Lybrand).

CURTIS, B., KELLNER, M.I. and OVER, J. (1992) Process modelling. *Communications of the ACM. 35* (9) Sep:75–90.

GOODMAN, J. (1993) Change of direction. *Computer Weekly.* Sep 16th, p.30. [discussion of Oasis Group's methodology].

GUHA, S., KETTINGER, W.J. and TENG, J.T.C. (1993) Business process reengineering: Building a comprehensive methodology. *Information Systems Management. 10* (3) Summer:13–22. [discusses 'process reengineering life cycle' as methodology].

HARRISON, D.B. and PRATT, M.D. (1993) Transforming the enterprise. *Canadian Business Review. 20* (2) Summer:22–25. [on the methodology of A T Kearney Canada Inc].

HARRISON, D.B. and PRATT, M.D. (1993) A methodology for reenginering business. *Planning Review.* Mar/Apr:6–11.

HUCKVALE, T. and OULD, M. (1993) Process modelling: Why, what and how. Chapter 6 In *Software assistance for business re-engineering,* edited by SPURR, K. and others (Chichester: John Wiley) op.cit.

PFRENZINGER, S. (1992) Reengineering goals shift toward analysis, transition. *Software Magazine. 12* (14) Oct:44–46, 50–58. [discusses IS techniques for BPR].

SMITH, G. (1994) *The business process approach – placebo, panacea or poison?* (London: Organisation Consulting Partnership). [describes OCP's methodology and cites 5 client case studies].

STILLWAGON, W. and BURNS, R. (1993) Improving manufacturing competitiveness through the application of Human Performance Engineering. *International Journal of Technology Management. 8* (3–5):411–421. [discusses 'Human Performance Engineering' as methodology].

TSANG, E. (1993) Business process re-engineering and why it requires business event analysis. *CASE Trends. 5* (2):8–15.

7. Journals Dedicated to BPR

Focus on Change Management: Cases in Business Process Reengineering (UK) 1st Issue Jan 1994.

Insights Quarterly. The Journal of Strategy and Re-engineering. (Cambridge, MA: Computer Sciences Corporation). Quarterly since

Summer 1989 (Limited circulation) [a wealth of case studies and articles. CSC Index is headed by James Champy q.v., co-author of Re-engineering the Corporation, op cit].

IOPener. Newsletter of the IOPT Club for the introduction of Process Technology, (c/o Messrs Praxis, UK: iopt@praxis.co.uk).

Journal of Strategic Change. Bi-monthly. (Chichester: John Wiley & Sons). (44) 1243 770351.

The Journal of Business Change and Reengineering. Quarterly since Summer 1993. Via Cornwallis Emmanuel Ltd. PO Box 163, Guildford, Surrey, GUI 2YP.

8. Experience-Sharing Forums

THE INSTITUTE OF BUSINESS PROCESS RE-ENGINEERING; founded in Jan 1994 and to be officially launched in Sep 1994. Membership inquiries to: 1 Cecil Court, London Road, Enfield, Middlesex, EN2 6DD. Tel & fax: (44) 181 366 6718.

STRATEGIC PLANNING SOCIETY; Re-engineering & Radical Change Special Interest Group. Monthly seminars; quarterly workshops. Tel: (44) 171 636 7737.

BRITISH COMPUTER SOCIETY; various sectoral and regional Special Interest Groups are addressing BPR. Tel: (44) 1793 417417.

BPR conferences, seminars, workshops and exhibitions, at a range of prices, are regularly available, nationally and internationally. Typically, these are publicised via leaflets in quality journals. Advance information can also be obtained by subscribing to electronic discussion groups such as those mentioned in the introduction.

9. Forthcoming Publications (as at June 1994)

BETTERIDGE, J. (1994, forthcoming) *Managing BPR.* (London: Cambridge Market Intelligence).

BRODDLE, M. and HOBLER, B. (1994, forthcoming) *BPR: Tools and technologies report.* (London: Cambridge Market Intelligence).

GALLIERS, R. (expected 1994) *Information systems, operational research and business reengineering.* International Transactions of Operations Research.

KEEN, P.G.W. and KNAPP, E.M. (expected 1994) *Business process investment: Getting the right process right.* (Harvard Business School Press).

WHITE, T.E. and FISCHER, L. (eds) (expected 1994) *New tools for new times.* (Alameda CA: Future Strategies Inc).

10. Background Reading

APPLEGATE, L., CASH, J.I. and QUINN MILLS, D. (1988) Information technology and tomorrow's manager. *Harvard Business Review.* Nov/Dec:128–136.

BAUER, COLLAR, and TANG (1992) *The Silverlake project: Transformation at IBM.* (Oxford University Press).

BEER, M. (1990) *The critical path to corporate renewal.* (McGraw-Hill).

CLOUGH, A.J. (1992) *Choosing an Appropriate Process Modelling Technology.* Communications of the ACM. Aug.

COULSON-THOMAS, C. (1992) *Transforming the company: Bridging the gap between management myth and corporate reality.* (London: Kogan Page).

DANIEL DUCK, J. (1993) Managing change: The art of balancing. *Harvard Business Review.* Nov-Dec:109–118.

DAVIES and LEDINGTON, P. (1991) *Information In Action – Soft Systems Methodology,* Macmillan ISBN 0–333–56539–8 [contains a comprehensive reference bibliography of Soft Systems Methodologies; starting with Checkland, P.B. (1981). Systems thinking, systems practice. (Chichester: John Wiley)].

GOLDRATT, E. and COX, J. (1989) *The goal.* (Aldershot, Gower Publishing Co.).

HASTINGS, C. (1993) *The new organisation: Growing the culture of organisational networking.* (McGraw-Hill).

KEEN, P.G.W. (1991) Redesigning the organization through information technology. *Planning Review. 19* (3):4–9.

MITCHELL, V.L. (1993) *An exploration of the relationship between business process redesign and information technology infrastructures.* (Diss: Florida State).

MOSS KANTER, R. (1992) *The challenge of organizational change: How people experience and manage it.* (NY: Free Press).

NADLER, D.A., GERSTEIN, M.S. and SHAW, R.B. (1992) *Organizational architecture: Designs for changing organizations.* (San Francisco: Jossey-Bass).

NAISBITT, J. and ABURDENE, P. (1985) *Re-inventing the corporation.* (New York: Warner Books Inc.).

SEMLER, R. (1993) *Maverick.* (McGraw-Hill).

STALK, G. and HOUT, T. (1990) *Competing against time.* (NY: Free Press).

TAPSCOTT, D. AND CASTON, A. (1993) *Paradigm shift: The new promise of information technology.* (New York: McGraw-Hill).

Business Week, US 1993. *The technology payoff: A sweeping reorganization of work itself is boosting productivity.* June 14th, Special report; various authors, pp.37–48.

Index